Ontogenesis Beyond Complexity

This book is based upon the collaborative efforts of the Ontogenetics Process Group (OPG) – an interdisciplinary, multi-institutional, multi-national research group that began meeting in 2017 to explore new and innovative ways of thinking the problem of complexity in living, physical, and social systems outside the algorithmic models that have dominated paradigms of complexity to date.

For all the descriptive and predictive power that the complexity sciences offer (the ability to compute feedback systems, recursive networks, emergent dynamics, etc.), they also presume that the living world in all of its modalities (biological, semiotic, economic, affective, social) can be reduced to finite schema of description that delimits in advance all possible outcomes. What is proposed in this volume are conceptual architectures for the living that are not only irreducible to physico-mathematical frames of reference, but that are also as vital as the phenomena they wish to express. In short: life is more complex than complexity. What emerges from this engagement is not the ascendance of a new transcendental principle (or, what amounts to the same thing, a foundational bedrock) derived from the physico-mathematical sciences, but just the opposite: a domain in which the ontological and the epistemological domains enter a zone of strange (and unavoidable) entanglement.

The chapters in this book were originally published as a special issue of *Angelaki*.

Cary Wolfe is Bruce and Elizabeth Dunlevie Professor of English at Rice University, USA, where he is Founding Director of 3CT: Center for Critical and Cultural Theory. His books and edited collections include *What Is Posthumanism?* and *Ecological Poetics, or, Wallace Stevens's Birds*. In 2007 he founded the series *Posthumanities* at the University of Minnesota Press.

Adam Nocek is Assistant Professor in Philosophy of Technology and Science and Technology Studies in the School of Arts, Media and Engineering at Arizona State University, USA. Nocek is the Founding Director of the Center for Philosophical Technologies at ASU and the author of *Molecular Capture: The Animation of Biology*.

Angelaki: New Work in the Theoretical Humanities

New Work in the Theoretical Humanities is associated with *Angelaki: Journal of the Theoretical Humanities*, a leading international interdisciplinary journal that has done much to consolidate the field of research designated by its subtitle and which has been at the forefront of publication for three decades. This book series publishes generous edited collections across the humanities as informed by European philosophy and literary and cultural theory. It has a strong interest in aesthetics and art theory and also features work in those areas of the social sciences, such as social theory and political theory, that are informed by *Angelaki's* core disciplinary concentration. This broad latitude is disciplined by a strong sense of identity and the series editors' long experience of research and teaching in the humanities. The *Angelaki* journal is well known for its exceptionally substantial special issues. **New Work in the Theoretical Humanities** publishes vanguard collections on current developments in the energetic and increasingly international field of the theoretical humanities as well as volumes on major living thinkers and writers and those of the recent past. Volumes in this series are conceived as broad but integrated treatments of their themes, with the intention of producing contributions to the literature of lasting value.

Alien Vectors
Accelerationism, Xenofeminism, Inhumanism
Edited by James Trafford and Pete Wolfendale

The African Other
Philosophy, Justice and the Self
Edited by Abraham Olivier

Institutional Transformations
Imagination, Embodiment, and Affect
Edited by Danielle Celermajer, Millicent Churcher and Moira Gatens

Sentient Subjects
Post-humanist Perspectives on Affectz
Edited by Gerda Roelvink and Magdalena Zolkos

Relationality
Edited by Simone Drichel

Love and Vulnerability
Thinking with Pamela Sue Anderson
Edited by Pelagia Goulimari

Nuclear Theory Degree Zero
Essays Against the Nuclear Android
Edited by John Kinsella and Drew Milne

Tranimacies
Intimate Links Between Animal and Trans* Studies
Edited by Eliza Steinbock, Marianna Szczygielska and Anthony Clair Wagner

Ontogenesis Beyond Complexity
Edited by Cary Wolfe and Adam Nocek

For more information about this series, please visit:
www.routledge.com/New-Work-in-the-Theoretical-Humanities/book-series/ANG

Ontogenesis Beyond Complexity

Edited by
Cary Wolfe and Adam Nocek

LONDON AND NEW YORK

First published 2022
by Routledge
2 Park Square, Milton Park, Abingdon, Oxon OX14 4RN

and by Routledge
605 Third Avenue, New York, NY 10158

Routledge is an imprint of the Taylor & Francis Group, an informa business

Introduction, Chapters 2–8, 10 and 11 © 2022 Taylor & Francis
Chapter 1 © 2020 Stuart Kauffman. Originally published as Open Access.
Chapter 9 © 2020 Giuseppe Longo. Originally published as Open Access.

With the exception of Chapters 1 and 9, no part of this book may be reprinted or reproduced or utilised in any form or by any electronic, mechanical, or other means, now known or hereafter invented, including photocopying and recording, or in any information storage or retrieval system, without permission in writing from the publishers. For details on the rights for Chapters 1 and 9, please see the chapters' Open Access footnotes.

Trademark notice: Product or corporate names may be trademarks or registered trademarks, and are used only for identification and explanation without intent to infringe.

British Library Cataloguing in Publication Data
A catalogue record for this book is available from the British Library

ISBN: 978-0-367-70545-9 (hbk)
ISBN: 978-0-367-70547-3 (pbk)
ISBN: 978-1-003-14685-8 (ebk)

DOI: 10.4324/9781003146858

Typeset in Baskerville
by Newgen Publishing UK

Publisher's Note
The publisher accepts responsibility for any inconsistencies that may have arisen during the conversion of this book from journal articles to book chapters, namely the inclusion of journal terminology.

Disclaimer
Every effort has been made to contact copyright holders for their permission to reprint material in this book. The publishers would be grateful to hear from any copyright holder who is not here acknowledged and will undertake to rectify any errors or omissions in future editions of this book.

Contents

Citation Information vii
Notes on Contributors ix

Introduction 1
Cary Wolfe and Adam Nocek

1 Eros and Logos 7
  Stuart Kauffman

2 The Epimedial Landscape 22
  Adam Nocek

3 The Digital Sublime: Algorithmic Binds in a Living Foundry 39
  Gaymon Bennett

4 Alienated Life: Toward a Goth Theory of Biology 51
  Phillip Thurtle

5 The Square Root of Negative One is Imaginary 62
  Sha Xin Wei

6 The Singularity Has Come and Gone: The Beginning of Organization 81
  Helga C. Wild

7 In-Kind Disruptions: Circadian Rhythms and Necessary Jolts in Eco-Cinema 95
  Erin Espelie

8 Relational Realism and the Ontogenetic Universe: Subject, Object, and Ontological Process in Quantum Mechanics 106
  Michael Epperson

9 Scientific Thought and Absolutes: For an Image of the Sciences, Between Computing and Biology 118
  Giuseppe Longo (translated by David Gauthier)

10	What "The Animal" Can Teach "The Anthropocene" *Cary Wolfe*	129
11	Ontogenesis Beyond Complexity: Conversations	144
	Index	182

Citation Information

The chapters in this book were originally published in *Angelaki*, volume 25, issue 3 (2020). When citing this material, please use the original page numbering for each article, as follows:

Introduction
Editorial Introduction
Cary Wolfe and Adam Nocek
Angelaki, volume 25, issue 3 (2020), pp. 3–8

Chapter 1
Eros and Logos
Stuart Kauffman
Angelaki, volume 25, issue 3 (2020), pp. 9–23

Chapter 2
The Epimedial Landscape
Adam Nocek
Angelaki, volume 25, issue 3 (2020), pp. 24–40

Chapter 3
The Digital Sublime: Algorithmic Binds in a Living Foundry
Gaymon Bennett
Angelaki, volume 25, issue 3 (2020), pp. 41–52

Chapter 4
Alienated Life: Toward a Goth Theory of Biology
Phillip Thurtle
Angelaki, volume 25, issue 3 (2020), pp. 53–63

Chapter 5
The Square Root of Negative One is Imaginary
Sha Xin Wei
Angelaki, volume 25, issue 3 (2020), pp. 64–82

Chapter 6
The Singularity Has Come and Gone: The Beginning of Organization
Helga C. Wild
Angelaki, volume 25, issue 3 (2020), pp. 83–96

Chapter 7
In-Kind Disruptions: Circadian Rhythms and Necessary Jolts in Eco-Cinema
Erin Espelie
Angelaki, volume 25, issue 3 (2020), pp. 97–107

Chapter 8
Relational Realism and the Ontogenetic Universe: Subject, Object, and Ontological Process in Quantum Mechanics
Michael Epperson
Angelaki, volume 25, issue 3 (2020), pp. 108–119

Chapter 9
Scientific Thought and Absolutes: For an Image of the Sciences, Between Computing and Biology
Giuseppe Longo (translated by David Gauthier)
Angelaki, volume 25, issue 3 (2020), pp. 120–130

Chapter 10
What "The Animal" Can Teach "The Anthropocene"
Cary Wolfe
Angelaki, volume 25, issue 3 (2020), pp. 131–145

Chapter 11
Ontogenesis Beyond Complexity: Conversations
Angelaki, volume 25, issue 3 (2020), pp. 146–183

For any permission-related enquiries please visit:
www.tandfonline.com/page/help/permissions

Notes on Contributors

Gaymon Bennett is an anthropologist and Associate Professor of Religion, Science, and Technology at Arizona State University (ASU). He studies how modernity has become a problem for both science and religion: in shifting relations of power, destabilized regimes of disenchantment, and uncertain subjectivities. He pursues these questions in active collaboration with scientists, technologists, and entrepreneurs through collective empirical inquiry, concept work, and sustained attention to the politics of productivity.

Michael Epperson is a research professor and founding director of the Center for Philosophy and the Natural Sciences at California State University, Sacramento, and the founding director of the university's History and Philosophy of Science Program. Epperson did his doctoral work in philosophy of science and philosophy of religion at The University of Chicago and earned his Ph.D. there in 2003.

Erin Espelie is a filmmaker whose works have been shown at the New York Film Festival, the British Film Institute, the Whitechapel Gallery, Anthology Film Archive, the San Francisco Museum of Modern Art, and more. Her writing has appeared in SciArt magazine, Labocine, The Brooklyn Rail, and Natural History magazine. She is Co-director of NEST (Nature, Environment, Science & Technology) Studio for the Arts and an Assistant Professor in the Department of Cinema Studies & the Moving Image Arts and the Department of Critical Media Practices at the University of Colorado Boulder.

Stuart Kauffman is a medical doctor, theoretical biologist, and complex systems researcher. He has held professorships at the University of Chicago and the University of Pennsylvania and was awarded a MacArthur Fellowship in Evolutionary Biology in 1987. He is the author of multiple seminal works including *Origins of Order* (1993), *At Home in the Universe* (1996), *Investigations* (2002), and *Humanity in a Creative Universe* (2017).

Giuseppe Longo is Directeur de Recherche (DRE) CNRS, Centre Interdisciplinaire Cavaillès, Ecole Normale Supérieure, Paris and Adjunct Professor, School of Medicine, Tufts University, Boston. He is former Professor of Mathematical Logic and, later, of Computer Science at the University of Pisa.

Adam Nocek is Assistant Professor in Philosophy of Technology and Science and Technology Studies in the School of Arts, Media, and Engineering at Arizona State University (ASU). He is also the Founding Director of the Center for Philosophical Technologies at ASU. Nocek has published widely on the philosophy of media and science, speculative philosophy (especially Whitehead), design philosophy, and on critical and speculative theories of computational media.

Phillip Thurtle is Professor in History, Chair of the Comparative History of Ideas Department, and Adjunct Professor in Digital and Experimental Arts at the University of Washington. He received his Ph.D. in History and the Philosophy of Science from Stanford University. His research focuses on the material culture of information processing, the affective-phenomenological domains of media, the role of information processing technologies in biomedical research, and theories of novelty in the life sciences.

Sha Xin Wei is Director of the Synthesis Center for experimental art, philosophy, and technology, Director of the School of Arts, Media, and Engineering at ASU, and Fellow of the ASU–Santa Fe Center for Biosocial Complex Systems. Sha teaches at the European Graduate School and is Senior Fellow at Building21 at McGill.

Helga C. Wild studied Experimental Psychology and Neurophysiology at the University of Innsbruck, Austria. After postdoctoral studies in Systems and Automata Theory she went to the United States with a Schrödinger Fellowship to carry out research at the Neuropsychology Lab at Stanford University. Her theoretical work is anchored in phenomenology and fueled by the experience with real-world problems and issues.

Cary Wolfe is Bruce and Elizabeth Dunlevie Chair in English at Rice University, where he is Founding Director of 3CT: The Center for Critical and Cultural Theory. He is founding editor of the Posthumanities book series at the University of Minnesota Press, which has published nearly sixty volumes to date by noted authors such as Donna Haraway, Roberto Esposito, Isabelle Stengers, Michel Serres, Vilem Flusser, Jacques Derrida, Siegfried Zielinski, and others.

INTRODUCTION

cary wolfe
adam nocek

ONTOGENESIS BEYOND COMPLEXITY
the work of the ontogenetics process group

This special issue is the result of multiple years of collaboration among a diverse group of scholars, scientists, and practitioners. This group came to be known as the Ontogenetics Process Group (OPG). From the outset, what distinguished this unruly collective seemed to be a shared nostalgia for an intellectual space where scientists, humanists, and artists could engage in theoretical exchange without the pressure of superficial "outputs" to satisfy administrators, mixed with an insatiable hunger for the formation of an interdisciplinary conceptual frame capable of responding to pressing questions emerging not just from biological and computational systems (explored here in the essays by Longo, Nocek, Thurtle, and Wolfe), but also from the domains of social and cultural practice (plumbed in the work of Kauffman, Bennett, Espelie, and Wild). As the "roundtable" conversation shows, while the focus of this issue is tilted toward the sciences, the group has a keen interest in asking after the system dynamics, principles of organization and development, and modes of coherence that might obtain in the domains of law, the economy, and so on – and the extent to which those might be illuminated by models from the mathematical and biological sciences.[1]

This kind of interdisciplinary theoretical endeavor has a long history, of course, one that, in recent decades, has been largely occluded by the rise of Big Data, the neo-Darwinian paradigm and its obsession with the genome as an engineerable "book of life," and the assumption that "hard," tenurable scientific knowledge is fundamentally quantitative in nature. It's entirely possible, however, that that hegemony will, in the longer view, prove to be misguided or, at the very least, oversold, and in that longer view, the OPG might be situated genealogically somewhere between the intellectual investments of the Theoretical Biology Club in the 1930s (organicism), the interdisciplinary ambitions of the Macy Conferences in the 1940s and 1950s (that included figures as diverse as Warren McCulloch, Gregory Bateson, and Margaret Mead), and the restless game-changing and institution-building work of the Santa Fe Institute in the 1980s and 1990s. From the very beginning, Stuart Kauffman, one of the original members of Santa Fe Institute, and a founding member of the OPG, would often remark (and we're paraphrasing), "there is really something here that the complexity scientists over there at the Institute won't be able to get their heads around."

What Kauffman is referring to is the fundamental challenge that OPG researchers pose to what has become the lingua franca of theoretical biology: complex systems theory, on a quantitative and mathematical template. For all the descriptive and predictive power that the complexity sciences offer (the ability to compute feedback systems, recursive networks, emergent dynamics, etc.), they also presume that the living world in all of its modalities (biological, semiotic, economic, affective, social) can be reduced to finite schema of description that delimits in advance all possible outcomes. The mathematics of complexity function like a "grid of intelligibility" for physicists, biologists, economists, information scientists, sociologists, and now many humanists; they permit the sciences of the living and nonliving to speak the same language. What distinguishes this group of researchers, and this special issue of *Angelaki* in particular, is the breadth of disciplinary and methodological frameworks brought to bear on the possibilities and limitations of this proposition. More than this, what is proposed here are conceptual architectures for the living that are not only irreducible to physico-mathematical frames of reference but that are also as vital as the phenomena they wish to express. In short: life is more complex than complexity.

In a sense, this may not seem like an entirely new proposition for the theoretical humanities. There is a rich genealogy of continental thought that engages with the contemporary biosciences through the vital materialist philosophy of Nietzsche, Bergson, Deleuze, Guattari, Simondon, Canguilhem, and others (see Ansell-Pearson; Grosz; Braidotti; Thacker). Bennett, Nocek, Thurtle, and Epperson address these touchstones in their articles, with different angles of emphasis, to be sure. However, several features of the OPG's treatment of the biosciences and related scientific fields resist some of the unfortunate clichés that have come to characterize humanist engagements with science, particularly under the broad rubric of "materialism."

On the one hand, and in the interest of a more robust and rigorous form of interdisciplinarity, this collection opposes the pervasive tendency to keep scientific abstraction and mathematical formalism at a safe distance from philosophical and critical reflection, even or especially when the former are essential to engage head on. For example, Bergson's vitalist critique of Darwinian mechanism (via the *élan vital*) has served as a rallying cry for many neo-vital materialists and contemporary biophilosophers, but it has very little to say about the actual work of evolutionary and developmental biology as such. Rather, this abstract principle of vital force contributes to an overly general critique of scientific abstraction that privileges a metaphysics of vitality over and against what is already an often rudimentary understanding of mechanism. Similarly, the Deleuzoguattarian fad of drawing on von Uexküll's ethology, Leibniz's calculus, and Jacob and Monod's *lac* operon involves only the loosest appropriation of the hard sciences. This may tell us about continental philosophy's motivations and interests in engaging the sciences, but it tells us very little about the practices of working scientists and how philosophy and theory can learn from them. The point is that the conceptual work of continental theorists is often sanitized from the concerns of working scientists and what counts as success in their respective fields. These immunization strategies are undercut at every turn in this special issue, and this is nowhere more evident than in the work of Longo, Kauffman, Epperson, and Sha. Indeed, the methods, problems, and concerns of scientists and mathematicians (from theoretical biology, information theory, physics, and topology) are on full display in their work. These perspectives augment the "second-order" observations and ramifications of scientific work for the larger social context in the articles by Espelie, Wolfe, Nocek, and Bennett, adding another layer of critical urgency to the many issues raised about the computational sciences and algorithmic styles of reasoning generally.

There is, on the other hand, another tendency in the theoretical humanities from which this project also wishes to steer clear. In the wake of the so-called speculative turn in the humanities, which has undergone a number of facelifts since its inception in the mid-2000s, we find a persistent, if entirely overblown, faith placed in the hard sciences as a "foundational" enterprise. The wager is that the theoretical sciences (which de-correlate thought from being) can deliver the "great outdoors" (Meillassoux) that has been apparently missing from post-Kantian philosophy. Of course, these realisms and materialisms, as well as their many offspring, were by no means the first philosophical programs to privilege scientific and mathematical abstraction (e.g., Badiou; DeLanda), but their efforts have contributed to a decisive shift in orientation within the humanities in the name of the "real."

This story has been told many times, and there is no use recycling the history of its emergence here (see Mackay; Gratton; Harman), but what is nonetheless worth underscoring is that the "scientific turn" in the speculative humanities has less to do with philosophers and cultural theorists working alongside theoretical scientists, or engaging in genuine debate about scientific and mathematical reason, than with good old-fashioned humanists cherry-picking from the hard sciences (mostly physics, mathematics, and computer science). Frustrated theorists and philosophers have managed to negate one set of organizing principles (those that underlie the situated practices of humans) and replace it with another: mathematical formalism (Meillassoux), or lifeless matter (Brassier), or abstract universalism and computational intelligence (Negarestani), or automation and Promethean design (Bratton).

This is not to say that scientists, social scientists, and humanists have not been assembled in recent years to address the limitations of the computational sciences. An excellent example is the edited collection, *Beyond Mechanism: Putting Life Back into Biology* (Henning and Scarfe). At the center of this work is a commitment to using the underlying principles of process philosophy (and related conceptions) as the basis for addressing what computational practices have so far been unable to explain: in particular, the *self* in biological self-organization. On the one hand, it is remarkable that theoretical biologists are drawing (and not superficially) on Whitehead, Peirce, and even Kant for conceptual clarity. But on the other hand, the topics they explore are circumscribed by the presupposed relevance of a process-based metaphysics of life. What's more, continental genealogies of nonhuman process, ecology, and subjectivity are entirely missing from the collection. Other collections and volumes have attempted to explore similar themes, most notably, *Life and Process: Towards a New Biophilosophy* (Koutroufinis), but here too we find the already-presumed sufficiency of process philosophy, and a complete lack of engagement with other conceptual histories.

Instead, the work done in the OPG meetings, and showcased in this issue, revolves around a genuine concern for scientific styles of reasoning, and in particular for the problems, concerns, and assumptions that animate scientific work. (Here, for example, a problem internal to the discipline of biology – the fact, as Denis Noble has suggested, that for decades theoretical biologists and experimental biologists have had almost nothing to say to each other – has stakes and implications that can be *better* illuminated, perhaps, from outside the discipline itself, when philosophy and anthropology shed light on what counts as "real" "science" and how that, in turn, overdetermines what counts as "life" (Noble 169, 235–37).) And what emerges from this engagement is not the ascendance of a new transcendental principle or (what amounts to the same thing) foundational bedrock, derived from the physico-mathematical sciences, but just the opposite: that theorists working in these scientific fields are searching for conceptual frameworks that can express the fact that certain material and energetic systems (living systems) exceed the computational and conceptual systems designed to understand them, a domain in which the ontological and the epistemological domains enter into a zone of strange (and unavoidable) entanglement.

As Alicia Juarrero asks,

> Does emergence therefore simply come down to an *epistemological* ignorance, to our human inability to exhaustively list every *ceteris paribus* and disjunctive condition (even though such an exhaustive set of conditions in fact exists and there is a 1:1 correlation between each fully specified set of conditions and corresponding emergent property?). (518)

And Kauffman's answer, in short, is that "it is impossible to predict emergent properties even in principle because the categories necessary to frame them do not exist until after the fact" (qtd in Juarrero 518). And this is where, as Wolfe suggests, what one might think of as the astringent force of a fundamentally deconstructive sensibility is crucial to doing justice to the challenge of complexity and resisting the temptation to extract yet another "final" version (whether realist or idealist, transcendental or foundational) that anchors the thinking of complexity and, in the process, evacuates it. This detotalizing impulse may take the form of deconstruction proper, or it may be found in Bennett's attention to the thick description of the practice-based entanglement of minding and mattering and the worlds they create (both micro and macro), in Longo's insistence on the specific boundedness of time and place of the biological organism, or in the theorization of the unentailed evolution of the biosphere and the fundamentally circular and recursive logic of living systems that we find in Kauffman and fellow travelers such as Anna Soto, Alicia Juarrero, and, of course, Longo himself.

The site on which these investigations converge, then, isn't just complexity, but constitutively *irreducible* complexity, of the sort increasingly mitigated against in the WEIRD (Western, Educated, Industrialized, Rich, and Democratic) world ruled by "governmentality" and "medicalization" (to use Foucault's well-known terms), where "science" is increasingly seen *tout court* as *applied* science. That complexity may be converged upon from various directions, of course. From one orientation (the one given "goth" voice in Thurtle's essay), difference, alterity, the chaotic, "noise," and so on is a desideratum, something to be liberated from falsely reductive forms of identity, recovered and valorized. For another orientation, it is a problem that systems of organized complexity have to figure out a way to solve if they are to persist in the world: not "problem" in the sense of "bad" but rather in the adaptive and pragmatic sense, as a puzzle or a challenge. Either way, yet another turn of the screw here is to recognize that this domain of alterity, "noise," and chaos is itself an enormous asset in the larger gambit called "complexity."

Order and noise (to use shorthand) are not opposites but are rather co-implicated, and the liminal zone where they converge is, for us, the zone of interest, one that requires a new kind of dynamic, non-reductive theory whose most familiar shibboleth in contemporary continental philosophy is probably "repetition with difference" and its variants. As Yuk Hui puts it,

> Recursivity is not only a mechanism that can effectively "domesticate" contingency [...]; it is also a mechanism that allows novelty to occur, not simply as something coming from outside but also as an internal transformation [...] [T]he recursive mode can effectively integrate contingency in order to produce something new; in other words, it demands constant contingencies. (138)

But since the alterity or negativity of temporality is at the (non)core of this process on both the micro- and macro-levels – hence our emphasis on "dynamic" – we are dealing here not with "the identity of identity and non-identity" (as in Hegel), but rather "the *non*-identity of identity and non-identity," a logic that is "heterogeneous" (as Derrida puts it) "to the dialectic and the calculable" (116), to the logic of any identitarian scheme, one that Epperson's essay explores in cross-mapping theoretical physics and the work of Whitehead and Simondon on the processes of "ontogenesis" and "individuation."

If this introduction reads like it is preparing the genealogical and intellectual ground for the claims made by the OPG, then it is because spaces for such theoretical engagement do not yet exist. Rarely, if ever, do we see an information scientist, a complexity theorist, a design and organizational theorist, a mathematician, a historian of science, an experimental filmmaker, an anthropologist of science and religion, a philosopher of physics, and a couple of theoretical humanists assemble in order to contemplate modes of living that are *more complex* than complexity. At the heart of this shared inquiry is a deep and sustained interest in biology, in questions of self-organization, morphogenesis, epigenetics, cultural inheritance systems (soft inheritance), downward and distributed causation, as well as the implications of quantum physics in these domains. But in taking these questions on board, especially in light of the work Longo and Kauffman have done on the limitations of complex systems science, two things become startlingly clear: (1) that cultural, political, and economic systems cannot be isolated from the physicochemical emergence of living phenomena; and (2) that the reigning models of complexity need to be paired with non-computational and non-algorithmic modes of inquiry in order to better express the unfolding of living worlds. And yet, just what relevance these extra-biological systems have and what modes of (non-algorithmic) inquiry are most appropriate (ethnography, mathematics, conceptual art, philosophy, speculative design) are not agreed upon and remain open for debate.

This lack of agreement should not be treated as a limitation, however. Where other anthologies, volumes, or working groups would demand a clear path forward, and might even insist upon formulating a "new science" out of the non-algorithmic study of the living, we maintain that this is precisely the style of thinking that leads to the metaphysics of life that we aim to critique. We therefore see the radical plurality of views, which do not always sit comfortably together, as a strength that forcefully demonstrates the resistance of the living to metaphysical capture.

note

1 Somewhere along the away, OPG researchers realized that these conversations were too important to go unrecorded. But because we did not intend for these meetings to yield specific outcomes (like a publishable roundtable conversation), many conversations went unrecorded. We would like to pay tribute to those individuals who were essential to the development of the Ontogenetics Process Group, but whose utterances are not transcribed here. These individuals include: Erin Espelie, Helga Wild, Giuseppe Longo, Patricia Pisters, Wim Hordijk, and Peter Sloot.

bibliography

Ansell-Pearson, Keith. *Germinal Life: The Difference and Repetition of Deleuze*. London: Routledge, 1999. Print.

Badiou, Alain. *Being and Event*. Trans. Oliver Feltham. London: Continuum International, 2006. Print.

Braidotti, Rossi. *The Posthuman*. Cambridge: Polity, 2013. Print.

Brassier, Ray. *Nihil Unbound: Enlightenment and Extinction*. Basingstoke: Palgrave Macmillan, 2007. Print.

Bratton, Benjamin. *The Stack: On Software and Sovereignty*. Cambridge, MA: MIT P, 2015. Print.

DeLanda, Manuel. *Intensive Science and Virtual Philosophy*. London: Bloomsbury, 2002. Print.

Derrida, Jacques. *Limited Inc.* Trans. Samuel Weber et al. Evanston: Northwestern UP, 1990. Print.

Gratton, Peter. *Speculative Realism: Problems and Prospects*. London: Bloomsbury, 2014. Print.

Grosz, Elizabeth. *Becoming Undone: Darwinian Reflections on Life, Politics, and Art*. Durham, NC: Duke UP, 2011. Print.

Harman, Graham. *Speculative Realism: An Introduction*. Cambridge: Polity, 2018. Print.

Henning, Brian G., and Adam C. Scarfe, eds. *Beyond Mechanism: Putting Life Back into Biology*. Lanham: Lexington, 2013. Print.

Hui, Yuk. *Recursivity and Contingency*. London: Rowman, 2019. Print.

Juarrero, Alicia. "What does the Closure of Context-Sensitive Constraints Mean for Determinism, Autonomy, Self-Determination, and

Agency?" *Progress in Biophysics and Molecular Biology* 119 (2015): 510–21. Print.

Koutroufinis, Spyridon. "Introduction: The Need for a New Biophilosophy." *Life and Process: Towards a New Biophilosophy.* Berlin: De Gruyter, 2014. Print.

Mackay, Robin James, ed. *Collapse: Speculative Realism.* Vol. 2. Falmouth: Urbanomic, 2007. Print.

Meillassoux, Quentin. *After Finitude: An Essay on the Necessity of Contingency.* Trans. Ray Brassier. London: Continuum International, 2008. Print.

Negarestani, Reza. *Intelligence and Spirit.* London: Urbanomic Media, 2018. Print.

Noble, Denis. *Dance to the Tune of Life: Biological Relativity.* Cambridge: Cambridge UP, 2017. Print.

Thacker, Eugene. "Biophilosophy for the 21st Century." *Critical Digital Studies: A Reader.* Ed. Arthur Kroker and Marilouise Kroker. Toronto: U of Toronto P, 2008. Print.

Cary Wolfe

Adam Nocek

1 introduction

I wish to show that the becoming of the world is both entailed by the natural laws of physics and is also a becoming beyond any law at all. Three hundred and thirty years after Newton in 1687 published his *Principia*, in which the world is an entailed becoming, my statement that the world is a becoming beyond any law at all is revolutionary. In fact, we live in a world that is both: law and story, entailed becoming and narrative. We have come to know that C.P. Snow's "Two Cultures," Art and Science, are in fact, one world.

We inhabit and make that world with the rest of life on the planet, but at the same time, we are destroying that planet. We face a crisis our species has not seen in our 300,000 years of existence. Our $100 trillion global economy is growing at 4 percent a year. It will be tenfold larger in AD 2100. Our economy lifts millions from poverty, reduces childhood death rates, increases literacy, links our nations in trade, and is the means by which we earn our livings and find much of our meaning. But the same global economy is driving climate change with sea level rise, flooding, severe weather, and ocean acidification, as we have come to know in 2020. The same growing global economy is driving a mass extinction event. By 2050, thirty years from now, 1,000,000 species, 20 percent of the standing diversity, will be extinct. As we speak, wildlife populations dwindle. Humanity uses about 40 percent of the planet's land surface to grow our food. Over 50 percent of the terrestrial biomass of the planet is humans and our domestic products, cows, pigs, chickens, wheat, rice, sorghum. We are almost ten billion in abundance. For mammalian species, a population of a million is vast. We are 10,000-fold more abundant than each single member of such a species.

Our issues are global in both scale and existential magnitude. We are badly out of balance with the biosphere. Our species, for the first time in its history, will either come together and piece together a way forward to survive sustainably on our finite planet, or, driven by our growing juggernaut global economy, we will fail. If we

stuart kauffman

EROS AND LOGOS

This is an Open Access article distributed under the terms of the Creative Commons Attribution-NonCommercial-NoDerivatives License (http://creativecommons.org/licenses/by-nc-nd/4.0/), which permits non-commercial re-use, distribution, and reproduction in any medium, provided the original work is properly cited, and is not altered, transformed, or built upon in any way.

fail, we fail the evolving life that spawned us: the rest of life on this planet. The story we need is a new narrative of our becoming on our planet, a new origin myth, and from it a transnational mythic structure by which we can orient ourselves anew. It is our story to construct.

2 the ancient greeks

We mirror the ancient Greeks in their appreciation of Eros and Logos, creative chaos and the law. For the ancient Greeks, Eros was the god of creativity from whom the world emerged from primal chaos. The events on earth consisted of chaos mixed with fate and the intervention of man and the gods. Ancient Greece is the Bronze Age, some 40,000 years after our ancestors in Indonesia painted the hunt with half mythical beasts, 20,000 years after Cro-Magnon painted the walls of Lascaux with aurochs killed with the atlatl, and seven thousand years after the onset of agriculture in the Near East. Early animistic gods of the volcano, lake, stream, dancing stone, and the hunt, gave way to the Greek Pantheon – Zeus, Athena, Diana, Mercury – who, having killed the Titans, ruled heaven and earth, played tricks on one another, fought, were jealous of one another, loved, laughed with and at humanity below, and arranged the world as they would.

What brought the storms, the whirlpools that come and go, sinking ships, the failure of rain and crops, the blights, but at the same time the olives and olive oil to trade around the Aegean? Could humans avoid their Fate or shape it? Oedipus did not as Athenians were told. The *Iliad* and *Odyssey* were founding civilizational myths of sword, love, loyalty, and war – epic tales of this struggle. The heavens with the ordered patterns of the stars in their constellations, the sun and moon, were the abode of order, and the first hint of natural law, of order and perfection, of Logos.

Aristotle taught that the circle was the perfect form, hence that the universe was a set of concentric spheres. The sun, moon, and the fixed stars were on these spheres rotating about the earth. The irregular motions of the five planets, the "wanderers," worried the Greeks, particularly Plato. Two thousand years later, Kepler, knowing the circle was the proper orbit for a planet, surrendered that conviction to find the ellipse later predicted by Newton.

The first real steps toward science itself arose in Ionia with Thales of Miletus, a city in Asia near the island of Samos. Thales, about 540 BC, was the first to seek a common "principle" underneath all things that might explain the world without invoking the gods. What we now say of quarks and gluons, electrons and photons, he said of water. Anaximander, friend of Thales, determined the length of the year and made the first sundial. Empedocles, holding closed the openings to a clepsydra filled with water, showed that no water flowed out, so the clepsydra must be filled with an invisible stuff, air, made of invisible particles (Sagan 175–85). The single substance of Water slowly became earth, air, fire, and water. In 430 BC, Democritus argued that, rather than earth, air, fire, and water, the world was made of uncuttable units, atoms, moving and colliding randomly in the void of empty space. All atoms were of different shapes and all complex things made by combining atoms of different shapes. Centuries later, Lucretius, 94 BC in *De Rerum Natura*, introduced the random "swerve" to avoid the determinism in the universe of Democritus. Democritus and Lucretius 2,000 years ago presage the determinism of classical physics and the indeterminism of quantum physics of today.

So, for ancient Greece, the world was one of Eros and Logos, Creativity and Law, the Muse and the Ruler with its ordered line.

Foundational to the Ruler was number. Pythagoras, 570–495 BC, and his school of mathematics, discovered that for a right triangle, the length of the hypotenuse could not be a ratio of whole numbers such as 23/17. This discovery shattered the certainty in the Greek world that all numbers could be expressed as ratios of whole numbers, hence "rational numbers." The length of the hypotenuse is not a rational number, nor is the famous "pi," the ratio of the circumference to the diameter of a circle. The Greeks discovered irrational numbers.

An even more compelling result due to Pythagoras was his discovery that the different musical notes of a plucked string were different stable patterns of vibration of the string: Fundamentals, Thirds, Fifths, Octaves. Quantitative physics grows from this to this day.

"*All is Number*" proclaimed Pythagoras. This view, the Pythagorean dream, underlies most of contemporary physics, both in classical and quantum physics. It is the "Dream of a Final Theory" *down there*, voiced by Steven Weinberg some years ago, that entails and explains by such deduction from a fundamental law all that arises in the evolution of the universe. This dream is Reductionism, the "Dream of a Final Theory."

> The world of physics is the world of Logos. All is Logos. Eros is dead.
>
> What a brave brilliant Age was Ancient Greece.

3 the origin and evolution of life: the rebirth of eros

We now turn to the origin and evolution of life here on earth – and perhaps more widely in the universe. There are 100 billion galaxies, each with 100 billion stars. Most stars have solar systems, so there are some 10^{22} solar systems. If life arises easily, as I will suggest, the universe is rife with life. Stunningly, the evolution of life on our, or any, planet, the evolution of biospheres, is entirely beyond entailing law. Evolution beyond Law, beyond Logos, *is* Eros. Our planet and the universe are rife with Eros and Logos. The Greeks were right.

My statement that no law entails the becoming of our, or any, biosphere is indeed revolutionary. Such a bold claim needs careful presentation, and careful criticism. I believe the claim is correct (Kauffman, *Reinventing* 120–49; *Humanity* 64–81; *A World* 115–28). If so, it transforms our understanding of science, of reality, and our place in the cosmos. It bounds the Pythagorean dream. *Caveat lector*, I may be wrong.

4 the universe is non-ergodic above the level of atoms

Our first step beyond entailing law will seem odd: can the universe in its 13.7-billion-year history create all possible proteins 200 amino acids in length? Recall that a protein is a linear string of twenty different kinds of amino acids strung together by peptide bonds. A typical protein in us is about 300 amino acids long. How many possible proteins are there of length 200 amino acids? Well, at each position there are twenty choices, so the total number of possible proteins length 200 is 20 raised to the 200th power. Twenty to the 200th power is 10 raised to the 260th power. This is a hyper-astronomical number.

Can the universe have made all 10 to the 260th possible proteins length 200? There are 10 to the 80th power particles in the known universe. The shortest timescale is 10 to the −43 seconds, the Planck timescale. So if all 10 to the 80th particles were operating in parallel for each 10 to the −43 seconds to make proteins length 200, and the universe is 13.7 billion years old, which is about 10 to the 17th seconds, it would take the age of the universe raised to 10 to the 37th power to make all possible proteins length 200 just *once*.

This fact is fundamental. Since the Big Bang 13.7 billion years ago, the universe has made all 102 stable atoms: hydrogen, helium, carbon, to uranium and beyond. But the universe can have made only an infinitesimal fraction of the possible complex molecules, each with many atoms. A protein length 200 amino acids, for example, has about 4,000 atoms. The physicist's phrase, "ergodic," means, rather roughly, that the system does all that is possible in the time available. For example, if a drop of milk is placed at the center of a cup of coffee, rather shortly thereafter the drop will have diffused all throughout the cup of coffee to a homogeneous distribution. This is the well-studied subject of equilibrium statistical mechanics, invented by L. Boltzmann in 1884. (This is the famous "Second Law of Thermodynamics" that C.P. Snow said too few people in the world of literature understood.)

Our simple example shows that, above the level of atoms, the universe is vastly non-ergodic. This has physical meaning. History enters when the space of what can possibly happen is vastly larger than what does happen.

History is child of the non-ergodicity of the universe. The enormous non-ergodicity of the universe means that *most complex things will never exist*. This fact raises a profound puzzle. Every human reading this article has a human heart. Human hearts are very complex things. Then, why do hearts exist in the non-ergodic universe above the level of atoms?

We know the outline of the answer. Human hearts pump blood, whose circulation in the body helps keep the human alive. Humans have children, so our species propagates in the biosphere. As this happens, surviving humans carry along the hearts that sustain their lives, and heritably pass the heart to their offspring down the generations.

The central conclusion is that hearts exist in the non-ergodic universe above the level of atoms by virtue of the fact that by pumping blood the heart keeps the organism alive and propagating descendant organisms that carry with them their hearts.

The biological *function* of the human heart is to pump blood. But the heart also makes heart sounds and jiggles water in the pericardial sac. These latter causal consequences of the heart are NOT the function of the heart. Thus, the function of an organ is typically a *subset* of its causal consequences. Here the function of the heart is its causal pumping of blood, not its making heart sounds or jiggling water in the pericardial sac.

In sum, hearts exist in the universe in virtue of their *function* in sustaining the whole organism of which the heart is a part. The whole organism propagates offspring that bring with them the hearts by which the whole organism is sustained (Kauffman, *A World* 13–16).

5 kantian wholes

A foundational concept is that of a "Kantian Whole." The amazing philosopher, Immanuel Kant, in about 1790 wrote, "In an organized being, parts exist for and by means of the whole." This is a Kantian Whole (Kant; Kauffman, *Humanity* 67–69; *A World* 8). Given such a system, the *function* of a part is its causal consequence that sustains the whole. If this is true, then already biology cannot be reduced to physics. Functions pick out subsets of the causal consequences of parts. Physics talks about *all* the causal consequences of a "thing" but cannot pick out any preferred subset of these.

The origin of life *is* the origin of Kantian Wholes.

I now introduce the fifty-year-old concept of "collectively autocatalytic sets" (Kauffman, *A World*; "Cellular"; "Autocatalytic"; Farmer, Kauffman, and Packard 50–67). Consider a set of three small proteins: peptides, say thirty amino acids in length. Catalysts speed up chemical reactions in their approach to chemical equilibrium. Let peptide 1 catalyze the formation of peptide 2 by ligating (gluing) two fragments of peptide 2 together to create a second copy of peptide 2. Let peptide 2 catalyze the formation of a second copy of peptide 3 by ligating two fragments of peptide 3 to create that second copy of peptide 3. Let peptide 3 catalyze the formation of peptide 1 by gluing two fragments of peptide 1 to create a second copy of peptide 1. This is a "collectively autocatalytic set" of three peptides. Note that no peptide catalyzes its own formation. The set as a WHOLE collectively catalyzes the formation of all three peptides.

This three-peptide collectively autocatalytic set is a very simple example of a Kantian Whole. Each peptide exists for and by means of the whole set of three peptides. The function of each peptide is to catalyze the formation of the next peptide in the set. Each peptide also jiggles water in the Petri dish. Jiggling water is not the function of each peptide. So again, the function of a part is a *subset* of its causal consequences.

Such collectively autocatalytic sets of peptides have been created experimentally. Gonen Ashkenasy at the Ben Gurion University in Israel has a nine-peptide collectively autocatalytic set reproducing in his laboratory (Wagner and Ashkenasy). His set is a Kantian Whole where, indeed, the function of each peptide is to catalyze the formation of the next peptide around the cycle of nine peptides. A powerful implication of this set of nine reproducing peptides is that molecular reproduction does *not* depend upon nucleic acid polymers such as DNA or RNA, as described further below. Life need not be based on nucleotide polymer replication as commonly held.

6 living cells are collectively autocatalytic sets, hence kantian wholes

The cell is the minimal unit of life. Already in Newton's time, Joseph Hooke studied a thin slice of wood under an early microscope and noted what he called "cells." Cells are bounded by a membrane which is a bilipid structure with pores that control what molecules enter and leave the cell, and receptors on the membrane recognize such molecules. Transmembrane pumps control influx and efflux. Inside the cell are the chromosomes housing the famous DNA double helix. The genes of a cell are encoded in the specific sequences of the four bases: A, T, C, and G, along the DNA strand. Triplets of these bases – for example, CCA – code for specific amino acids in the famous "genetic code." The DNA encoded genes are copied, or transcribed, into a sister molecule, RNA. The triplets along the RNA specify sequences of amino acids that are linked together by peptide bonds to form the newly synthesized protein. The ribosome, a structure of peptides and RNA, creates these peptide bonds.

Thousands of different small molecules are linked in the metabolism, where the reactions among these molecules are catalyzed by protein enzymes encoded by genes. Among the thousands of protein products, some form linear structures, or fibrils. Molecular motors hold and transport other molecules, like cargo across the cell, to defined destinations.

Genes turn one another on and off. The protein specified by one gene can transcribe another gene into its RNA or help or block that transcription into RNA. Bacterial cells have some 3,000 genes. Humans have about 23,000 genes coding for proteins. Thus, the human cell links about 23,000 genes into a network in which genes turn one another on and off, rather like twinkling Christmas tree lights. Humans have about 300 distinct cell types: nerve, liver, muscle, and so on. We know that each cell type is a different stable pattern of the genes blinking on and off, or in different patterns of steady on or off activity (Kauffman, *Origins* 441–522; Huang, Emberg, and Kauffman). Living cells are Kantian Wholes. No molecule alone creates a second copy of itself. In dividing cells, thousands of metabolic and other "tasks" are collectively achieved, hence are Kantian Wholes. The *function* of each such process is the causal consequence that sustains the whole living reproducing cell. Functions are real in the universe.

7 the origin and evolution of life

Life on earth started about 3.7 billion years ago. The Hadean earth had an ocean and volcanoes that created land masses above the ocean, rather like Hawaii today. On land, rainfall led to shallow pools near volcanoes, draining to the ocean. Such environments were rich in a high diversity of many thousands of small organic molecules, metals, and so forth. The atmosphere was largely nitrogen, with no oxygen (Deamer).

No one knows how life started. A first favorite theory is that life started with long double stranded RNA molecules that could copy themselves by template replication. This is the RNA World hypothesis (Gilbert). A second hypothesis (Kauffman, "Autocatalytic"; Farmer, Kauffman, and Packard; Hordijk and Steel) is that life started with the spontaneous formation of collectively autocatalytic sets of small organic molecules, then peptides and RNA, followed by the emergence of long double stranded RNA or DNA that could template-replicate. Plausible sites for life's origin are deep water hydrothermal vents, rich in organic matter, or volcanic hydro-fields with freshwater pools subject to repeated evaporation and refilling. Such wet–dry cycles add energy to the system that can drive the linking of amino acids together to form peptides, or nucleotides to form long

RNA polymers. Such polymers, housed in hollow lipid vesicles called "liposomes" which can grow and bud, may be the origin of early protocells. Experiments on all these fronts are underway (Deamer).

This 3.7-billion-year process of evolution has created on earth the most complex system of which we know. If life is abundant among the 10 to the 22 solar systems, life is a major feature in the evolution of the universe. Life may well be abundant. By five billion years ago, the universe had "cooked up" a high diversity of organic molecules, perhaps 60,000 or perhaps millions of molecular species of the organic atoms, CHNOPS: carbon, hydrogen, nitrogen, oxygen, phosphorus, sulfur. Such diversity is found on a meteorite, the Murchison, which fell in Australia. The Murchison was formed five billion years ago as the solar system formed. Today, on Enseladus, a moon of Jupiter, a similar diversity is found.

If small-molecule, collectively autocatalytic sets form easily in such rich mixtures, the universe was everywhere ripe for life five billion years ago. A group led by Joana Xavier and Bill Martin (Xavier et al.), have recently reported finding small-molecule, collectively autocatalytic sets in bacteria and archaea from more than two billion years ago, before oxygen was in the atmosphere. Each set has no polymers, no DNA, RNA or proteins, yet it reproduces.

Each set has about 1,500 types of molecular diversity and 1,500 reactions. The two sets, bacteria and archaea, overlap in a collectively autocatalytic metabolic set of about 800 molecular species. This suggests that this group of about 800 autocatalytic sets precedes the divergence of bacteria and archaea billions of years ago, and that highly diverse soups of small molecules can indeed form self-reproducing collectively autocatalytic sets. The universe may indeed have everywhere cooked up molecular reproduction eight billion years after the Big Bang. The universe may be rife with life.

We can imagine, then, how early life on earth propagated and organized itself through a process involving non-equilibrium living cells. This created the three great branches of life: bacteria, archaea, and eukaryotes – cells with nuclei. For the first two billion years, life consisted of single-celled bacteria, archaea, and more complex eukaryotic cells with nuclei housing their chromosomes. Among these, stentor are amazing. A single-celled organism, it lives attached to rocks as a filter feeder. If confronted by toxic molecules, it averts its "mouth" area. Confronted a second time, it averts its "mouth" more rapidly. If still confronted with toxins, it "vomits" by turning its insides out. Yet more toxin, and the stentor inverts its "stomach" and crawls off to a new safer location. As Peil points out, the stentor samples its world, evaluates it "good or bad for me," and acts. Such evaluation – good or bad for me – is the onset of value in the universe. The stentor has values. So do all living things. Acting in the world is "agency." All living things are agents: self-reproducing, non-equilibrium systems doing thermodynamic work cycles, able to choose and act on their own behalf in their worlds: "yuck" vs. "yum" (Kauffman, *Investigations*; *A World*). This is how we begin to move from "matter to mattering." Sensing the world, evaluating "good or bad for me," and acting is, Peil suggests, the first sense, which is emotion. Later, as life evolves, more fully developed emotions evolve, and with it, eventually, our ethics.

Multicellular life arose six times, about 1.4 billion years ago. In sexual multi-celled organisms, most cells give up propagating progeny forever, and die with the organism. Only sperm and egg pass on down the generations. With multicellularity, about 650 million years ago in the Ediacaran, rather complex worm-like organisms, among others, arose. The stunning Cambrian Explosion was 550 million years ago, well studied from the Burgess Shale (Gould). Almost all later phyla arose in the Cambrian. Vertebrates arose in the next, Ordovician period. This plethora of multi-celled life branched into the phyla and lower taxonomic groups. Today, there are millions of species, many dying in the mass extinction our growing global economy is causing.

Organisms create niches for one another. The trunk of a tree has a hole that houses a woodpecker. Life's branching organisms create new niches faster than new organisms arise to live in those new niches. The biosphere explodes in diversity. Organisms "make a living" with one another: my refuse is your food. My solid surface affords a place on which you can crawl or run. Reindeer run on the permafrost. The permafrost now melts, the reindeer stagger, the Lapps lose their herds after thousands of years of a stable lifestyle. We all make our livings with one another.

Evolution is not all increasing diversity. Small and large extinction events have dotted the past 550 million years. There have been five large extinction events. The largest, the Permian, some 255 million years ago, wiped out 94 percent of all species. It is thought that this extinction was caused by increased atmospheric CO_2 which increased over several hundred thousand years. Current climate change is increasing CO_2 dramatically by the decade. If one million species will be extinct by 2050, how large will this mass extinction be, quantitatively speaking? Qualitatively, we are in the process of destroying the collective knowhow, hard-won, of millions of species that have come into existence over 3.7 billion years, creating niches for and making their livings with one another. In destroying accumulated life on this planet, we know not what we do – and, so far, we seem not to care.

8 no laws entail the becoming of the biosphere: logos bounded, eros unbounded

I turn now to my major claim: no entailing law governs the becoming of our, or any, biosphere in the universe – a universe of perhaps 10 to the 22nd in size, flowering in abundance. The context of this claim and its prospective importance reaches all the way back to Pythagoras and his dream. Aristotle said that scientific explanation is deduction. All men are mortals. Socrates is a man. Therefore, Socrates is a mortal. This basic model, in which the logical force of the premise, if true, entails the conclusion, later becomes classical and then quantum physics.

Modern physics begins with Copernicus and his advocacy of a heliocentric world view, in 1543. Kepler, using the data of Tycho Brahe, showed that planetary orbits are ellipses, not circles, with his three mathematical laws. In 1621, Galileo watched swinging chandeliers in church and saw that the period of the oscillation was independent of the amplitude. The same Galileo, around 1630, diluted gravity using shallow incline planes and found that by rolling balls down the plane, the distance covered increased as the square of the time elapsed. Pythagoras had claimed "All is Number." Here was the Pythagorean dream 2,000 years later. The motions in the heavens and on earth were governed by mathematical laws.

Then the claw of the lion: Newton, with his three laws of motion, universal gravitation, and his invention of the calculus, differential and integral, soon after reading Euclid. Newton is probably the greatest scientist in history, surely in physics. From him comes the foundation of classical physics. In 1684, he united the motions of heaven and earth and indeed, those of the entire universe. Newton's laws are entirely deterministic. Given initial and boundary conditions, integration of his differential equations yield the deduced, hence entailed, future behavior of the system. That behavior, the trajectory of the system, is fixed forever. The universe is a clockwork. With Newton, the struggle between science and religion increased because on this view, God could cause no miracles. By the Enlightenment, the Theistic God had disappeared in learned Europe, replaced by a Deistic God. God set up the universe and stepped aside for Newton's laws to govern what would happen, forever. God became the God of the Gaps where science had not yet reached.

Even more importantly, perhaps, Newton taught us how to think within the Newtonian Paradigm: (1) Write down laws of motion for your system in differential equation form. (2) State the initial conditions. For billiard balls on a table, these are the positions and momenta of all the balls on the table. (3) State the boundary conditions. For billiard balls, the boundary conditions are the shape of the edges of the table. These boundary conditions specify the "phase space" of the system. For the billiard balls, the phase space is the set of all positions and momenta of the balls on the table. In the physics of the Newtonian Paradigm, it is always essential to state ahead of time the phase space of the system. The behavior of the system in time is a flow, or trajectory, in that state space. (4) Integrate the differential equations to yield the logically deduced, hence entailed, trajectory of the system in its state space. For billiard balls, this entailed trajectory is the motion of the balls for all time, ignoring friction – and also, their motion backward in time, for Newton's laws are time reversible.

The Newtonian Paradigm stands astride all of physics. Between Planck's discovery of the quantum of action in 1900, and the formulation of the Schrödinger linear wave equation in 1927, physics confronted a major crisis. The moment when a radioactive decay occurs is entirely random. Thus, there can be no determinate cause in the Newtonian sense. Similarly, in quantum mechanics, it is extremely well confirmed that randomness cannot be eliminated from events. That randomness is not epistemological uncertainty, as in classical physics, but ontological. If this is true, the becoming of the world, even at the level of physics, is not deterministic. This was a major crisis for science. Determinism had to be abandoned. Einstein never accepted this. As he famously quipped, "God does not play dice with the universe."

For all of that, however, quantum mechanics remains entirely within the Newtonian Paradigm. The Schrödinger linear wave equation is entirely deterministic. However, instead of determining the trajectories of balls in a phase space, the Schrödinger differential equation, upon integration, yields a determined trajectory of a probability distribution. The probability distribution is the probability that a given quantum event happens at some time and place in the universe.

In fact, all of contemporary physics and chemistry are within the Newtonian Paradigm. Weinberg's "Dream of a Final Theory" is within the Newtonian Paradigm. The dream is to unite the four fundamental forces – gravity, electromagnetism, the Weak Force and the Strong Force – in a single theory. Much has been done. Weinberg himself played a major role in uniting the electromagnetic and the Weak Force. Gell-Mann and Zweig discovered quarks and gluons binding quarks in atomic nuclei. Quantum Chromo Dynamics describes this Strong Force. The current standard model of particle physics unites all three quantum forces and is amazingly confirmed by work at CERN and elsewhere. The Higgs particle has recently been discovered, bringing the standard model to completion. All are within the Newtonian Paradigm. So too is Einstein's magnificent Theory of General Relativity. But the search for a means to unite the classical physics of General Relativity with quantum mechanics, the twin pillars of twentieth-century physics, has so far met with no success. This union would be Weinberg's fulfilled "Dream of a Final Theory": Pythagoras redux.

I am about to tell you that the evolution of our, or any, biosphere in the universe is entailed by no law at all. We can now say, probably for the first time in science since Pythagoras and Newton, that the becoming of biospheres falls entirely outside the Newtonian Paradigm. The reason, as we shall see, is that the very phase space of biological evolution – which includes biological functions – persistently evolves in ways that we cannot even prestate, let alone predict. Without a prestated phase space, we can write no law of motion in the form of differential equations, hence we cannot integrate the equations we do not have. Thus, no laws at all entail the stunning unfolding of our, or any, biosphere in the universe. But our biosphere is the most complex system we know. So, no *law* is required for the amazing, ever-creative becoming of biospheres. Reality is not what we have thought – quite the contrary. Moreover, Weinberg's "Dream of a Final Theory" is dead. Biospheres are part of the universe, of course, and if no law entails the becoming of biospheres, then no final theory entails all that unfolds in the universe. There is and can be no Final Theory. With this realization, Logos is bounded, and Eros unleashed. As did the ancient Greeks, we live with the creativity of Eros, seen in the ever-creative becoming, beyond any entailing law, of biospheres. The world of Eros is embedded in the laws of physics, but it is also a world beyond physics. The third crisis for physics, then, beyond the indeterminism of quantum mechanics that remains firmly in the Newtonian Paradigm, is that *no law* "governs" the ebullient unfolding of a biosphere.

9 eros anew

The universe, then, is truly non-ergodic above the level of atoms. Most complex things will never get to exist. One way to get to exist as a complex entity in the non-ergodic universe is to be a living evolving "Kantian Whole." As Kant said, "In organized beings, the parts exist for and by means of the whole." Vertebrates with hearts, for example, are Kantian Wholes. And as we saw earlier, the function of the heart is a subset of its causal consequences: pumping the blood that helps keep the whole organism alive. The essential issue, however, is that hearts only get to exist in the non-ergodic universe by virtue of their causal role in sustaining the whole organism of which they are parts. The evolving vertebrate lineage since the Ordovician some 500 million years ago propagated Kantian Wholes, and with them their evolving hearts, in all their complexity.

Or, think of cells and organisms. Hearts exist in the universe by virtue of their functional role in sustaining the organism. But so too, do the fibrils traversing cells and the molecular motors that do thermodynamic work to crawl back and forth along these fibrils carrying their needed freight around the non-equilibrium reproducing cell. So too, do the flagellar electric motors with a rotor and a stator, rotating the flagellum clockwise or counterclockwise to move up a sugar gradient for food. The stripes of the zebra, the eye of the octopus, the loop of Henle in vertebrate kidneys that concentrates urine: all exist in the non-ergodic universe by virtue of their functional causal roles in sustaining the Kantian Whole, the living, evolving organisms of which they are parts. The issue, then, is this: can we have a deductive theory that, like those of Newton and Schrödinger, entails the becoming of these adaptations since the origin of life 3.7 billion years ago? The answer is NO. And the reason is what I call "Tinkering."

Nobel Laureate François Jacob wrote about evolution as a process of ongoing tinkering, or "bricolage" in French. Evolution stumbles upon new uses for structures and processes that already exist and grafts these new uses into the organisms in which they arise. The amazing flagellar motor in bacteria arose precisely in this way. This motor is a jury-rigged, tinkered-together contraption of the unused causal features of the several initial molecules that came together to form a new combination and found a new function. And from their new combination, the new stator–rotor electric motor system emerged.

Evolution is rife, of course, with Jacob's tinkering, in which unused causal features of parts of organisms come to be used for novel functions. Such new uses arise due to what are called Darwinian "pre-adaptations," or by Stephen Gould, "exaptations." Consider again the heart. Darwin would tell us that the heart evolved, hence exists in the non-ergodic universe, by virtue of its function of pumping blood. But again, the heart makes heart sounds and jiggles water in the pericardial sac. Darwin brilliantly pointed out that such "unused" causal features of an organ might, in some different environment, come to be of selective value. Darwin did not mean by "pre-adaptation" that evolution had foresight, but rather that some causal feature of no selective and functional use for an organism in a first environment, might, by chance, have selective value in another environment.

A favorite example of a pre-adaptation is the swim bladder. Some fish have a swim bladder where the ratio of air and water in the bladder tunes neutral buoyancy in the water column. Paleontologists think the swim bladder evolved from fish with lungs. Water got into a fish's lung, which was now partially filled with air and water. Such a lung was poised, in turn, to evolve into a swim bladder. Once the swim bladder evolved as a new causal consequence of a sac filled with air and water, a new function (detecting neutral buoyancy) came to exist in the evolving biosphere. The swim bladder is a complex structure that gets to exist in the non-ergodic universe by virtue of the function it performs in the Kantian Whole: the fish with a swim bladder that lives and propagates over generations.

Something stunning is happening here. Once the swim bladder exists, it affords what I will call a new "Adjacent Possible" empty niche. A worm or a bacterium could evolve to live only in swim bladders. Now let's ask: did natural selection play a role in crafting a functioning swim bladder? Of course, natural selection played a role (crafting) such that functioning swim bladders evolved. But did natural selection craft the swim bladder *so that* it could constitute an Adjacent Possible empty niche into which a worm or bacterium could evolve? NO. This means that evolution is creating its own future opportunities without selection (in the Darwinian sense) *determining* them. Without selection achieving it, evolution creates its own future pathways of becoming. Evolution, due to variation and natural selection, is then "sucked into" the very opportunities it creates, only to create yet more opportunities (Kauffman, *Humanity* 64–98; *A World* 115–38). This is a kind of magic.

Let's now ask whether we could anticipate, or prestate, *all* possible Darwinian pre-adaptations for *all* organisms – or even merely humans in the next three million years. How would we do this? What new environments might arise, calling for new uses tinkered together to "solve" some adaptive problem? What are these uses, or tasks? How might they be met by the particular, and changing, features of existing organisms? We cannot answer these questions exhaustively. We cannot "prestate" all possible Darwinian pre-adaptations.

To make the impossibility of "prestating" all such pre-adaptations clearer, I now present what I call "The Screwdriver Argument" (Kauffman, *Humanity* 64–82; *A World* 115–22). I hand you a screwdriver, say in New York, in 2020. You tell me all the things you can do with a screwdriver, by itself or together with other things. Well, you can screw in a screw, open a can of paint, stab someone, scrape putty off a window, wedge a door open, wedge a door closed, smash a window, tie the screwdriver to a stick and spear a fish, rent the spear to the locals for 5 percent of the catch, and so on. My favorite use of a screwdriver is to lean it against a wall, prop up a plywood board on the end of the screwdriver and place a wet oil painting beneath the plywood board to keep the painting dry in case of rain.

So, is the number of uses of a screwdriver in New York in 2020, by itself or in conjunction with other things, a specific finite number like 16? Is the number infinite? Is the number "indefinite?" In fact, the number of uses of a screwdriver is not a specific finite number, but neither is it infinite, for there is no iterative process of counting its possible uses, like N and $N+1$ to infinity. The number of uses of a screwdriver is, in fact, indefinite.

Next point: there are four ordering relations in mathematics: a nominal scale in which there is no ordering; a partial ordering in which X is greater than Y and Y is greater than Z, so X is greater than Z; an interval scale, like a thermometer, in which 3°C is greater than 2°C by the same interval as 2°C is greater than 1°C; and a ratio scale where two meters is twice the length of one meter. The different possible uses of screwdrivers are merely on a nominal scale. There is no ordering relation between the different uses. These features of indefinite and unordered uses of things (e.g., screwdrivers) implies the following: no rule-following procedure – that is, no algorithm – can list all the uses of a screwdriver alone or with other things, nor compute the next new use of a screwdriver. Finding new uses of screwdrivers is not an algorithmic problem. Neither is evolution. The evolution of the biosphere is rich with jury-rigged pre-adaptations (new uses of the screwdriver). But as we have just seen, we cannot deduce that new use! We cannot logically or algorithmically derive all the new uses of things, or all the new functions, that come to exist in the evolving biosphere.

For example, all that has to happen in the evolution of some bacterium in a new environment is that some molecular screwdriver "find a use" that enhances the fitness of the bacterium in that new environment. Then, thanks to heritable variation and natural selection operating on the Kantian Whole of the bacterium, that new use, hence new function, may come to exist in the evolving biosphere. The molecular screwdriver and its new function – and the organism housing it – will get to exist for some period of time in the non-ergodic universe. But because we cannot list all the uses of screwdrivers, nor deduce the possible new uses of a screwdriver, we cannot *PRESTATE* what those uses will be. The issue here is vastly different from the difficulty of *PREDICTING*. Consider throwing a fair coin 100 times. We do not know if it will come up heads fifty-five times. But we can use the binomial theorem to calculate the probability it will come up fifty-five times. Critically, in the case of the coin flip, we know all possible outcomes of 100 flips of a coin. We know the "sample space" of the process, in which any particular outcome itself is a random process. But in the case of the evolution of the biosphere into the Adjacent Possible that it itself creates, we do *not* know the sample space of the process. We not only do not know what *will* happen, we do not even know what *can* happen. We cannot say what is "in" the Adjacent Possible of the evolution of the biosphere. Our incapacity to prestate possible future pre-adaptions is not a failure to predict; it is something far more profound. Because we do not know the sample space of the process of evolution, we cannot even define "random." Such a definition requires that the space of possibilities can be specified first, and then a process can contain random outcomes in that space of possibilities. But here, we can form no probability calculus for the becoming of the biosphere into its unprestatable Adjacent Possible.

10 no law entails the becoming of a biosphere

In physics, we always prestate the phase space: for example, as we saw earlier, the phase space of the billiard balls on a specified table. But, as we just saw with our screwdriver example, we cannot prestate the ever-changing phase space of biological evolution – and for reasons that reach far beyond the "unpredictable" and the "random." Because we cannot prestate the ever-changing phase space of the evolving biosphere, we can write no laws of motion for that evolution in the form of differential equations. Therefore, we cannot integrate the equations we do not have. And therefore, *NO LAW* entails the evolution of our, or any, biosphere (Longo, Montévil, and Kauffman). No Law. No deducing of all new uses of all things for all unprestatable tasks and functions. The rotation of flagella, molecular motors pulling cargo along fibrils, swim bladders, flight feathers, hearts that pump blood: all are part of the ever-changing phase space of evolution. Is it any wonder that no one could have predicted, three billion years ago, that the capacity of an elephant to spray water on itself via its trunk would help it survive three billion years later?

Kant said there would never be a Newton of a blade of grass, and he was right. We cannot "do Newton" for the evolution of biospheres. Three hundred and thirty years after his *Principia*, we are, with evolving life, beyond the Newtonian Paradigm. And we are beyond Pythagoras. It is not true that All is Number, and the dream of a "final theory" that will entail all that becomes is dead. Life is based on physics, Logos, but is a world beyond it. The becoming across time of biospheres is one of untellable creativity in which evolution creates and becomes into the opportunities that it itself, unprestatably, creates.

11 story

The becoming of life for 3.7 billion years is a Raphael tapestry richly interwoven, one that tells the story of millions of species and their populations that strut and fret their hour upon their stages and then, indeed, are heard no more. Shakespeare was right, as ever. The widely branching Tree of Life, entailed by no law, is the stuff of story, of narrative. If we cannot deduce what will happen, we can only tell the tale afterwards. We can reconstruct the history of life, as we have done with Darwin and paleontology. Story is needed where deduction fails us. So, here are the same facts, again, but a different story. From 3.7 billion years ago: protocells, single-celled prokaryotes and eukaryotes, multi-celled organisms, the Cambrian explosion, the Phanerozoic with thirteen phyla, the vertebrate lineage with fish, amphibians, reptiles, mammals. The hominid lineage branched from the broader Primate lineage about three million years ago with *Australopithecus*, followed by *Homo erectus*, *Homo habilis*, and us, *Homo sapiens*, with our cousin, *Neanderthal*.

We are social primates; our behaviors and ethics evolved with us. Franz de Waal did a wonderful experiment with two capuchin monkeys. The two were in adjacent cages and could see one another. For days, de Waal gave each monkey a slice of cucumber in the morning. One day he gave a grape to one monkey and a slice of cucumber to the second. Enraged, the second monkey spat out the cucumber, shook the cage door, and screamed out his anger: "It isn't fair!" Thence our evolved sense of justice, or so de Waal surmised. From single-cell stentor to all organisms, emotion has evolved with the increasing complexity and diversity of the worlds we make with one another, our *Umwelt*s (Hoffmeyer). As biosemiotics stresses, the bat lives in a "bat world," the dog in a "dog world," the trout in a "trout world," and we, in a "human world." Life has evolved from "approach or avoid" to the rich filigreed structure of our own legal systems.

The first of the hominid lineage, *Australopithecus*, was the first to fashion stone tools, some dozen in number and crudely made. Hundreds of thousands of years passed, and tools improved at a glacial pace. Knife blades grew longer by a few centimeters over hundreds of thousands of years. Compound tools, such as knife blades grafted to a bone handle, emerged about 300,000 years ago, perhaps with the emergence of *Homo sapiens*. In many ways, we are the same species we were 300,000 years ago. Our technology evolved at the same glacial pace again for another 200,000 years, with a gradual increase in the number of tools and their gradual differentiation into more and more complex tools. *Cro-Magnon* inhabited the Périgord region in the south of France and the north coast of Spain some 30,000 to 15,000 years ago. The *Cro-Magnon* museum in Les Eyzies has a magnificent collection of superb pressure-flaked stone tools, arrow heads, needles, fishing hooks, spears, axe heads, bracelets, chisels, and polishing stone; the atlatl, the compound spear thrower that allowed *Cro-Magnon* to hurl spears at aurochs from meters away; and shallow stone hollows and shells to hold dried fern wicks for candlelight. The cave wall paintings at Lascaux, world famous, rival Picasso for line and form. What rites were held there? *Neanderthal* buried their dead and had needles and flutes 60,000 years ago.

With this evolution of simple to more complex and valuable tools, inequality also arose. Tim Kohler and his colleagues studied sixty-seven Neolithic sites from about 30,000 years ago and found clear evidence of inequality in the divergent distribution of living quarters (Kohler et al.). Another Neolithic site shows many graves, three with adolescents buried with complex necklaces comprised of thousands of beads brought from several hundred miles away. These bespeak inequality and inherited wealth. In *The Great Leveler*, Walter Scheidel pursues such clues in the larger context of 10,000 years of violence and collapse: a history of inequality.

The agricultural revolution was some 8,000 years ago. In the Near East, wild grasses were domesticated. Food diversity shrank, as did human stature, but food could be reliably stored. The plow transformed agriculture. The first empires arose: Egypt, Mesopotamia, in the Indus Valley, and China 5,000 to 4,000 years ago. Thus, about 7,000 years after hunter-gatherer *Cro-Magnon*, with its few hundred tools ranging from simple to more complex – we find in Mesopotamia perhaps 1,000 tools, ranging from the needle Neanderthal had 60,000 years ago to something as complex and laden with value as the chariot.

Ancient Greek culture flourished 2,500 years ago: Eros and Logos, the gods, the Fates, chance and contingency, Thales, Anaximander,

Democritus, Socrates, Plato, Aristotle, Sophocles. From 4,000 years ago, the Jews and the monotheism of the Abrahamic Traditions arise. From 1,000 to 500 BC, the Axial age (Bellah and Jonas): Buddha, Confucius, Socrates, Plato, Jeramiah. Humanity seeking something beyond the god of the hunt. And then, the Roman Empire, from 300 BC to about AD 300: Lucretius and *De Rerum Natura*, and Emperor Constantine's adoption of Christianity for the Empire in AD 313, Ptolemaic astronomy with its hypercycles to explain the wandering orbits of the planets.

St Augustine AD 400: The City of God, that founds much of Church Doctrine. And for almost 1,000 years in post-Rome Europe, people ignored this life, seeking their salvation in the next. Aristotle is lost in the West but survives in the Islamic world from AD 632 on, brought to Spain by Maimonides to Andalusia. With the reintroduction of Aristotle in the West, Aquinas, in *Summa theologicae*, argues in AD 1268 that both the Old and New Testaments (but also Nature) are God's work. It becomes permissible to study this world. The Scholastics flourish, and universities are founded in Paris and Padua. Cervantes writes *Don Quixote* in 1615.

The earth is at the center of the universe, surrounded by the celestial spheres carrying the moon, the sun and the stars. God is above, below are the angels, below is Man, below Man are large animals, then worms, then the concentric levels of Hell. Humanity is the center of all things, enjoined by God, who commands Adam to name the animals and take dominion over all things. Then Copernicus, using the data of Tycho Brahe, proposes that the earth revolves around the sun, a heliocentric view last suggested by the ancient Greeks but lost. Galileo, using a simple telescope, sees the four moons of Jupiter. If the tiny moons revolve around giant Jupiter, why not tiny earth around the giant sun?

Consider the Church. Its cosmology for over 1,000 years was Ptolemaic, with the earth at the center of the universe, as Cervantes had written. All revolved around Man poised between God, heaven, and the deepest level of hell. If the views of Copernicus and Galileo held, the moral order of the Church and Western World would be lost. Galileo faces the Inquisition formed to block such moral insurrection; he faces house arrest and mutters "*E pur si muove.*" "And still it moves." Galileo's courage becomes the moral rallying cry of science: truth. Then Kepler, Newton, and Laplace and his demon, who, knowing the positions and momenta of all the particles, could compute the entire future and past of the universe. This is the birth of modern Reductionism. And Nobel Laureate Steven Weinberg dreams of a "Final Theory" in which Logos, law, is all. But this, as we have seen, is only half the story.

So where are we now? Our toolkit has grown exponentially, from a glacial pace over millennia to an explosion: hundreds of tools in the global economy ten millennia ago, billions today. For millennia, the needle Neanderthal had 60,000 years ago and its modest improvements; today, the Space Station. Our $100 trillion growing juggernaut global economy overwhelms the planetary biosphere that has flourished for 3.7 billion years. And here we are in the so-called Anthropocene, with global warming and a mass extinction event underway. Humanity has never faced such a crisis, either in scale or in existential terms.

What will the 7.7 billion of us do? What can our diverse civilizations weave together in the face of this crisis? We have, perhaps, a new origin myth: our becoming in the long flowering of our biosphere. We *are* of Nature, not above Nature. Life, our selves among it, is magical, is sacred. A transnational mythic structure is subtended by our membership and participation with all of life.

The Gospel of John begins:

In the Beginning was the Word.
The Word was with God
The Word was God
The Word became flesh and dwelt among us.

I prefer to read this passage with a different sense of the sacred. What more could we want from all the gods of our past 300,000 years – the gods of the stone, the stream, the willow, the volcano, the moon, the sun, Zeus, Athena, Diana, Mercury, Thor, Woden, the God of Abraham and the Axial Age – but that the gods afford us the opportunity to co-create our shared reality?

disclosure statement

I have no grants and am free to publish this work.

bibliography

Bellah, Robert, and Hans Jonas. *The Axial Age and its Consequences*. Cambridge, MA: Harvard UP, 2012. Print.

Deamer, David. *Assembling Life*. Oxford: Oxford UP, 2019. Print.

Farmer, J.D., S.A. Kauffman, and N.H. Packard. "Autocatalytic Replication of Polymers." *Physica D* 2 (1986): 50–67. Print.

Gilbert, Walter. "Origin of Life: The RNA World." *Nature* 319 (1986): 618. Print.

Gould, Steven J. *Wonderful Life*. London: Norton, 1989. Print.

Hoffmeyer, Jesper. *Biosemiotics*. Scranton: U of Scranton P, 2008. Print.

Hordijk, W., and M. Steel. "Chasing the Tail: The Emergence of Autocatalytic Networks." *Biosystems* 152 (2017): 1–10. Print.

Huang, Sui, I. Emberg, and S. Kauffman. "Cancer Attractors: A Systems View of Tumors from a Gene Network Dynamics and Developmental Perspective." *Seminars in Cell & Developmental Biology* 20.7 (2009): 869–76. doi:10.1016/j.semcdb.2009.07.003. Print.

Jacob, François. "Evolution as Tinkering." *Science* 196 (1976): 1161–66. Print.

Kant, Immanuel. *Critique of Judgement*. 1892. Trans. J.H. Bernard. New York: Hafner, 1951. Print.

Kauffman, Stuart. *Humanity in a Creative Universe*. Oxford: Oxford UP, 2017. Print.

Kauffman, Stuart. *Investigations*. Oxford: Oxford UP, 2000. Print.

Kauffman, Stuart. *Origins of Order*. Oxford: Oxford UP, 1993. Print.

Kauffman, Stuart. *Reinventing the Sacred*. New York: Basic, 2008. Print.

Kauffman, Stuart. *A World Beyond Physics: The Emergence and Evolution of Life*. Oxford: Oxford UP, 2019. Print.

Kauffman, S., and P. Clayton. "On Emergence, Agency and Organization." *Biology and Philosophy* 21 (2006): 501–21. Print.

Kauffman, S.A. "Autocatalytic Sets of Proteins." *Journal of Theoretical Biology* 119 (1986): 1–24. Print.

Kauffman, S.A. "Cellular Homeostasis, Epigenesis, and Replication in Randomly Aggregated Macromolecular Systems." *Journal of Cybernetics* 1 (1971): 71–96. Print.

Kohler, T., et al. "Greater Post-Neolithic Wealth Disparities in Eurasia than in North America and Mesoamerica." *Nature* 551 (2017): 619–22. Print.

Longo, G., M. Montévil, and S. Kauffman. "No Entailing Laws, but Enablement in the Evolution of the Biosphere." *Proceedings of the Fourteenth International Conference on Genetic and Evolutionary Computation Conference Companion*, 2012. 1379–92. doi:10.1145/2330784/2330946. Print. Also: <http://dl.acm.org/citation.cfm?id=2330163>.

Peil, K.T. "Emotion: The Self-Regulatory Sense." *Global Advances in Health and Medicine* 3.2 (2014): 80–108. Print.

Sagan, Carl. *Cosmos*. New York: Random, 1980. 175–85. Print.

Scheidel, Walter. *The Great Leveler*. Princeton: Princeton UP, 2018. Print.

Snow, C.P. *The Two Cultures*. Cambridge: Cambridge UP, 1959. Print.

Wagner, N., and G. Ashkenasy. "Systems Chemistry: Logic Gates, Arithmetic Units, and Network Motifs in Small Networks." *Chemistry: A European Journal* 15.7 (2009): 1765–75. Print.

Weinberg, Steven. *Dreams of a Final Theory*. New York: Pantheon, 1992. Print.

Xavier, J., W. Hordijk, S. Kauffman, M. Steel, and W. Martin. "Autocatalytic Chemical Networks Preceded Proteins and RNA in Evolution." *Proceedings of the Royal Society B: Biological Sciences*, 11 Mar. 2020.

Stuart Kauffman

Although the term "epigenetics" has been around in its current form since geneticist Conrad Hal Waddington introduced it in 1940, interest in this scientific field has spiked dramatically in the past several decades. Scholarly books on the topic proliferate. The field appeals to so many because it seems to have a wide range of potential applications. To researchers interested in social, racial, and gender justice, the epigenetic dimension seems to hold exciting promise to free us from the idea that we are what our genes make us and enable us instead to identify those factors beyond genetics that shape us to become who we are [...] Did our grandmothers face starvation during pregnancy, leaving us a legacy of weight problems or undernourishment? Did a toxic physical or social environment limit our lung capacity or stress us so that we became vulnerable to depression? Epigenetics seems to reach from the body to society, holding out hope to illuminate issues as diverse as the development of gender identity; the intergenerational impact of slavery, war, or starvation; the range of factors that make us more vulnerable to depression or psychosis [...] (Susan Merrill Squier 1–2)

This epigraph is taken from the first lines of Susan Merrill Squier's 2017 book *Epigenetic Landscapes: Drawing as Metaphor*. She uses it to frame and undermine the hype surrounding epigenetics. Not unlike genomics in the early 2000s and the genome editing technology CRISPR-Cas9, the potential for epigenetic research is seemingly unlimited. For once development and inheritance systems are no longer reduced to the mechanistic programs of the modern evolutionary synthesis, all of a sudden

adam nocek

THE EPIMEDIAL LANDSCAPE

old questions about soft inheritance (Lamarckism) and organic selection (the Baldwin effect) that had long been disqualified seem tenable and raise much broader questions about social, cultural, and political inheritance systems (Jablonka and Lamb; Gissis and Jablonka). While this may satisfy the desires of certain media-consuming publics, it also squares with the research of an increasing number of scholars in the theoretical humanities and social sciences who work on epigenetics (Squier; Bono; Grosz; Malabou) and critical genealogies of inheritance systems that exceed gene-centric programs of human and nonhuman evolution (Stiegler; Leroi-Gourhan; Simondon). In short, epigenetics opens up domains of research at the intersection of the biosciences, theoretical humanities, cultural anthropology, media and technology studies, and more.

Accompanying this wave of excitement is an equally strong, and not unrelated, surge of interest in complex dynamical systems. Increasingly, epigenetics researchers are modeling with complex dynamical systems. This is largely because epigenetic regulation is proving to be too complex, which is to say, involves too many levels of nonlinear self-organization over multiple scales of time, to rely on the tried and tested methods of wet experimentation and linear models of information exchange (Ringrose; Hall). Consequently, in the last few decades research on epigenetic regulation has increasingly become a subset of mathematical complexity: emergent regulatory systems are modeled using nonlinear differential equations that run on sophisticated computer software. This turn toward complexity is not lost on the theoretical humanities either. The connection running between epigenetics and complexity has proven to be fertile ground for theorists in the humanities searching for different models of theoretical rigor (DeLanda; Protevi), systems of vital and energetic exchange that overturn the hegemony of cultural and linguistic paradigms of knowledge production (Grosz; Malabou), or alternative genealogies of cultural and critical theory (Marks). Whatever the case, epigenetic complexity has come to dominate both the scientific and humanistic discourses on the extra-genomic regulation of development and evolution.

One of my interventions into this expanding discourse on epigenetics is that the theoretical humanities require a critical frame for assessing the relation between epigenetics and complex dynamical systems. More than this, they need to think critically about the computability of epigenomic regulation (proposed by the complexity sciences), as well as speculatively about the possibility of an epigenomics beyond complexity. Save mild skepticism issuing from the analytical tradition of process philosophy (see Henning and Scarfe; Koutroufinis, "Teleodynamics"),[1] there is little in the literature from the biological turn in continental thought indicating a deep conceptual grasp of the dynamical systems view of epigenetics. This stems not only from a failure to engage with the mathematics of complexity, but also from a failure to engage with its history.

Both epigenetics and the application of complex dynamical systems to biology originate in the mid-twentieth-century work of Conrad Hal Waddington. In what follows, many of the uses and abuses of Waddington's work will be discussed, as well as how they inform contemporary paradigms of epigenetic complexity. What will become clear from this genealogical analysis is that Waddington's thought continues to shape the dynamical systems view of epigenetics, although for reasons that often undermine the original spirit of his work. The use of nonlinear differential equations to calculate the probability of developmental and evolutionary trajectories will solidify this point. What will emerge in the course of this discussion is that the so-called original spirit of Waddington's thought is largely derived from the work of Alfred North Whitehead, and that it is ultimately Whitehead (in close proximity to Waddington) who helps to reinvigorate a philosophical conception of epigenomics beyond the mathematics of complexity. What will also become clear is that this vision of epigenomics is made possible by engaging with the mediating function of the epigenome. This will bring media philosophy right into the center of critical and speculative work on the development and evolution of biological systems. Ultimately, the "epimedial landscape" serves as a first pass at a media philosophical revision of the complex dynamical systems view of the epigenetic landscape.[2]

In order to gain critical perspective on the role of mediation within epigenetic research, we first need to understand the genesis of a certain style of mathematical and computational reasoning about the epigenetic landscape in Waddington's work. From there, difficulties surrounding the meaning and extension of epigenetic computability begin to take shape, as does the attendant need for a philosophical conception of epigenetic mediation.

epigenetics: a complex landscape

Epigenetics is a term coined by the theoretical biologist C.H. Waddington. Elsewhere, I have written about Waddington's thought in the context of contemporary theoretical biology, focusing on how it is central to understanding onto-epistemological tensions within the complexity sciences (see Nocek, "Transcendental Biology"). Part of this piece demonstrated that Waddington is most often remembered today for his pioneering work on two interrelated fields: epigenetics and complex dynamical systems. The fact that these domains of research are thoroughly entangled in twenty-first-century bioscientific research says very little about historical causality. In fact, biologists embraced neither epigenetics nor complexity in Waddington's day, leaving each field to have its own, albeit deeply interwoven, reception history.

Epigenetics, for its part, was originally conceived in order to account for Waddington's experiments with developing embryos. Waddington discovered that the induction of certain phenotypic variations (e.g., the crossveinless phenotype) through environmental changes could be passed on, even in the absence of the original stimulus (see Waddington, "Canalization of Development"; "Genetic Assimilation"). What this meant is that nongenetically produced traits could be inherited (reactivating Lamarckian schemes of soft inheritance) and that neo-Darwinian causal schemes could not explain evolution and development *tout court*. The epigenotype was coined in order to explain how extra-genetic environments (gene products, as well as other cellular and noncellular environments) mediate the communication between genes and traits. As Angela Oliveira Pisco and her colleagues explain in relation to the confusion over the meaning of epigenetics today, "Waddington focused on development in his quest for a [...] basis of the genotype–phenotype correspondence and in this context he first coined the notion of the 'epigenotype' as a mediator between the two" (Pisco, Fouquier d'Hérouël, and Huang 9). The epigenotype, Waddington explains, is "the entirety of the developmental processes through which the genes produce the phenotype," and this is a developmental reality that undermines the strict genetic determinism guaranteed by the modern evolutionary synthesis ("The Epigenotype" 10).

It is well known that Whitehead's "philosophy of organism" was an important inspiration for Waddington's theory of epigenetics. Not only did Waddington reportedly give up the study of geology for biology after reading *Science and the Modern World* (Peterson, "Excluded Philosophy"), but many of the most important features of his epigenetic system are also derived from Whitehead's philosophy of organism. For instance, the idea that genetic and epigenetic systems are not isolated or entirely separate is very much in line with Whitehead's proposal for an organic cosmos. For Whitehead, entities do not influence each other by bumping up against one another as they do in the history of Western metaphysics; rather, they actually enter into the constitution of each other. Entities become what they are because of the way they incorporate other entities into their own becoming (*concrescence*). Hence, there is no dualistic opposition between self and other: the self just is its integration of others. This is why Whitehead explains that his philosophy of organism is "mainly devoted to the task of making clear the notion of 'being present in another entity'" (*Process and Reality* 50). For Waddington, this meant that genes and environments are thoroughly entangled systems that enter into the constitution of the developing or concrescing system: "In the cells of higher organisms," Waddington notes, "we are not usually, if ever, confronted by the switching on or off of single genes. What we find is a whole complex cell becoming either a nerve or a kidney or a muscle cell" ("An Autobiographical Note" 9).

Waddington offers a concrete illustration of this non-dualistic theory of development in his epigenetic landscape. The epigenetic landscape is both a visualization and a conceptual diagram that maps the unfolding relation between genes and environments by tracing their production of developmental pathways (or creodes) for an undifferentiated cell.

Waddington's well-known depictions of a landscape of diverging valleys illustrate how an undifferentiated cell can move in and out of a developmental trajectory depending on the depth of the valley. The steepness of the slope corresponds to the degree to which the system has been "canalized": a concept borrowed from Whitehead (who borrowed it from Henri Bergson) that indicates the degree to which a developing system can withstand perturbations from its environment (*Process and Reality* 104). Finally, the depth and course of each valley is determined by the unfolding relation between genes (represented by pegs and guy ropes in the diagram) and extra-genetic factors (Waddington, *The Strategy of Genes* 29, 36).

The fact that the wider biological community did not warmly embrace Waddington's epigenetic landscape should not come as a surprise: the climate of bioscientific research in the first half of the twentieth century was such that all evidence for extra-genetic inheritance was cast aside, and anything left behind was swiftly absorbed by the gene-centered programs of the modern evolutionary synthesis (see Dobzhansky). What's more, Waddington's theories were tainted by the organicism of Whiteheadian metaphysics, which did not sit well with the Newtonian physics underwriting neo-Darwinian mechanism (Peterson, "Excluded Philosophy"; Bono). In the last few decades, however, epigenetics has taken center stage in evolutionary and developmental biology. One explanation for this is that gene-centered research programs could no longer make the promises they once could in the pre-genomics era. This story has been rehearsed many times in the historical and scientific literature (Trewavas; Bruggeman and Westerhoff; Stevens), but it bears repeating that in the wake of the Human Genome Project where experimental and theoretical biology are now dominated by the use of Big Data analytics in omics-wide research programs (i.e., genomics, proteomics or metabolomics), genetic regulatory networks (GRNs) and certain extra-genetic materials have been shown to mediate (by regulating) gene products and undermine older commitments to genome-centered theories of evolution and development (Saunders; Champagne et al.; Tebbich, Sterelny, and Teschke; Ringrose).

However, the so-called "return" of epigenetics has less to do with a return to a forgotten theoretical paradigm than it has to do with the evolution of its conceptual architecture. What Waddington meant by epigenetics is not what contemporary bioscientists mean by epigenetics (see Pisco, Fouquier d'Hérouël, and Huang; Hall). This is true even though references to Waddington in the scientific literature have sharply spiked in the last several years (Bateson 198). If for Waddington, epigenetics refers to the wider environment of extra-genetic processes that mediate gene expression, then for most contemporary biologists, epigenetics means something far more circumscribed: namely, the molecular regulatory machinery responsible for DNA methylation and histone modification. Today, molecular epigenetics bears only a vague resemblance to the holistic conception that we find in Waddington (Pisco, Fouquier d'Hérouël, and Huang), and in most cases the former has done little to dispense with the old Newtonian mechanism that dominated molecular biology (more on this below).

There is an entire history that explains the rise of molecular epigenetics (which passes through the work of Holliday and Pugh, and Riggs on DNA methylation and the research on covalent modifications of histone proteins), as well as the more recent attempts to supplement strictly molecular accounts of epigenetic regulation with broader and more functional conceptions of the epigenome (echoing Waddington's original notion). These latter conceptions are prominent in the works of Eva Jablonka, Marion J. Lamb, and others, which contend that there are multiple inheritance systems, and that there may even be evidence to suggest that development can make heritable modifications to the DNA sequence (Jablonka and Lamb). But as Adam Scarfe is quick to point out, even if these latter conceptions of epigenetic regulation seem far from mainstream (even "avant-garde"), they still endorse the mainstream effort to identify the precise *mechanisms* of epigenetic regulation, even when these mechanisms include behavioral and symbolic systems (377–78). In short, contemporary epigenetics is still bound by the metaphysics of mechanism; it's just that the mechanistic account has gotten more complex.

It is largely this search for causal mechanisms that has led to the widespread use of complex dynamical systems in epigenetics research (Ringrose; Hall; Pisco, Fouquier d'Hérouël, and Huang). But like epigenetics, the complexity sciences have their own complicated reception history in the biosciences. As I discuss elsewhere,[3] mathematical formalism was met with hostility in most domains of biological research laboring under an experimental paradigm for much of the nineteenth and twentieth centuries (Keller). This is true of early efforts to formalize morphological and developmental complexity in D'Arcy Wentworth Thompson and Alan Turing (ibid.; Gould; Longo); but it is also true of mid-century efforts to apply cybernetic systems and information theory to evolutionary and developmental biology (Kay), as well as later attempts to model "fitness landscapes" (Kauffman and Johnsen). The early successes of experimental genetics and molecular biology made it hard for mathematical formalism to make inroads: the latter seemed largely incapable of dealing with the messy realities of wet systems (Keller).

However, the post-genomics era has ushered in a new appreciation for mathematical modeling. The inundation of molecular and cellular data has left molecular biologists unequipped to connect molecular parts to intracellular and extracellular wholes. In this new data-intensive landscape (which has also given new life to epigenetics) differential equations capable of modeling nonlinearity and self-organization over multiple timescales are now required in order for biologists to understand the context of their work (Trewavas). Thus, if the complexity sciences made waves in mathematics, engineering, and physics throughout the twentieth century (Érdi), then it would take a data deluge for them to be genuinely useful to working biologists.

If there is still any lingering doubt over whether Waddington's concept of the epigenome is still meaningful to contemporary biologists, then there is little question about his epigenetic landscape: it is a crucial early example of a complex dynamical system. In Waddington's own terms, the epigenetic landscape is a "multidimensional phase space" that involved a level mathematical abstraction biologists were not accustomed to at the time (*The Strategy of Genes* 27). This has not been lost on contemporary biologists either (Saunders; Gunawardena; Tronick and Hunter). As the complexity theorist Peter T. Saunders writes,[4]

> Waddington was aware that one should think of development in dynamical terms and he even wrote down some equations as an indication of how this might be done [...] For we can define a dynamical system as a manifold with a vector field defined on it. In other words, we describe a dynamical system by specifying the complete set of possible states, the phase space, and then providing rules that tell us at each point in the space where to go next.[5] (46)

Waddington realized that in order to model the developmental and evolutionary trajectories of an organism, he could not rely on the theoretical dogma that accounted for evolution in terms of small genetic changes (the modern synthesis). He needed a model of organization that was robust enough to demonstrate the exact opposite: namely, that "a small change in the landscape can have a significant effect on the organism if it occurs just where it can divert the ball down a different path," and that "the mode of evolution suggested by the epigenetic landscape is precisely that of punctuated equilibria" (45). Ultimately, "[t]here is nothing mysterious about the properties that Waddington identified as typical of developmental systems," explains Saunders, "they are likely to be found in any complex system which can be modeled by non-linear differential equations" (48).

And so if the mid-twentieth century was largely inhospitable to Waddington's approach to systems modeling, then the climate of data-intensive biology is now such that complex dynamical systems are at the center of efforts to understand the mechanisms regulating the development and evolution of organisms. According to the physicist Paul Davies, epigenetics is a natural fit for complex systems modeling. This is because the epigenome displays

> a web of causation, both upward and downward in length scale, with complex feedback loops leading to many possible stable and unstable states. Generally, an explanation for a biological process will entail both upward causation – such as when a gene is switched on and makes a protein that affects cell and organismal behaviour – and downward causation – when a change in the environment triggers a response all the way down to the gene level [...] The necessity to consider organisms as systems subject to both upward and downward causation complicates causal reasoning and presents a challenge to physical scientists used to thinking of step-by-step cause and effect. The subject of systems biology attempts to get to grips with this fundamental and unavoidable characteristic of life. (Davies 43)

nonlinearity in biological systems modeling

While it would be impossible here to provide an overview of modeling epigenetic systems using complex dynamical systems (with nonlinear differential equations), it is nevertheless useful to review some basic features of nonlinearity, largely because the possibilities and limitations of nonlinear mathematics are widely misunderstood in the overzealous endorsement of complexity in the theoretical humanities. In doing so, I wish to pay special attention to what it is possible to model and understand about epigenomic systems when nonlinear differential equations are used. For if the prevailing scientific conception of epigenomics is framed by nonlinear mathematics, then we need to get clear on what these mathematical tools make it (im)possible to say about epigenomic mediation.[6] For the sake of clarity, I will limit myself to a narrative description of nonlinearity without introducing another layer of abstraction by using mathematical notation.[7]

As a point of comparison, note that linear ordinary differential equations (ODEs) tend to have one critical point and are very often solvable. Nonlinear differential equations, on the other hand, which tend to be the most important type of differential equations for modeling epigenetic systems, have multiple stable points and trajectories and cannot be solved so easily, if at all. In fact, there are only a few exact solutions to nonlinear differential equations, although solutions are often possible if the equations are linearized (see Kadiyala). The linearization of nonlinear differential equations is commonly practiced in epigenetic modeling (Saunders 48). In any case, one of the consequences of having multiple stable points and trajectories, and Waddington knew this decades ago, is that a system headed on a trajectory can withstand a certain amount of perturbation without changing its course. This is the significance of canalization in Waddington's landscape model.

However, where many stable trajectories coexist in the same phase space (which is a space that maps all possible states of a system), it is possible for systems to move between trajectories given the right circumstances. But these circumstances do not have to be large perturbations to the system. In fact, an essential feature of modeling with nonlinear differential equations is that very small changes in the environment can induce large-scale effects. This has proven to be especially useful to biologists trying to understand how organisms change their developmental and evolutionary trajectories even after being exposed to slight variations in the environment. As Waddington observed, *Dorsophilia* can pass on the crossveinless phenotype after being exposed to small doses of heat shock ("Canalization of Development"; "Genetic Assimilation"). Nonlinear differential equations are useful because they are especially good at modeling how large effects can be induced by small changes.

What's more, an essential feature of nonlinear systems is that these large effects cannot be traced back to specific causes. What this means is that an effect may have multiple sources. This is particularly relevant to efforts in theoretical biology to overcome neo-Darwinian causal schemes: phenotypic transformations cannot be traced back to specific gene mutations. Rather, nonlinear equations express how the same phenotypic transformation can be induced by different genetic and epigenetic sources. (This also explains why there can be consistency of organismic development despite genetic and epigenetic differences – different causes, same effect.) But in order for small changes to produce large-scale effects the system has to become less stable somehow. This is what permits small and otherwise inconsequential perturbations from having a major effect on the overall system – e.g., speciation (Saunders 49–50). The prevailing assumption in evolutionary and developmental biology is that genes that were silent are now "switched on" (via GRNs), although according to this model of epigenetic regulation, genes are always on, it's just that the epigenetic system is now vulnerable to very small changes shaping the developmental trajectory of an organism (50).

We can now summarize several basic features of using nonlinear differential equations to model epigenetic systems. Essentially, they model systems that: have multiple stable points and trajectories; that are capable of undergoing large-scale changes (change of trajectory) induced by relatively small changes in the environment; that have effects with multiple causes; and that are irreducible to their parts (the whole is greater or less than the sum of its parts). Of course, there are many aspects of using nonlinear differential equations to model epigenetic systems that are not captured in this description, although this rudimentary characterization suffices for the analysis that follows.

It's clear that Waddington intuited many features of nonlinear dynamical systems with his epigenetic landscape.[8] Despite its importance, scientists note that his model is largely unequipped to explain the complexity of actual epigenetic systems. This has less to do with a flaw in his thinking about dynamical systems,[9] than it does a limitation in the two-dimensionality of his model (Saunders 49). Because Waddington was not computing in higher dimensions, he was not able to model how a developing system can have many "neighboring" trajectories.[10] In other words, the epigenetic landscape is deceptively simple. However, today's biologists are modeling multidimensional systems, and as such they are able to describe systems that have many neighbors at once. It's as though each valley in the epigenetic landscape were surrounded by multiple (instead of two) trajectories (Saunders uses the example of a "multi-core electric cable"), and only a few of them are viable paths (Waddington's two-dimensional model cannot depict this). This ultimately increases the model's ability to make predictions about the course of development. And for epigenetic researchers (from the molecular to the holistic), predicting the likelihood that the presence of *this* chemical gradient will induce *that* heritable phenotypic change is foundational to understanding the causal mechanisms that underlie epigenetic regulatory systems. What morphological events are likely to happen given certain conditions are met? Can a probability distribution be calculated for them? Can these developments be controlled and redesigned (see Davila-Velderrain, Martinez-Garcia, and Alvarez-Buylla)?

It's crucial to note here that making predictions using differential equations ultimately depends upon the relation set up between constants and variables in the mathematical model.[11] The constants are the parameters whose values are set in advance and limit the system's ability to develop. This is something that Waddington clearly understood: "[a] system can be completely defined by a set of parameters and the functional relations between them. These parameters may stand for concentrations, quantities, rate constants, temperature, time, distance, volume, etc." (*The Strategy of Genes* 224). What this means is that if parameters are the carefully selected constants that limit the development of the system, then differential equations are the "rules" that allow us to say at every point in the phase space where the developing system will most likely go (see Saunders 46).[12] Thus, given the selection of certain parameter values, the phase space of the system can be constructed, and the probability of one event occurring over another can (ideally) be calculated (see Longo and Montévil, "Extended Criticality").

I bring this up in order to show how the complexity sciences may not be able to make good on many of their promises to map the regulation of phenotypic development. As evidence for this claim, let me emphasize that *scientists* determine the parameters of the system and not the systems modeled. This is significant because if you vary the parameters over time, then the system tends to behave differently. Waddington notes this phenomenon in *The Strategy of Genes* and writes that in many cases changing parameter values will create "initial effects" that,

> set into operation a chain of further effects whose outcome is the eventual cancellation (or partial cancellation) of the initial effect. Thus, its main characteristic is that of the feed-back. An important aspect of its operation is that there is a time-lag between the onset of the change and the completion of the compensatory process. The range of this time-lag extends from fractions of seconds to years, and on this basis important distinctions between "physiological responses" and "acquired characters" have been made. (227–28)

What this illustrates is that parameters are artifacts of the modeling environment that affect how systems behave in that environment. This is obvious enough to anyone who models with nonlinear differential equations (the art of parameter selection is essential to model design), but their effect on our understanding of the developing organism is rarely noted. It is much more common to celebrate the many affordances of complex dynamical systems, as well as the design of algorithms to solve nonlinear differential equations (Khan), than it is to get bogged down in ontological and epistemological questions concerning the (non-)computability of organismic development.

But when we do get bogged down in these messy questions Waddington reappears as someone to whom we should pay close attention. At the outset of *The Strategy of Genes* he notes that biological and physical systems differ in their relation to time: "to provide anything like an adequate picture of a living thing," writes Waddington, "one has to consider it as affected by at least three different types of temporal change, all going on simultaneously and continuously. These three time-elements in the biological picture differ in scale," and they are: evolution, life history, and physiology (6). The trouble is that it is impossible to parameterize so that the effects that these vastly different scales of time have on the regulation of gene products are brought to bear at every point in phase space. Saunders notes just this problem in his study of complex epigenetic systems. He explains that the time of development lies at the intersection of evolutionary and physiological change, but that, "[b]iologists, faced with the immense complexity of organisms have naturally tended to look at the three time scales separately, and physiology, developmental biology and evolution exist as separate disciplines" (Saunders 61).

These are convenient abstractions for mathematicians. However, they obscure the fact that all three scales of time interact, and development in particular is in the crosshairs of the other two.[13] Saunders' response to this problem is telling: "it is certainly hard to imagine how biology could progress if we had to take absolutely everything into account all the time. The subject is hard enough as it is" (ibid.). This pragmatism has its consequences though: biological systems are treated as if they were physical systems. Developing systems are modeled as if these vast differences in rates of change were not ingredients in the determination of phenotypic trajectories in phase space; such differences are thought to be negligible for running a computer simulation. Developing embryos are regarded as though the extra-genetic factors mediating development can be isolated and predictions can be made.

These are just some of the useful fictions that biologists working with complex dynamical systems must leverage. These fictions conceal their own artifice by rhetorically reframing Waddington's epigenetic landscape as a mere metaphor (or an unscientific fiction of organic holism), rather than as a harbinger of the complex organization of the living (see Pisco, Fouquier d'Hérouël, and Huang). That Waddington drew so heavily on Whitehead's "philosophy of organism" for his epigenetic landscape should come as no surprise then. If for Whitehead there is no entity in isolation, then this means every entity is connected to every other one in some degree of relevance. Such metaphysical connectionism proves unbearable for models of epigenetic regulation whose reliability (which is to say, ability to compute the probability of certain outcomes) depends upon eliminating from mathematical relevance that from which the model abstracts.

In recent years, a handful of theoretical biologists have tempered the excitement over the complexity sciences. In particular, Giuseppe Longo, working in the close company of Maël Montévil, Stuart Kauffman, Francis Bailly, and others, has shed light on the fact that no theory of biological systems currently exists (Longo and Montévil, *Perspectives on Organisms*). This is not to say that there are no theories of biological organization. It's to say that they reduce biological organization to systems of physico-mathematical organization, and this does not square with the organization of actual living systems. For if modeling the behavior of a nonlinear dynamical system requires that all its possible trajectories are determined in advance by selecting relevant parameters, then these methods cannot capture the behavior of actually existing biological systems. Determining which interacting scales of temporal change, or which transformation in temperature or pressure concentration over which periods of time, are going to be relevant to a developing system, and in which ways, has to be resolved by the developing system at each point in phase space. According to Longo and Montévil ("Protention and Retention"), this is why the internal dynamics of a living system cannot be externalized in a physico-mathematical model of complexity.

What this means is that the models of mathematical complexity used to describe the behavior of physical systems are not adequate for describing the behavior of biological systems.

As Koutroufinis writes, mathematical models of biological systems would need to be able

> *to calculate a significant part of [their] parameters* – namely, to dynamize those quantities which in today's modeling are kept constant, or in other words, to convert most of the parameters into variables and let the overall system's dynamics calculate their value. ("Teleodynamics" 324)

Given that such computational systems do not exist (even if some think that they may one day), scientists must settle for solving the problem of what is left constant and dynamic in an epigenetic model in advance of the system solving it for itself. As a consequence, calculating the probability that one trait is more likely to be produced than another given the influence of predetermined environmental factors tells us more about the model than it does an actual organism (Davila-Velderrain, Martinez-Garcia, and Alvarez-Buylla). What an epigenetic landscape means for an organism is decided in the process of the organism's development; it is in continuous variation and therefore cannot be known in advance. If the pertinent environmental mediators have to be predetermined in order to run a successful computer simulation, then in actual living systems the conditions of developmental potentiality are immanently constructed from out of the material and energetic constraints of the organism. In short: what the epigenome is for an organism remains ontologically underdetermined.

The physicist Paul Davies writes that "the epigenome is a useful concept," but he cautions us against using the notion like we do the genome: namely, an operating system that regulates the expression of proteins (48). This is a very different story than we typically hear from epigenetic researchers, some of whom even suggest that there is a "histone/epigenetic code" that complements the so-called "genetic code" (Jenuwein and Allis). For Davies, however, the epigenome has a much more complicated ontological status: it is neither physical nor mechanical; it is not even an actual object. Rather, it is "a virtual object (in contradistinction to the genome), as there is no identifiable 'command-and-control' centre, or instructions set or programme, etched into a physical system, from which epigenetic control ultimately emanates" (Davies 48). This does not mean that the epigenome is somehow less "real" because it is "virtual" and not computable; rather, and just the opposite: the epigenome is the real condition for the production of gene–trait relations. Davies also adds that complex dynamical systems are currently not in a position to accommodate the virtuality (or what amounts to the same thing, "reality") of the epigenome, since the latter involves "[a] more radical, strongly emergent description [that] would entail introducing an explicit coupling between dynamical laws and information-rich states" (ibid.). Davies explains that this would grant

> higher level entities, such as contextual information, with direct causal efficacy on matter alongside intermolecular forces. Although such a proposal represents a decisive break with the normal formulation of the theory of dynamical systems, a rich variety of self-organizing emergent behaviour is likely. So far, theories of this sort remain largely unexplored. (Ibid.)

Davies' proposition that the epigenome is a virtual object comprising a field of contextual relations that exceed the computational capabilities of nonlinear dynamical systems is likely to be a tough pill for theoretical biologists to swallow. But for theorists engaged in critical ontologies of the biosciences, this proposition announces the possibility of a critical philosophy of epigenetics. Of course, Davies invokes neither Deleuze nor any other philosophical framework to support his thesis about the virtuality of the epigenome. Yet, in many ways, his thesis serves as a conceptual bridge between the limits of nonlinear dynamical systems discussed by an increasing number of theoretical biologists, information theorists, and physicists (as noted above) and the affirmation of irreducible difference as the condition for the immanent genesis of potentiality (virtual conditions) that has been the abiding concern for many scholars working in the critical humanities and post-humanities.

For critical media philosophers in particular this conception of the epigenetic landscape sheds important light on the mediating function of the epigenome: mediating the relation between the genotype and phenotype is an entire field of material, energetic, and temporal forces. This is not a new proposition of course: Waddington knew it, and experimental and theoretical biologists have known this for some time. In fact, the mediating function of the epigenome is what scientists working with nonlinear differential equations are trying to understand: namely, the probability that the environment will interfere with the expression of certain traits (see Pisco, Fouquier d'Hérouël, and Huang). For this reason, I would argue that a media theory of epigenomics is deeply engrained in the working practices of the biosciences. But the proposition that epigenomic mediation is not transparent, and that its comprehension via sophisticated computational models is forever differed, does not square with the conception of mediality currently entertained by theoretical biologists. But if this less transparent, or even murkier, conception of mediation is implicit in the critical work of Longo, Kauffman, Davies, and others, as well as some of Waddington's work on the epigenetic landscape, then it needs to be made explicit in a fresh conception of epigenomic mediality. What I call the epimedial landscape is a first attempt at such a conception.

from mediality to epimediality

Before I conclude, I want to sketch some relevant features of the epimedial landscape, as well as the conceptions of media that are likely to be of service in our articulation of it. I noted that this murkier conception of media abandons the idea that there is a direct communication between gene and trait through an epigenetic medium. This is not the conception of media currently entertained in the biosciences. For if many bioscientists have given up on the fantasy of unmediated communication between genotype and phenotype (the Central

Dogma of molecular biology), then they have not lost faith in the idea that mediation between these two registers can become transparent to thought. This is largely the job of nonlinear dynamical systems: to clear up the murky waters of epigenomic mediation and enable scientists to understand the mechanisms by which mediation occurs. Among other things, complex systems modeling permits scientists to map feedback systems, demystify causal relations, and calculate probabilities, all of which ensure that predictions can be made. While this surely oversimplifies matters, it nonetheless serves the heuristic function of illustrating how the chasm that separates genotype and phenotype in the wake of molecular reductionism is less substantial because of a third term: the epigenome is what brings these heterogeneous domains into closer proximity.

In media theoretical terms, dynamical systems theory frames the epigenome as a medium that brings two heterogeneous orders into a communicative relation. Following Sybille Krämer's conceptual genealogies of media, current epigenetics research would seem to fall somewhere within a history of media that does not erase the medium (which is to say, treat it as disruptive to the transmission event that occurs between sender and receiver), but embraces its essential function in bringing about the communicative relation as such. In this view of the communication, the medium is central to information exchange: it is, in short, its generative condition. Yet, in managing to bridge the gap between material systems something curious happens to the medium in Krämer's view: it disappears. To understand why, note that in the act of putting two heterogeneous systems into relation the medium overcomes the distance that separates them. If distance and separation are presupposed for the communicative act, then mediation is what allows the divergent system not only to hold something in common, but also, and more fundamentally, to unify previously "impenetrable inner worlds" (Krämer 23). According to Jürgen Habermas, who is perhaps the most well-known advocate of this position, the medium transforms heterogeneity into homogeneity, difference into identity, such that no distance, heterogeneity, or irreducible excess remains. But in this case, the medium itself is no longer essential to the relation. Here's Krämer:

> media are peripheral and negligible vehicles that provide undistorted and unmediated access to something that they themselves are not, much like transparent window panes. Because the dialogical relationship results in the annihilation of distance and the direct experience of reciprocal understanding, which happens precisely when two individuals in their own inner worlds agree and "merge," there is no more space for a mediator or a medium. (Ibid.)

While the comparison between the dynamical systems view of epigenetics and Habermas' theory of communicative action may seem exaggerated, there are nevertheless certain advantages to making it. For one, it allows us to reflect on how the prevailing view of epigenetics does not get us far beyond (or perhaps not at all) the models of linear information transfer that dominated the previous era of molecular biology. If the epigenome mediates between heterogeneous systems (systems whose heterogeneity has become especially clear in the wake of the Central Dogma), then it is in order for genes and gene products to become legible to one another. Insofar as there is an abyssal line separating the genotype and phenotype – and any attempt to map one onto the other in the post-genomics era makes this separation shockingly clear – then the epigenome is a theoretical–mathematical entity that crosses this line for scientists. Indeed, the reason to map epigenetic regulation through nonlinear differential equations is to overcome division, to reduce heterogeneity, and ultimately to make these two realms (more) transparent to one another. While this model of transparency is surely a fantasy inherited by Western scientific modernity, it still animates the dynamical systems view of epigenetics. This fantasy plays itself out every time a mathematical model fails to accommodate the fact that: (1) the epigenetic landscape is not an epistemological object that resolves the difference between heterogeneous series; and (2) the paradox of epigenetic mediation is that in connecting heterogeneities it does not stop reestablishing their separation. So far, mathematical modeling has not been able to accommodate this paradoxical form of mediation.

In her assessment of media philosophical frameworks, Krämer proposes a more radical genealogy of mediality that connects Walter Benjamin's theory of translation, Jean-Luc Nancy's notion of community, Michel Serres' conception of communication, Régis Debray's theory of the immaterial ideas, and John Durham Peters' theory of non-reciprocal communication. The points of convergence among these otherwise unrelated theories is that they all affirm conceptions of mediality in which: there is always presumed to be an unbridgeable "difference between communicants"; media do not overcome this difference (for the sake of identity), but rather connect by maintaining the difference between them; and communication is always a non-reciprocal act (Krämer 72). While there are other principles of mediality that Krämer derives from these five conceptions, suffice it to say that these are the ones that ground her notion of media that resonates most explicitly with the mediating function of the virtual epigenome. In particular, the epigenome is not a transparent windowpane, and it does not resolve the difference that exists between genotype and phenotype. Connections are borne out of a mediating relation that does not pre-exist the terms of the relation. As such, every connection is singular, which means that the heterogeneity of these two orders does not stop being reestablished in epigenetic mediation. Epimediality is characterized by the fact that heterogeneity is renewed with each act of mediation.

dis/connecting: epimedial landscapes

I want to end here by noting a possible philosophical partner in our sketch of the epimedial landscape: namely, Whitehead. If Waddington's epigenetic landscape is largely indebted to Whitehead's philosophy of organism, then I think we can close the circle by underscoring Whitehead's influence on an updated theory of the epigenome. While an overview of Whitehead's metaphysics is well beyond the scope of this conclusion, I simply want to gesture toward a possible line of philosophical research on mediation in epigenetics.

In *Process and Reality*, Whitehead sets himself the task of overcoming the modern presumption that the world is ultimately composed of disconnected substances (substance metaphysics). However, he also wanted to articulate a speculative philosophy that could accommodate the fact that there are real experiences of disconnection. The world is experienced as both deeply connected and radically isolated. To neglect or reduce either one of these poles of experience would be to commit the "fallacy of misplaced concreteness," which is the "accidental error of mistaking the abstract for the concrete" (Whitehead, *Science and the Modern World* 52). The conjunction of these twin intuitions (connection and disconnection) is perhaps best captured in Whitehead's well-known formula: creativity "is the ultimate principle by which the many, which is the universe disjunctively, become the one actual occasion, which is the universe conjunctively" (*Process and Reality* 21). In short: "The many become one, and are increased by one" (ibid.).

What this is supposed to capture is how the world is experienced as both divergent and convergent, and this duality is expressed in every occasion of experience, also known as an actual occasion of experience. To show this, Whitehead argues that every actual occasion (or entity) is a concrete integration of the many, which is another way of saying that an occasion *just is* the integration (or prehension) of diversity. The disjunctive many *become* one. This is how Whitehead overcomes the duality between the many and the one at the heart of Western metaphysics: the wealth of diversity over "there" enters into the constitution of what is most immediate right "here": "Actual entities," Whitehead explains, "involve each other by reason of their prehensions of each other" (*Process and Reality* 20; see also *Science and the Modern World* 69). However, causal efficacy is not only what is at stake here, since there is no bare repetition of the other's experience in the prehending occasion. If this were the case, nothing would happen, the world would not move. Difference cannot be overcome in identity (*pace* Habermas). If one entity actually enters into the constitution of another (which is required if Whitehead is to overcome metaphysical isolationism), then it would have to do so in a *novel* way (hence, the many "are increased by one").

What guarantees this divergence of perspectives is that one entity prehends another through the mediation of eternal objects. Without getting into a lengthy discussion of the metaphysics of these strange entities, suffice it to say that they function as pure potentials for definiteness (Whitehead, *Process and Reality* 22), which essentially means that eternal objects index a realm of potentials for feeling or integrating heterogeneity into experience. In short, eternal objects are potentials for *how* an entity might incorporate what is heterogeneous to it. These potentialities are what make the integration of heterogeneous perspectives possible without falling into the trap of dead repetition: they give what the other shares of itself a quality or tonality that is absolutely singular to *that* experience of sharing. This mediation ensures that the integration of another into experience is possible without it being subsumed under the umbrella of the same. What Whitehead spells out for us then, although it requires much further elaboration, is that what makes the coordination of divergent systems possible – potentials for feeling another – is also what guarantees that these systems maintain their heterogeneity.

Whether the mediation performed by eternal objects is similar enough to the mediation performed by the epigenome is for another discussion. There is a good chance that Deleuze's conception of virtual potentiality is closer to the epigenomic potentiality that we are looking for, though it would be worth examining the overlaps between Deleuze and Whitehead on potentiality and where they converge with epigenetics.[14] At a more abstract level, however, there is an implicit philosophy of media in Whitehead (that resonates in important ways with Krämer's theses on mediality) that illustrates how mediation occurs by means of actualizing potentials for the simultaneous connection and disconnection of systems. Thus, media conceived as the genesis of convergence and divergence is central not only to Whitehead's metaphysics (or at least that is what I am proposing), but also to any theory of epigenomics that wishes to grapple with how the separation between genetic and phenotypic systems does not stop being produced through the epigenetic systems that connect them.

Waddington was an early promoter of Whitehead's metaphysics. His enthusiasm (which was not shared by many other biologists at the time) had much to do with the philosophy of organism's insistence that there can be no disconnected systems. This relational holism helped Waddington critique the essentialism of the modern synthesis and propose that genes and their wider environments cannot be disarticulated in the development and evolution of phenotypes. If Waddington's work was not well received in the mid-twentieth century, then in the last few decades it has been warmly embraced. Despite this, metaphysical determinism is still at the heart of the discourse and practices of the biosciences: the epigenome is conceived as an operating system whose rules can be understood through differential equations. Advances in epigenetics promise to reveal how divergent series relate. The game is the same as it has always been; it's just that the rules have changed slightly. Now, the epigenome is a necessary mediator and complex dynamical systems theory is the language of mediation.

The trouble with this story, like all good modern scientific fantasies, is that it conceals the artifice that makes its determinism possible. But then what is the mediating function of the epigenome? Where is it and how does it function? If the epigenome is not an epistemic object with determinate rules that allow scientists to make predictions, then how is it going to be theorized? Ultimately, our detour through the philosophy of media is what allowed us to find our way back to Whitehead. But if Whitehead was called upon in the mid-twentieth century in order to ensure that the connection of systems (genetic and epigenetic) was not explained away in the service of mechanism, then he is called upon in the twenty-first century for a slightly different reason (still with the goal of undermining mechanism): to produce a philosophy of epigenetic mediation that maintains the heterogeneity of systems. Taken together, these two Whiteheadian moments in epigenetic thought illustrate the speculative service that his metaphysics can offer the biosciences generally: they ensure that both sides of the epigenetic system are kept together (convergence and divergence) so that bioscientists do not continue to commit the fallacy of misplaced concreteness in their comprehension of developing systems.

disclosure statement

No potential conflict of interest was reported by the author.

notes

1 This is not to diminish the contribution of analytical approaches to process philosophy. Increasingly, this work merges with the questions and concerns of theorists trained in the continental tradition. The overlaps have become most explicit in shared research on Whitehead's "philosophy of organism."

2 There are several conceptual genealogies that link biology, philosophy, and media that closely intersect what I am proposing with the "epimedial landscape." Epimedia is a neologism that brings together the science of epigenetics and media theory. By adding landscape to epimedia, I am also deliberately invoking the biological philosophy (or biophilosophy) implied by Waddington's epigenetic landscape. For this reason, and not unintentionally, the epimedial landscape is a notion that fits into a lineage of biophilosophy. Of course, biophilosophy itself has contested histories and meanings. On the one hand, it combines philosophy and biology, which gives it a natural affinity with the philosophy of biology in the analytical tradition (see Koutroufinis, *Life and Process*). On the other hand, biophilosophy is also thought to range over a much broader conceptual genealogy of living systems that "deal[s] with questions that arise out of biology but which biology cannot answer [...]" (Koutroufinis, *Life and Process* 3). If the philosophy of biology is a subset of biophilosophy, which Koutroufinis and others maintain, then biophilosophical thought is an umbrella term with diverse discourses and methods, indebted to a wide range of intellectual and disciplinary frameworks. Yet, epimediality is also related to notions of media and mediation that directly engage biological systems: namely, "biomedia" and "vital media," as well as related media theoretical constructions. These notions are both theoretical and practical responses to difficult questions (and anxieties) posed by the rapid development of biotechnology, bioinformatics, and BioArt/Design in the last several decades: what conceptions of life and media are adequate when biological organisms are media for technological, economic, and artistic intervention (Thacker; Mitchell)? The concept of epimediality shares many of these concerns (especially insofar as it fabricates a concept of media adequate to non-computable modes of organismic development and evolution), although it eventually draws on a different genealogy of media for its formation.

3 In my forthcoming monograph, *Molecular Capture: The Animation of Biology* (U of Minnesota P, 2021), I examine how experimental biologists were hostile toward mathematical formalism and systems theoretical analysis for most of the nineteenth and twentieth centuries. There are of course exceptions to this rule: Ludwig von Bertalanffy's work on systems biology was incredibly influential, and the musings of the Theoretical Biology Club also helped shape the intellectual trajectory of systems theoretical analysis in biology (Peterson, *The Life Organic*). In the main, however, it would take decades – after sequencing the human genome – for the methods and practices of systems biology to become relevant to working biologists.

4 Peter T. Saunders' chapter, "The Organism as Dynamical System," in Wilfred Stein and Francisco J. Varela's collection, *Thinking About Biology*, is one of the most systematic examinations of the relation between Waddington's epigenetic landscape and the mathematics of dynamical systems theory.

5 Saunders goes on to note that it is not entirely accurate to say that the epigenetic landscape is a

dynamical system, since the landscape merely illustrates some general features of developing systems. Rather, "[t]he epigenetic landscape represents a class of dynamical systems which share a number of important properties which are typically found in developmental systems. The mathematical problem," Saunders continues, "is to determine the properties of this class" (46).

6 Here I follow Saunders' discussion of nonlinear differential equations, mainly because the connections to Waddington's work come into full view.

7 For a thorough examination of nonlinear differential equations in biology, see J.D. Murray's *Lectures on Nonlinear Differential Equation Models in Biology*; and Guy-Bart Stan's course at Imperial College London, *Modelling in Biology*: <http://www.bg.ic.ac.uk/research/g.stan/2010_Course_MiB_article.pdf>.

8 As Saunders insists, "Waddington was aware that one should think of development in dynamical terms and he even wrote down some equations as an indication of how this might be done" (46).

9 As evidence for the usefulness of Waddington's conception of a dynamical system today, see NetLand: <http://netland-ntu.github.io/NetLand/>.

10 According to Saunders, Waddington's model is ultimately insufficient because

> each valley has only two neighbours, but in higher dimensions a path can have many neighbours: imagine a multi-core electric cable. This means, for instance, that there can be a very large number of dead ends and still a few viable pathways, which is not obvious from the picture. (49)

11 Spyridon Koutroufinis has an exceptional discussion of parameters and variables in complex dynamical systems modeling in his chapter, "Teleodynamics: A Neo-naturalistic Conception of Organismic Teleology."

12 For instance, using Lewis, Slack, and Wolpert's (1977) model of tissue development based on the concentration of a specific gene product, Saunders demonstrates that given a transition between states, one direction is more probable than another. What's more, the model even shows that phenocopying will only occur in one direction (Saunders 55, 62).

13 Here's Saunders: "[i]t is not simply a matter of the slowly varying quantities acting as parameters for the fast processes, of evolution setting the framework for development [...] fast process can profoundly affect the nature of a slow one" (61).

14 See James Williams' chapter, "Deleuze and Whitehead: The Concept of Reciprocal Determination," for an extended discussion of potentiality in Deleuze and Whitehead.

bibliography

Bateson, Patrick. "The Rise and Rise of Epigenetics." *The Systems View of Life: A Unifying Vision.* Ed. Fritjof Capra and Pier Luigi Luis. Cambridge: Cambridge UP, 2014. Print.

Bono, James. "Perception, Living Matter, Cognitive Systems, Immune Networks: A Whiteheadian Future for Science Studies." *Configurations* 13.1 (2005): 135–81. Print.

Braidotti, Rosi, and Simone Bignall, eds. *Posthuman Ecologies: Complexity and Process After Deleuze.* Lanham: Rowman, 2018. Print.

Bruggeman, F.J., and Hans Westerhoff. "The Nature of Systems Biology." *Trends in Molecular Biology* 15.1 (2007): 45–50. Print.

Champagne, Frances A., et al. "Variations in Maternal Care in the Rat as Mediating Influence for the Effects of Environment on Development." *Physiology and Behavior* 79 (2003): 359–71. Print.

Davies, Paul. "The Epigenome and Top-Down Causation." *Interface Focus* 2.1 (6 Feb. 2011): 42–48. Print.

Davila-Velderrain, Jose, Juan C. Martinez-Garcia, and Elena R. Alvarez-Buylla. "Modeling the Epigenetic Attractors Landscape: Toward a Postgenomic Mechanistic Understanding of Development." *Frontiers in Genetics* 6 (Apr. 2015): article 160. Web.

DeLanda, Manuel. *Intensive Science and Virtual Philosophy.* London: Bloomsbury, 2002. Print.

Dobzhansky, Theodosius. *Genetics and the Origin of Species.* 1937. New York: Columbia UP, 1982. Print.

Érdi, Péter. *Complexity Explained.* Berlin: Springer, 2008. Print.

Gissis, Snait B., and Eva Jablonka. *Transformations of Lamarckism: From Subtle Fluids to Molecular Biology.* Cambridge, MA: MIT P, 2011. Print.

Gould, Stephen Jay. "D'Arcy Thompson and the Science of Form." *New Literary History* 2.2 (1971): 229–58. Print.

Grosz, Elizabeth. *Becoming Undone: Darwinian Reflections on Life, Politics, and Art.* Durham, NC: Duke UP, 2011. Print.

Gunawardena, Jeremy. "Biological Systems Theory." *Science* 328.5978 (2010): 581–82. Print.

Hall, Brian K. "Epigenesis, Epigenetics, Epigenotype: Toward an Inclusive Concept of Development and Evolution." *Beyond Mechanism: Putting Life Back into Biology.* Ed. Brian G. Henning and Adam C. Scarfe. Plymouth, UK: Lexington, 2013. Print.

Henning, Brian G., and Adam C. Scarfe, eds. *Beyond Mechanism: Putting Life Back into Biology.* Plymouth, UK: Lexington, 2013. Print.

Holliday, R., and J.E. Pugh. "DNA Modification Mechanisms and Gene Activity during Development." *Science* 187 (1975): 226–32. Print.

Jablonka, Eva, and Marion J. Lamb. *Evolution in Four Dimensions: Genetic, Epigenetic, Behavioral, and Symbolic Variation in the History of Life.* Cambridge, MA: MIT P, 2005. Print.

Jenuwein, Thomas, and C. David Allis. "Translating the Histone Code." *Science* 293 (2001): 1074–80. Print.

Kadiyala, R.R. "A Tool Box for Approximate Linearization of Nonlinear Systems." *IEEE Control Systems Magazine* 13.2 (1993): 47–57. Print.

Kauffman, Stuart, and Sonke Johnsen. "Coevolution to the Edge of Chaos: Coupled Fitness Landscapes, Poised States, and Coevolutionary Avalanches." *Journal of Theoretical Biology* 149.4 (1991): 467–505. Print.

Kay, Lily E. *Who Wrote the Book of Life? A History of the Genetic Code.* Stanford: Stanford UP, 2000. Print.

Keller, Evelyn Fox. *Making Sense of Life: Explaining Biological Development with Models, Metaphors, and Machines.* Cambridge, MA: Harvard UP, 2002. Print.

Khan, Yasir. "An Algorithm for Solving Nonlinear Differential-Difference Models." *Computational Mathematics and Modeling* 25.1 (2014): 115–23. Print.

Koutroufinis, Spyridon. "Introduction: The Need for a New Biophilosophy." *Life and Process: Towards a New Biophilosophy.* Berlin: De Gruyter, 2014. Print.

Koutroufinis, Spyridon. "Teleodynamics: A Neo-naturalistic Conception of Organismic Teleology." *Beyond Mechanism: Putting Life Back into Biology.* Plymouth, UK: Lexington, 2013. Print.

Krämer, Sybille. *Medium, Messenger, Transmission: An Approach to Media Philosophy.* Trans. Anthony Enns. Amsterdam: Amsterdam UP, 2015. Print.

Leroi-Gourhan, André. *Gesture and Speech.* Trans. Anna Bostock Berger. Cambridge, MA: MIT P, 1993. Print.

Longo, Giuseppe. "Letter to Turing." *Theory, Culture, and Society* 36.8 (2018): 73–94. Print.

Longo, Giuseppe, and Maël Montévil. "Extended Criticality, Phase Spaces and Enablement in Biology." *Chaos, Solutions & Fractals* 55 (Oct. 2013): 64–79. Print.

Longo, Giuseppe, and Maël Montévil. *Perspectives on Organisms: Biological Time, Symmetries and Singularities.* Berlin: Springer, 2014. Print.

Longo, Giuseppe, and Maël Montévil. "Protention and Retention in Biological Systems." *Theorie in den Biowissenschaften/Theory in Biosciences* 130.2 (2011): 107–17. Print.

Malabou, Catherine. *Before Tomorrow: Epigenesis and Rationality.* Trans. Carolyn Shread. Cambridge: Polity, 2016. Print.

Marks, John. "Molecular Biology in the Work of Deleuze and Guattari." *Paragraph* 29.2 (July 2006): 81–97. Print.

Mitchell, Robert. *Bioart and the Vitality of Media.* Seattle: U of Washington P, 2010. Print.

Murray, J.D. *Lectures on Nonlinear Differential Equation Models in Biology.* Oxford: Oxford UP, 1978. Print.

Nocek, A.J. *Molecular Capture: The Animation of Biology.* Minneapolis: U of Minnesota P, forthcoming.

Nocek, A.J. "Transcendental Biology." *Philosophy Today* 63.4 (Fall 2019): 1153–78. Print.

Peterson, Erik L. "The Excluded Philosophy of Evo-Devo? Revisiting C.H. Waddington's Failed Attempt to Embed Alfred North Whitehead's 'Organicism' in Evolutionary Biology." *History and*

Philosophy of the Life Sciences 33.3 (2011): 301–20. Print.

Peterson, Erik L. *The Life Organic: The Theoretical Biology Club and the Roots of Epigenetics*. Pittsburgh: Pittsburgh UP, 2017. Print.

Pisco, Angela Oliveira, Aymeric Fouquier d'Hérouël, and Sui Huang. "Conceptual Confusion: The Case of Epigenetics." *BioRxiv: The Reprint Server for Biology* (May 2016): 1–56. Web.

Protevi, John. *Life, War, Earth: Deleuze and the Sciences*. Minneapolis: U of Minnesota P, 2013. Print.

Riggs, A.D. "X Inactivation, Differentiation, and DNA Methylation." *Cytogenetics and Cell Genetics* 14 (1975): 9–25. Print.

Ringrose, Leonie, ed. *Epigenetics and Systems Biology*. Amsterdam: Elsevier, 2017. Print.

Saunders, Peter T. "The Organism as Dynamical System." *Thinking About Biology: An Invitation to Current Theoretical Biology*. Ed. Wilfred Stein and Francisco J. Varela. Boca Raton: Taylor & Francis, 1993. Print.

Scarfe, Adam C. "Epigenetics, Soft Inheritance, Mechanistic Metaphysics, and Bioethics." *Beyond Mechanism: Putting Life Back into Biology*. Plymouth, UK: Lexington, 2013. Print.

Simondon, Gilbert. *On the Mode of Existence of Technical Objects*. Trans. Cecile Malaspina and John Rogove. Minneapolis: U of Minnesota P, 2017. Print.

Squier, Susan Merrill. *Epigenetic Landscapes: Drawing as Metaphor*. Durham, NC: Duke UP, 2017. Print.

Stan, Guy-Bart. *Modelling in Biology*. Course Notes, Imperial College London, 2010. Web. Jan. 2020. <http://www.bg.ic.ac.uk/research/g.stan/2010_Course_MiB_article.pdf>.

Stevens, Charles F. "Systems Biology Versus Molecular Biology." *Current Biology* 14.2 (2004): R51–R52. Web.

Stiegler, Bernard. *Technics and Time, 1: The Fault of Epimetheus*. Trans. Richard Beardsworth and George Collins. Stanford: Stanford UP, 1998. Print.

Tebbich, S., K. Sterelny, and I. Teschke. "The Tale of the Finch: Adaptive Radiation and Behavioral Flexibility." *Philosophical Transactions of the Royal Society of London, Series B* 365 (2010): 1099–109. Print.

Thacker, Eugene. *Biomedia*. Minneapolis: U of Minnesota P, 2004. Print.

Trewavas, Anthony. "A Brief History of Systems Biology: 'Every Object that Biology Studies is a System of Systems.' Francois Jacob (1974)." *The Plant Cell* 18.10 (2006): 2420–30. Print.

Tronick, Ed, and Richard H. Hunter. "Waddington, Dynamic Systems, and Epigenetics." *Frontiers in Behavioral Neuroscience* 10 (2016). Web.

Waddington, Conrad Hal. "An Autobiographical Note." *The Evolution of an Evolutionist*. Edinburgh: Edinburgh UP, 1975. Print.

Waddington, Conrad Hal. "Canalization of Development and the Inheritance of Acquired Characteristics." *Nature* 150.3811 (1942): 562–65. Print.

Waddington, Conrad Hal. "Genetic Assimilation of the Bithorax Phenotype." *Evolution* 10.1 (1953): 1–13. Print.

Waddington, Conrad Hal. "Reprints and Reflections: The Epigenotype." *International Journal of Epidemiology* 41 (2012): 10–13. Print.

Waddington, Conrad Hal. *The Strategy of Genes*. New York: Routledge, 1957. Print.

Whitehead, Alfred North. *Process and Reality: An Essay in Cosmology*. Ed. David Ray Griffin and Donald W. Sherburne. Corr. ed. 1929. New York: Free P, 1978. Print.

Whitehead, Alfred North. *Science and the Modern World*. 1925. New York: Free P, 1967. Print.

Williams, James. "Deleuze and Whitehead: The Concept of Reciprocal Determination." *Deleuze, Whitehead, Bergson: Rhizomatic Connections*. London: Palgrave Macmillan, 2009. Print.

Adam Nocek

This is an essay about digital biology and the vocational binds biotechnologists find themselves in today as they enter a third decade of sustained efforts to capture, in and as the living, what I propose to call the digital sublime. It is also an essay on the rising discontent that these binds are generating among a small but influential group of bioengineers living and working in key tech enclaves, and the inchoate but growing sense among them that a different mode of operation, one which carries a bit more weight, moves a bit more slowly, and reflects a bit more honestly, may be needed if biology – if biologists – are going to thrive, biologically and ethically.

Digital biology here refers to a fundamental transformation in the everyday life of molecular biology and her daughter sciences, which took hold over the first decade of the twenty-first century (Bennett, "Assembling the Living"). This transformation, which has far-reaching consequences for the ways in which living things get imagined and manipulated, was brought about by the adoption and use of computers at every stage of experimental work. Digital biology was, in this sense, a quotidian transformation. The steady seep of computers and computing into every corner of our lives, the insatiable appetite for data, and the algorithmic styles of reasoning and modes of governance which have taken hold of so much in the world, territorialized biology as it did just about everything else.

In retrospect, this shift might seem fated. As Evelyn Fox Keller has pointed out, from the outset molecular biologists have taken up living things using the language of codes and complexity. They have grasped living things as

gaymon bennett

THE DIGITAL SUBLIME
algorithmic binds in a living foundry

avatars of information processing. Yet what one might call the "practical metaphysics" of digital biology – the more or less self-conscious effort to reimagine the logic of life on the logic of the digital, and to build the infrastructures (the concepts, research programs, technical platforms, modes of expertise, funding streams, and ethos) needed to constitute that re-imagination and make it profitable – didn't really come into force until the human genome sequencing projects of the 1990s and its post-genomic legacy (Shapin). It was only when computers became a normal feature of normal science that biology, to crib Giuseppe Longo, found itself seduced by the potent but unsettling tendency to render living realities as encodable bits of discrete information: DNA as software running on hardware.

François Jacob mused that such computational metaphors were merely a matter of scientific bootstrapping and would one day fade out. Biology itself would push back and molecular biologists, perhaps inspired by an image of evolution-as-tinkerer, would find its proper language (Jacob). Yet something else happened, something closer to Nietzsche's blunt proposition that "unspeakably more depends on what things are called than on what they are" (69). It's in this Nietzschean sense that biology has become digital, that biotech has become tech. Biology has become part of a wider cultural economy, and thus now shares in the malaise of a data-centric world with its distractions, dependencies, ubiquitous surveillance, and algorithmic manipulations.

Importantly, as I describe in what follows, the shift has been less about discursive habits (though these certainly enter in) and more about the changing machinery of experimental practice (Deleuze and Guattari). It is not only a social fact, but a material one. Today, a simple condition of work prevails: virtually all biologists depend on data-centric research infrastructures to do their research. They have thus, together, laid down a major vocational bet. The bet is this: that transformations in biological reasoning and practice brought about by the use of algorithmic machines – despite the fact that such machines can only be used to ask and answer questions that conform to a computable view of reality – will, in the end, prove worth it (Bennett, "Assembling the Living").

I'll say more about this bet and why it matters. The point here is that the turn to digital biology, if at first a function of changes in infrastructure and expertise, has become a programmatic aspiration. Hence the digital sublime: the sense – usually tacit – that digital technologies, by rending life as information, information as machine-readable data, and data the fuel of machine learning, will allow biology to realize a level of excellence, even exaltation, otherwise unimaginable. At the same time, and expressed the other way around, the digital sublime also names the operative sense that living systems, if taken up as an engineering substrate for programmers, can provide an unparalleled future of computational power and creative possibility.

The digital sublime has left technologists breathless, to say nothing of their funders (Rajan). If life is information, and information algorithmic, then biology can be – is being – taken up by the same people that brought us integrated circuits, big data, smartphones, and social media. Yet if Google and Facebook have "broken democracy," as Carole Cadwalladr has forcefully put it, we should pause and take seriously what it means that big tech is now as powerful a force in the shaping of the biological imagination as big pharma and big ag.

In this paper, I take up the digital sublime in a more pragmatic (but therein more existential) register. The digital sublime has been essential to the rise of second-generation biotech, especially the explosion of energy and investment in and around genome editing. But just out of view of *Wired Magazine* and Goldman Sachs, in the atelier of actual biotechnical craftwork, the digital sublime is provoking what Jarrett Zigon has referred to as a "moral breakdown." "Moral" here does not mean good or bad, right or wrong. At least not in the first place. It refers, rather, to "the unreflective and unreflexive ways we are able to act [together] most of the time, ways that are, for the most part, acceptable to others in our social worlds [in a seemingly natural way]" (Zigon 9). For the biotechnologists I describe in this paper, the digital sublime has generated deep uncertainty about such taken-for-granted ways of living together. That uncertainty is causing them to rethink the work ethic required for actualizing digital biology – work ethic not in the older sense of "working hard," but in the sense of the best strategies for moving forward.

The question of digital biology and the digital sublime call to attention the ways biology, as a practice and an economy, changed when biologists started thinking about life algorithmically, which they did once they started using computers to organize so much of their work. In that light, the ethnographic reflections offered here can be cast as part of a broader effort to think through what a data saturated world means for the way we grasp ourselves as living beings – and what we want to know, what we want to do, and what we hope to be thereby.

The paper will proceed in a roughly genealogical fashion. I offer three stories. The first centers on a type of biotech startup called "biofabrication facilities" – biofabs. These startups produce made-to-order biological artifacts. Biofabs are sometimes called "living foundries." I am especially interested in that name – living foundries. It carries an intuition about what's really going on with the digital sublime and why I think we should care. The second two stories take the idea of living foundries as an index and provocation for reflecting on the binds of a digital biology.

a first story: the biofab

From an anthropological point of view, a biofab is a curious thing. It attempts to give form to multiple competing cultural impulses at the same time (Bennett, "The Moral Economy"; Balmer, Bulpin, and Molyneux-Hodgson). Biofab founders sometimes compare what they're doing to an older moment in industrial manufacturing when large-scale producers – like automobile makers – would hire lots of individual fabs to render parts for them (Stinson). This image of the fab carries a particular working-class vibe. At other times, founders compare what they're doing to the early days of personal computing – a generation of geeks who built their own machines using standardized parts (Balmer and Bulpin). This image also evokes a kind of maker's dignity: Home Brew computer clubs in the mythological age of personal computing. Both characterizations evoke images of solidarity, community, and invention.

If we view the biofab from a distance, it looks like lots of other contemporary experiments you find at the interface of biotech and information technology: an attempt to make living things more easily re-workable at a genetic level (Church). But if you look closer, if you actually watch the work getting done, something more subtle is going on. The scientists, engineers, and designers in biofabs are putting in the work needed to invent what might be called a "case-based" approach to engineering living systems – each fabrication problem is taken up as a "case" in an ever-growing series. Like other case-based approaches, the "case" itself must be made: the engineer (like a lawyer or an ethicist or a doctor) has to discern the difference between features of the case that are singular and those that are like other cases.

This recursive approach itself is not unique. What is unique, however, and what sets the biofab apart, is that the knowledge and know-how derived from each iteration is captured in the design and redesign of the biofab itself – in flexible workflows, dynamic techniques and equipment, evolving concepts, in the reconfiguration of the physical space. Superficially, the biofab is made up of the kinds of things one might find in any lab – computers, fridges, benches, technicians. Yet unlike most high-throughput facilities, the biofab is less about uniform methods or standardized design principles. Rather, it's about the buildup of capacities in the relation between work habits, materiality, and the particular problem at hand. It's about getting better, and capturing that improvement in and as the facility itself. The biofab has a liveliness that is the primary creative output of the collective labor – it's a kind of living thing; it has a sort of soul.

A few years back I visited what was then new fab space for a company called Ginko. Ginko has since opened other spaces, but at the time the space in the dockyards on the east side of Boston was a big scale-up for Ginko and represented a significant threshold of success. The value proposition at Ginko is unlike biotech more broadly. Usually in biotech – as in tech more broadly – you make money by turning a good idea into intellectual property (IP), starting a company, and then selling the IP and the company to someone else. In the biofab, value is more workaday and the enterprise is riskier. You have to be able to make stuff. And the stuff you make has to be tricky enough to build that other people can't do it, but reliable enough that you can do it in a more or less predictable fashion. For Ginko to be opening a new facility was a big deal. A collective exhale, and a "ok, here we go."

Jason Kelly, Ginko's CEO, welcomed me to the shop floor – arranged in the center of their converted warehouse space. At a superficial glance, the arrangement looked motley – half unpacked boxes, equipment partitioned into small clusters of activity. Watching the technicians, however, it was clear Ginko's most important operational successes turned on seemingly little things, small but vital innovations. They had figured out more flexible labeling systems for their samples, data formats for their repository, had put robotics on wheels to allow for a rearrangement of design stations and lab benches. All things that looked like old-fashioned process engineering. But there was also something more elemental going on in their relation to living things. Ginko had found a way to hold open workspace that was tensile but purpose-built, situated between the artisanal and the industrial. A kind of space where the rhythms of success depend on the interplay of craftsmanship and productivity.

It's not clear Jason saw things this way. Despite what I took to be the blue-collar quality of the enterprise, he used language – which in my West Coast prejudices – seemed straight out of digital culture: design–work–build cycles, workflow rationalization, biology and machine learning, automation, scalability. Yet as anthropologist Anne Hammang has pointed out, even a short conversation with those actually building the designer organisms offers something more grounded. The biofab as a collective endeavor whose workman-like energy stands in contrast with the popular imagination of synthetic biology as simply a project aimed at remaking biology in the image of computer science.

In the midst of his tour, Jason indirectly acknowledged that contrast. He kept coming back to the word "foundry" to describe what they were trying to do. I do not want to overplay the importance of that word. But it struck me then as now, as a valuable heuristic for making sense of what seems to be at stake in biofabrication. For all the tech-speak, and the desire for the digital sublime, biofabs have begun to embody a different way of approaching living systems, one consistent with talk of foundries.

The idea of a "living foundry" as an aspiration for biotech activates a range of cultural valorizations that are not quite nostalgic, but are laced with pathos. The idea vibrates with an unstated desire for deeper authenticity and more meaningful work in the midst of high-tech: molten metal, physical danger, transmutation, hard labor, and solidarity. It carries an intuition that something vital and life-giving is at stake in the making of living things – vital in the exchange between the maker and the made, in the iterative give and take of experimental practice – something easily hidden behind the antiseptic environment of the lab.

The word "living" in "living foundries" is important – even if it was initially chosen because it carries a certain cachet. It is important because it signals an older instinct about craftwork that often gets overlooked in tech settings (Barley and Orr). Well into the nineteenth century, foundries were considered to be places of an unusual vitality. In foundries, the material being worked with – the molten metal – was considered to be as lively as the foundrymen working with it: when it was hot, when it transmuted, it had the potential to transmute the one working with it. It changed who you are. It worked you, even as you worked it. If you didn't respect it and care for it, it wouldn't do what you wanted it to do. It might even kill you.

It is against that background and in view of that longing for an older energy that the pathos of the biofab – and indeed of the experimental life – shows itself. Taking a cue from Aby Warburg, anthropologists Rabinow and Stavrianakis have suggested that scholars of the contemporary need to attend to the "*Nachleben*" – the afterlife, survival – of repertoires of experiences and expressions that continue to exert force beyond the social worlds in which they were initially conceived. Talk of fabs and foundries constitute such *Nachleben* for biotechnology today. Such talk might easily be mobilized in tragic or ironic modes –

as a nostalgia for what has been lost, or a self-satisfied critique of the bourgeois longings of the millennial elite. Against these, Rabinow and Stavrianakis propose that *Nachleben* can be taken up more generatively through a form of pathos. A form in which "things break down all the time, but equally that there are momentary or short-lived reconciliations." Pathos, unlike tragedy or irony, demands sustained work on the self in order to take up and test "whatever margins of freedom exist under particular conditions" (410).

This style of limit-testing is both analytically and ethically apposite for a study of the digital sublime in biology. Analytically, attention to *Nachleben* brings into focus places where the prior ways of being and their relative externalization may become a point of critical limitation leading to breakdown and thereby a possible reconciliation. Ethically, it invites work on oneself leading to a potential difference.

The first story: the biofab as a lively place that dreams of being a foundry.

a second story: the table

In a paper titled "Information and Causality," mathematician and philosopher Giuseppe Longo gives systematic articulation to a question, which, in the unexamined everyday life of the lab, surfaces incessantly if operationally. The question is this: which mathematics is right for biology? Longo (to risk oversimplifying an otherwise subtle argument) concludes that the math needed to describe phase shifts in biology – shifts from one state of being to another – is different from the kind of calculative mathematics characteristic of computers and thus characteristic of most experimental regimes in biology. The calculative mathematics of the computer presumes and describes discrete states. Think 1s and 0s. Living systems and their elements, however, can only be rendered discrete by making a conceptual cut in the midst of a flow. Given this difference, Longo is worried that the aspects of biological life that can be captured on a computer do not tell us enough of the story to be faithful to what is really going on.

In view of this, Longo is critical of how analogies from computing get (sloppily) used in biology. He is especially critical of any talk that portrays organisms as avatars of computable information – cells as little computers. Longo is not against computation – his lab works on the mathematics of machine learning. But what he wants and what he calls for is an approach to biology + math + data that rejects what he sees as a mistaken assumption, borrowed from computing, whereby information gets treated as immaterial "software" that is conceptually separable from the underlying material "hardware." He wants a mathematically rich biology, but one that gives proper attention to "the spatiality, materiality, singularity and historicity of the living being, which can be always surmised as *this living thing here*, in *this* three-dimensional space, with *this* material body and *this* history" (Longo 88).

The trouble with Longo's critique, from an anthropological perspective, is that, while scientifically compelling, it does not help account for the fact that billions of dollars of infrastructure, all over the world, are now in place to do biology in just such a computer-mediated fashion. It does, however, raise and amplify a question: if Longo's right, then what's going on? If, from a mathematical point of view, biology has an unsettled relation to computation, then what are biologists really up to? How have they learned to think biology informationally? And what might it look like for them to think information biologically?

Contemporary biofabs, like Ginko, were not the first to propose that the future of biotech requires the invention of new facilities. Early manifestos in synthetic biology called for just that: the creation of venues with new methods and work habits, inspired by the powerfully successful legacies of computer engineering (Rabinow and Bennett). The manifestos turned on a mantra: build biology like you build computers.

An immediate predecessor to Ginko, which called itself just "the BIOFAB," was a pure play in these early manifestos. The BIOFAB was founded by two engineers – Drew Endy and Adam Arkin – who in the late 1990s were among the first to start calling their vision for bioengineering "synthetic biology." Endy and Arkin liked to frame their vision as a provocation: molecular biology and her daughter sciences were too hung up on understanding how biology works. They needed to focus on how it might be made to work differently. That difference, they argued, requires a fundamental shift in comportment: biologists needed to imagine living things as informational systems, and reimagine their work accordingly (Rabinow and Bennett).

For those who took this provocation seriously, it generated the kind of moral breakdown signaled by Zigon, which I described at the outset – a disruption in the normal course of expectations about how to conduct daily life in the lab together. The normal flow of things could no longer be taken for granted: reflexive and deliberate efforts were needed to establish an alternative normality.

The trouble was, it was unclear where the terms of that normality might come from. Lots of folks knew what it looked like to be successful at molecular biology. Lots knew what it looked like to thrive in the tech worlds of Cambridge, MA and Silicon Valley. But what it looked like to be a "good" bioengineer was up for grabs.

For those on the computer side of things, the uncertainty proved generative. Lots of things could be tried out: Endy, for example, asked what it would look like to "refactor" DNA (Chan, Kosuri, and Endy). Ron Weiss and Tom Knight tried rigging cells like integrated circuits (Weiss, Homsy, and Knight). George Church started multiple biotech companies that were essentially copy-changes of digital tech companies. What underwrote these experiments was a working assumption that the information "running" on biological stuff is basically like information *in silico* – or enough like it that the tricks of the trade needed to be good at engineering on one substrate can get you a long way down the road engineering on another.

The phrase "digital biology" predates synthetic biology. It was originally used to name how, in the wake of the genome sequencing projects, almost every aspect of laboratory life required a computer (Sleator). But with synthetic biology, digital biology became something else: a programmatic effort to link bioengineering to the digital sublime. "Digital" referred most obviously to stuff having to do with computers – sequencers, synthesis, databases. But more subtly, it began to refer to how, for synthetic biology, the aspects of living things that really count are those that could be "seen" by machines that generate data for manipulation on digital platforms. Machines that could translate biological objects into digital objects (Bennett, "Synthetic Biology").

For the folks at the BIOFAB, the "sublime" in digital sublime had two sides to it. First, digital technologies seemed to offer the way forward toward a biological future in which the horizons for bioengineering were limited only by the designer's imagination. This view of programming was put forward by the great MIT computer engineers Gerry Sussman and Hal Abelson. Sussman and Abelson argued that programming represents the only form of engineering in which there are no material constraints per se. You obviously can only do things that the machine can handle. But at the level of the manipulation of information, a finite set of moves can be used to express a potentially infinite array of commands.

At the same time, the "sublime" also refers to the felt sense that biological systems potentially represent the most lofty possibilities for information engineering. Early on, Sussman and Tom Knight did back-of-the-envelope calculations of how much information they thought a single cell could process at any given moment – and then what a collection of cells might achieve. In their view, cells far outstripped any silicon-based processing.

For the BIOFAB, the road to the digital sublime passed through "parts-based" engineering (Balmer and Bulpin). The idea was that complex biological systems could be reimagined as ensembles of hierarchically arranged components, with each ensemble functioning as a new "part" for further higher-order abstractions. To that end, Endy and Arkin (on the model of a program Endy had helped establish at MIT) proposed a registry of parts: built, characterized, and designed for interoperability by a parts-fab.

On one level, their efforts weren't successful. After two years, the BIOFAB shut its doors. Yet they provided a warrant for trying out other approaches to biofabrication, which others, like Ginko, took up. In view of that legacy, it is worth thinking through the BIOFAB's approach to the digital sublime, and how that approach cast into particularly sharp relief the moral uncertainty at the heart of digital biology. Two points are most important: the BIOFAB's efforts to construct a registry of standardized parts can be thought of as an expression of a particular "cosmological inclination" in digital biology; this inclination can be characterized by what I call "algorithmic complexity."

The cosmological inclination at the heart of the registry is one that approaches the biological world as fundamentally interoperable. "Cosmological" here refers not to "cosmos" in the physics sense, but cosmos in the sense characteristic of late-medieval thought. The medieval commonsense held that all parts of reality resembled each other in basic ways. Analogy – that something was like something else – was a strongly ontological category. Things in the world were assumed to hang together in such a way that the meaning and purpose of one part – say, the natural world – could tell you something essential about another part – say, the nature of the human world. This was not the simple idea that everything was connected (though it was that too). It was the more subtle idea that everything participated in a shared logic of being – that reality fits together in a harmonious way. It was presumed that one could therefore (eventually) reason from one part of reality to another (Yates).

Skipping over lots of time and details, by the end of the seventeenth century this cosmological sensibility began to shift. Inductive reason and experimental science had come to dominate in the scientific imagination over mathematical demonstration and deductive proofs. Yet the idea that all of reality all hung together had not gone away. The combination of a feel for cosmology, on the one side, and a turn to inductive reason, on the other, gave birth to what Michel Foucault termed the "classical episteme" – a framework for thinking about the world in which the goal and expectation of science was that all of reality – especially living reality – could be represented in its most simple, constitutive elements, within a single chart or table.

The project was compelling. Those who sought to represent reality this way believed science would, eventually, fill in all the blanks. What made it potentially powerful was that, if put together correctly, the table would allow scientists to specify the place of the most important and defining features of the living world – from smallest to most comprehensive – in their interrelations within the broader order of the cosmos. Dynamic, comprehensive, and scalar.

All of this is an over-simplification. But the point is that once you get to the registry at the BIOFAB, the equivalent of the elements in the classical table have changed, but not entirely. There is still something like a cosmological sensibility in play: a working assumption that the things in the table can be ordered in relation to each other because they are fundamentally like each other. Thus, standardization. The difference is they can be ordered in multiple ways based on the inclinations of the one doing the ordering. The elements in the table, in other words, are interoperable, but not because they fit into a representational picture of the world, not because they conform to the nature of the cosmos.

This contemporary version of the table is thus complex, but algorithmic. It shifts our thinking about biological systems toward a science of the artificial: it does not represent things "as they are," but as they might be made to be when recombined with other elements. The registry, as it was envisioned, would be made up of a finite number of digital motifs, which could be used and reused in an indeterminate number of ways. Biological systems on this point of view might be limited by the rules governing their material interfaces, but not by the functional play of the information encoded in them. The systems were taken to be algorithmic insofar as the rules governing the engineering of new biological functions could be made explicit and specified in advance.

The upshot is that the elements in the table – the registry – were imagined to be governed not by what they are in their nature (material or informational), but what they could be made to be by the designer. That imagination depended on the kind of duality Longo is worried about: information conceived on an analogy of software to hardware. The registry operationally assumed that information and thus biology possess an abstract logic – it can be programmed. That was the purpose of the registry: to capture the potency of vital systems – their ability to do lively things like respond to an environment, make choices, grow, react, and communicate – but in a manner consistent with algorithmic complexity.

The BIOFAB had plenty of detractors worried about conceptual issues with naming and characterizing parts. But the problem was more mundane. The effort to establish and scale up reliably standardized parts simply did not work. They found themselves in a bind in which the wily fecundity of living things, which made them so attractive to the engineering imagination, did not play nicely with an algorithmic view of complexity. The research team at the BIOFAB spent two years just sorting out the parameters for standardization. A basic and yet ultimately elusive task.

Yet there is a twist: when things failed to work as expected – when one set of measurements couldn't be reproduced and thus standardized – it was assumed to be the result of experimental failure. The lab meetings in which these perceived failures were discussed were marked by a restlessness to get on to the larger project. Yet no one suggested that maybe the measurements were, in fact, accurate and that what was different each time were the living things themselves. No one suggested that maybe they were getting the measurements right but that the measurements were different because they were capturing a faithful picture of *these* living beings right here, with *these* bodies, under *these* circumstances. That kind of biological singularity or biological unruliness could not enter into the algorithmic imagination of the BIOFAB. It couldn't be squared with the digital sublime.

The second story: an algorithmic fixation that dreams of harnessing a cosmos.

a third story: the computer and the organism

In October 2018, the European Bioinformatics Institute (EBI) held a meeting in its facilities at the Sanger Institute in the UK. Sanger is as close to idealized English country living as one can get while still being at the center of the scientific universe. The buildings are set on a rolling estate. The best of contemporary architecture's efforts to tie the indoor to the outdoor. When you're in the buildings, you're caught by a sense that you could, at any moment, simply walk out onto a path and under a tree. This is powerful because it creates a kind of vital reverberation across the glass walls – it gives you this feeling that the material you're working on in the lab is a kind of distillate of the vital energy of the verdant surroundings.

This tangle of the artificial and the atmospheric embodies a problem and possibility at the heart of the EBI enterprise, and points to a difference that can't quite be sorted out. EBI has become a clearing house for data produced by biologists across Europe. There's a strong push in Europe to make all data freely available ("open science") and, ultimately, interoperable. That effort is housed at, and coordinated through, EBI. This means that EBI's technologists are faced with the immense and complicated task of helping reconcile the ontologies needed to allow hundreds of databases to play nicely together.

It is an immense technical and political problem. But it is also a biological problem. And, curiously, it is that dimension of the problem that often gets neglected. Yet there is at least one place where the biological problem keeps reasserting itself, and has had to be dealt with. That is around gene regulation – the biological processes that work to induce and repress the expression of biological information.

Over the years, scientists at EBI, like those at the other major biological data platforms such as the Gene Ontology Consortium (GO) and elsewhere, have tried to capture biological data in a kind of snapshot fashion. They have asked: how should biological material and processes be conceptually cut – "ontologized" – so it can be fitted into the rows and columns in the databases? How do you characterize aspects of living things in a manner that can be used to create a category for specifying one bit of knowledge such that it can be stored and compared to other bits of knowledge?

For folks interested in gene regulation, the problem with this whole process is that it is way too static. Biology gets rendered like those old flip-books that Disney used to make: each page has a picture, you run your thumb along the edge, and it seems as if the image is moving. But it is not. Gene regulation is lively and active and in motion. The question is: how to capture that data without making it just one more static object in the database?

EBI, GO, and others are part of a working group trying to sort this out (GRECO – Gene Regulation Consortium). Hence the meeting. The program began with a presentation by a group of European computer scientists who have developed and are trying to implement what they call the FAIR data principles. FAIR – all caps – stands for: findable, accessible, interoperable, reusable (Wilkinson et al.). The principles seem self-evident and sensible. This was not the first time I had heard a presentation on FAIR, and usually everyone just nods along. But it turns out the principles are less obvious when one tries to turn them into a set of community-wide practices. FAIR may seem perfectly reasonable, but to quote Zigon again, when implemented, they force one "to reflect on the kind of person one wants to be in her social world" (9). They require ethical work in the sense of re-examining one's otherwise taken-for-granted practices.

For those who support them, the FAIR principles are about embracing a particular vision for the future of innovation. The presentation at the meeting made this clear. FAIR goes beyond "open science," the presenter said. "The grand challenge is nothing less than the ability to automatically uncover evidence that supports and disputes a hypothesis using the totality of available data tools and scientific knowledge." It is about fulfilling the latent scientific promise of data-driven biology. It is, to use my vocabulary, about the digital sublime.

On this view, FAIR is a matter of vocational obligation: if you really believe in science, you will learn to comport yourself in such a way that your data is made interoperable with standards shared by the community. In an age of data saturation, this will clearly be difficult. It will require a change in work habits, technical platforms, and resource allocation. In that regard, resistance to FAIR is perfectly understandable: who has the time to spare? But it is not – and the presentation made this absolutely clear – scientifically reasonable to resist. One might resist a given standard or a particular semantics. But resistance to the idea per se cannot be scientifically warranted.

When the talk concluded, the discomfort in the room felt palpable. I could see biologists shifting in their seats, whispering to their colleagues. Yet there was something about the way FAIR was being framed as a scientific obligation that made the biologists in the room hesitate in giving voice to their discomfort directly. Instead, they asked for clarification. What counts as a digital object? My whole database? The results of one round of experiments? A key finding?

The presenter was caught off guard. Not by the questions, but by the intensity of tone and body language. A feeling of defensiveness crept in. The questions became more sharply scientific. Won't standards for machine readability risk degrading scientific nuance? Won't uniform data standards risk reconciling data which really ought to be treated as only partially comparable? Might standardized semantics give a picture of self-consistency which cannot be expected from biological processes? Won't this trade quality for scale?

The presenter finally grew intransigent: you don't have to get on board with this; but if you want to be part of the scientific future, you do. The real problem, which could not be addressed in the charged atmosphere in the room, was really about what gets to count as a scientific vocation and who finally gets to decide. What does a scientifically excellent life look like in a zone of digital biology? What does it mean to be a good and responsible researcher at the interface of data science and biology? Equally, and in a connected fashion, what about the underlying ontology of computers and living systems: to what extent can the logic of the one be reconciled to the other? How do we give form to a scientific way of life that accounts, digitally, for the idiosyncrasies of living things?

In the elaboration of the FAIR principles, the computer itself is named as a stakeholder. The needs of the computer – how it reads the world – have to be taken into account. And while there is something reassuring about a policy document that incorporates the nonhuman into the ethical domain, for many in the room the emphasis on the needs of the computer generated a different problem. If the computer, then why not the organism? What would it look like to make the vitality of vital systems a stakeholder? Not just in the sense of something whose ethical value counts, but, like the computer, as a stakeholder whose specific material and immaterial way of existing in the world has to be accounted for as we build our data infrastructures, and as we adapt our scientific habits to those infrastructures. Put differently, how might we approach digital biology if we were not only interested in viewing living things informationally, but if we also wanted to view information biologically – with all the messiness, responsiveness, context-specificity, and singularity such a biological view of things might bring into play.

After the meeting, I stood outside with a small group enjoying the autumn cold. One of the biologists – Paul Veyen – was agitated and animated in his usual wry fashion. Waving his half-smoked cigarette, Paul exclaimed, "I don't even know how gene regulation works! How am I going to comply with these standards!" Paul didn't buy the idea that semantics are agnostic or neutral, that meta-data is indifferent to the realities he is trying to capture in his work. It is all part of a way in which we're asking and answering our questions. Crackling with energy, Paul pointed out that the difference between the noses of different dog breeds – so obviously dissimilar – cannot be accounted for in simple genetic terms. "They are too similar genetically! It's all about regulation! But how? Where does the information come from? How are we to account for it?" We all laughed. Paul finished his cigarette, and we went back inside.

The third story: the biological binds of the digital sublime.

a few concluding thoughts

From an anthropological point of view, the aspiration to create a living foundry is a value proposition not yet in full alignment with itself. It conjures images of heat, transmutation, and craft, alongside uncertainty, specificity, and materiality. Yet these images have yet to be squared with tech-talk of scale, machine learning, automation, and high throughput.

If you talk to the people at the lab bench in places like Ginko, you find a more interesting proposition, one in which the living thing being made has to be accommodated: cells must be coerced, cajoled, enticed into playing along with our biotechnical imaginations. Efforts to regularize such accommodation, make things a bit more standard, are not unwarranted – foundries have always required structure, predictability, and reliability. But such regularization must be tempered by the living quality of the things being made: they shape us and our practices as much as we shape them. To act differently turns out to be the real source of breakdown.

The technicians at the bench who live with the demands of this accommodation on a daily basis understand that they are being changed by their work. They feel the pathos of the experimental life and its longings. They may not talk about it in these terms. But they get that they are pouring themselves into their experiments. They give it their all – their energy, their time, their creativity – in the name of a possible future. And that is the real risk and the real exchange. By giving themselves over to their work, they are inviting their work to give them something back. It is a redemptive economy – a bet that they will receive something of higher value than what they put in.

This economy is usually thought of in instrumental terms: if I get the experiment right, if I interpret the data well, it will allow me to ... take the next step in my career; get into the right school; get the next contract. But think about what that means for the ontological exchange at play. If the work is treated as only instrumental, it will treat me the same way. The goods I get out of it will be limited to instrumental goods. Which might be fine if the experiment works. But if it fails, I get nothing. As centuries of craftsmanship testifies, if I do not also seek the intrinsic satisfactions of a job done well, I will not be able to sustain the quality of my work, and I will not have the passion required to keep it going (Sennett).

Foundries make more than metal. They made foundrymen. Shake the hand of anyone who works with metal for a living, and you know immediately how deeply they have been marked by their work. This reciprocity – I shape the work, the work shapes me – is as true for crafting information or cells as it is for crafting metal. The advantage with metal is that most of the dangers are obvious.

It is worth noting in conclusion that the origin of the word foundry – a derivative of the Latin word "to pour" – comes from the same root that gives us "alchemy" and then "chemistry." The word "gheu" – alchemy – carries with it the idea of pouring a libation to the gods. When the alchemists poured the heated metal, they were in part pouring a tribute to the gods. A kind of material prayer. They thought of it as a prayer because they lived in a world, not unlike the world of the medieval cosmos, in which they experienced themselves as inextricably bound to their work: in transmuting the metal, they released an energy that would transmute them. They understood that who they were – their ethical constitution – shaped what they were making.

They shaped the metal but the metal shaped them. The question today is what a digital biology might look like which takes seriously the stakes of such a moral exchange.

disclosure statement

No potential conflict of interest was reported by the author.

bibliography

Balmer, Andrew, and Kate Bulpin. "Left to their Own Devices: Post-ELSI, Ethical Equipment and the International Genetically Engineered Machine (IGEM) Competition." *BioSocieties* 8.3 (2013): 311–35. arizona-asu-primo.com. doi:10.1057/biosoc.2013.13. Print.

Balmer, A., K. Bulpin, and S. Molyneux-Hodgson. *Synthetic Biology: A Sociology of Changing Practices.* 1st ed. Basingstoke: Palgrave Macmillan, 2016. Print.

Barley, Stephen R., and Julian E. Orr. *Between Craft and Science: Technical Work in U.S. Settings.* Ithaca: IRL P, 1997. Print.

Bennett, Gaymon. "Assembling the Living." *Raisons Pratiques* 28 (2018). Print.

Bennett, Gaymon. "The Moral Economy of Biotechnical Facility." *Journal of Responsible Innovation* 2.1 (2015): 128–32. arizona-asu-primo.com. doi:10.1080/23299460.2014.1002169. Print.

Bennett, Gaymon. "Synthetic Biology and the Digital Imagination." *Human, Transhuman, Posthuman: Emerging Technologies and the Boundaries of Homo Sapiens.* Farmington Hills: Macmillan Reference USA, 2018. Print.

Chan, Ly, Sriram Kosuri, and Drew Endy. "Refactoring Bacteriophage T7." *Molecular Systems Biology* 1 (2005). arizona-asu-primo.com. doi:10.1038/msb4100025. Print.

Church, George. *Regenesis: How Synthetic Biology Will Reinvent Nature and Ourselves.* 1st ed. New York: Basic, 2014. Print.

Deleuze, Gilles, and Félix Guattari. *A Thousand Plateaus: Capitalism and Schizophrenia.* Minneapolis: U of Minnesota P, 1987. Print.

Foucault, Michel. *The Order of Things: An Archaeology of the Human Sciences.* New York: Vintage, 1973. Print.

Fox Keller, Evelyn. *Making Sense of Life: Explaining Biological Development with Models, Metaphors, and Machines.* Cambridge, MA: Harvard UP, 2002. Print.

GRECO – Gene Regulation Consortium. Web. 7 Jan. 2020. <http://thegreco.org/>.

Hammang, Anne. *Comprehensive Examinations.* Tempe: Arizona State U, 2019. Print.

Jacob, François. *The Logic of Life: A History of Heredity.* New York: Vintage, 1973. Print.

Longo, Giuseppe. "Information and Causality: Mathematical Reflections on Cancer Biology." *Organisms. Journal of Biological Sciences* 2.1 (2018): 83–103. Print.

Nietzsche, Friedrich. *The Gay Science.* New York: Vintage, 1974. Print.

Rabinow, Paul, and Gaymon Bennett. *Designing Human Practices: An Experiment with Synthetic Biology.* Chicago: U of Chicago P, 2012. Print.

Rabinow, Paul, and Anthony Stavrianakis. "Movement Space: Putting Anthropological Theory, Concepts, and Cases to the Test." *HAU: Journal of Ethnographic Theory* 6.1 (2016): 403–31. journals.uchicago.edu (Atypon). doi:10.14318/hau6.1.021. Web.

Rajan, Sundar. *Biocapital: The Constitution of Post-Genomic Life.* Durham, NC: Duke UP, 2006. Print.

Sennett, Richard. *The Craftsman.* New Haven: Yale UP, 2008. Print.

Shapin, Steven. *The Scientific Life: A Moral History of a Late Modern Vocation.* Chicago: U of Chicago P, 2008. Print.

Sleator, Roy D. "Digital Biology: A New Era has Begun." *Bioengineered* 3.6 (2012): 311–12. arizona-asu-primo.com. doi:10.4161/bioe.22367. Web.

Stinson, Liz. "Move Over, Jony Ive – Biologists are the Next Rock Star Designers." *Wired* Nov. 2015. Web. <https://www.wired.com/2015/11/move-over-jony-ivebiologists-are-the-next-rock-star-designers/>.

Sussman, Gerald Jay, and Harold Abelson. *Structure and Interpretation of Computer Programs.* 2nd ed. Cambridge, MA: MIT P, 1996. Print.

Weiss, Ron, George E. Homsy, and Thomas F. Knight, Jr. "Toward In Vivo Digital Circuits." *DIMACS Workshop on Evolution as Computation*, Feb. 1999. ResearchGate. doi:10.1007/978-3-642-55606-7_14. Web.

Wilkinson, Mark D., et al. "The FAIR Guiding Principles for Scientific Data Management and Stewardship." *Scientific Data* 3.1 (2016): 1–9. www.nature.com. doi:10.1038/sdata.2016.18. Web.

Yates, Frances A. (Frances Amelia). *Giordano Bruno and the Hermetic Tradition.* Chicago: U of Chicago P, 1964. Print.

Zigon, Jarrett. "Moral and Ethical Assemblages." *Anthropological Theory* 10.1–2 (2010): 3–15. Print.

Gaymon Bennett

And however hard I try to integrate, I'll always remain alien. (Lebanon Hannover)

Let's begin by discussing my death. Most of us think of dying in stark existential terms; either you are "alive" or you are "dead." In this existential view, death is like flipping a switch from "on" to "off." Once the switch is flipped, an organism passes from a life of restless activity to the mystery of non-existence. Life and death are thought to be antagonistic conditions, where the arrival of death indicates the cessation of life.

A physiological view of dying, however, is much more complicated than this existential view. In physiological processes, life and death exist simultaneously and continuously inform each other. The clearest example of this is programmed cell death, or apoptosis. From the Greek for "falling off" (think of leaves in autumn), apoptotic cell death is usually triggered as a part of growth and development (BioChemWeb.net; Morange; Ackerman and Malmusi; Gayon). This contrasts with necrosis, which is a form of cell death triggered by disease or injury and is unplanned. Apoptosis is necessary for the functioning of multicellular organisms and can even help give them form. The webbing between embryonic fingers, for instance, "falls off" before birth, giving human hands their characteristic appearance. Apoptosis is only one of the most well-known examples for how death always accompanies life.

Taking account of this physiological view of death then, changes how we think of the process of dying. When I die my body doesn't cease to exist – it actually undertakes many important changes. At first, the muscles in my body relax, my heart stops beating and blood pools in specific tissues. A few hours later, the muscles contract and my body stiffens. After this, bacteria and insects assist in breaking down the soft tissues of my body, eventually exposing the bones of my skeleton, which, given the right environment, can last for a number of years shorn from flesh. In this view of death, life and death occur simultaneously, as elements of our bodies change or disappear while others persist (Carey). For instance, the hardness of my bones supports my flesh for part of my body's existence but lingers on after my flesh has wasted away. Bones remain as a haunting reminder that not all of us cease to exist once our inner worlds have eclipsed and our flesh decayed.

phillip thurtle

ALIENATED LIFE
toward a goth theory of biology

The implication of this view of life and death is that what we call a body is anything but a unified entity. Although we tend to think of bodies as a single element, a sack of meat perhaps or a bundle of flesh, bodies are, in fact, congregations of complex processes choreographed across incongruent spaces, materials, and durations. Everything involved with our bodies — such as my flesh, my bones, my thoughts, my desires — depends upon interactions between atomic, molecular, organismic, familial, and social spaces. Given this incredible complexity, how do we even begin to make sense of our bodies and the multiple scales of time and space that they inhabit?

I've recently found the inspiration to address these questions from what at first might seem an unlikely source: post-punk goth music. I became interested in goth music as I contemplated why some music shares identifiable moods, such as a feeling of darkness, even if this music doesn't share similar melodic patterns, key signatures, compositional techniques, or rhythms. There was something to the sound of the notes themselves and how they combined, some characteristic, that evoked these moods. It was while reading Isabella van Elferen's discussion of goth music that I came to identify these characteristics of goth music as distinctive timbres. As van Elferen writes, "Timbre takes listeners into an unknown outside" and goth "is a specially poignant case of timbral aesthetics. With its penchant for shadows and veils, beyond and outsides, this genre had developed a sophisticated timbral aesthetic as its main musical vehicle" (38). I find van Elferen's discussion of timbre in goth music interesting as it provides a way to think about the coherence of organisms, how they are put together and how they operate, without reducing them to teleological principles, vital drives, or moments of systemic closure.

In the argument that follows, I refer to one specific capacity of goth timbre especially important for understanding contemporary biology: the ability to create dramatic tension by contrasting disparate elements. As Gilda Williams, scholar of contemporary gothic culture, has written:

> Always present in the Gothic is this: two things that should have remained apart — for example, madness and science; the living and the dead; technology and the human body; the pagan and the Christian; innocence and corruption; the suburban and the rural — are brought together, with terrifying consequences. (12)

As I argued above when discussing my death, the packaging of two disparate elements together, such as life and death, gives a much more accurate view of living processes than the idea of an organism as a singular and tightly bound entity composed of integrated parts. Life not only depends upon and generates coordination of different elements, it is built upon and produces drama as well. Too often this drama is dismissed as a by-product of life instead of an important constitutive element. Both my inner goth and my inner biologist recognize that multicellular life couldn't exist without drama.

Let me briefly explain what I mean. Too many biological stories center on successful outcomes. Evolutionary stories, for instance, often assume an adaptational fallacy that Stephen Jay Gould derided as "just-so stories" based on the "assumption that everything exists for a purpose" (xvii). "Scientists know that these tales are stories," continues Gould,

> unfortunately, they are presented in the professional literature where they are taken too seriously and literally. Then they become "facts" and enter the popular literature, often in such socially dubious forms as the ancestral killer ape who absolves us from responsibility for our current nastiness, or as the "innate" male dominance that justifies cultural sexism as the mark of nature. (xvii–xviii)

From a goth perspective, one of the problems with this type of argument is that it reduces an incredibly complex bundle of tendencies into a single "just-so" outcome. These stories strip the productive drama from life by reducing it to a set of clichéd outcomes.

I think this tendency is even more prevalent in biology than the simple adaptationist accounts that Gould ridicules. As I will argue by revisiting Kant's distinction between aesthetic and natural judgment, there is a tendency in theoretical biology to build just-so types of arguments into many forms of biological causality. Even textbooks, for instance, describe bodies in perfect working conditions (often under the guise of another under-interrogated assumption, that we are all "normal") instead of the embodied messes that most of us actually are. My goal here is not to disprove accounts predicated upon normal or idealized bodies or even successful evolutionary outcomes, as they are often explanatorily useful; rather, I hope to embellish and augment them by offering a disharmonious and temporal counterpoint. This, in effect, is the goth ethos. The last thing a goth would want is for the rest of the world to become goth with them. That would only reduce the oppositional tension, the deep sense of alienation, that gives goth music its vitality and characteristic drama. The implication of this observation is that despite its reputation as an art of darkness, the goth aesthetic is better characterized as an art of shadows that mixes dark and light elements. At its best, a goth aesthetic can operate like a shadow play that adds mystery to the more commonly illuminated stories of success that biologists more frequently share.

So, what can we learn by exploring biology's shadows? What happens, for instance, if we resist the siren song of organicism that biology inherited from German Idealism in order to explore our bodies' more goth tendencies? What happens if we view the interactions of parts of bodies as conflicting tendencies that don't always reach a synthesis to a higher function? Or, in terms of health and illness, what happens if we assume that pathology is a condition of health instead of its antithesis? I'm literally *and* figuratively sick of judging lives through the prism of success. It's time we came up with a biology for those of us who can't integrate, those of us who feel chronic pain or sickness, and those of us who have never felt normal. I'm glad that there is a biology built on idealism, normality, and success. It's just that its remit for biological knowledge is too narrow. It's time for a biology for the rest of us. It's time for a biology of the alienated, the disabled, the leaky, and the broken. It's time for a goth biology.

In what follows, I will use goth music as a way to explore gothic characteristics in order to begin an aesthetic analysis of biological processes. Not only will this allow for us to reconsider the role of aesthetics in health, development, and evolution; it will give us an ability to understand biological processes in greater complexity, while opening new ways of viewing how organisms relate to each other. Consequently, this article is not intended to be an extensive exploration of the ways that goth and the gothic have been studied in the humanities and social sciences (although I do draw on some of these studies). I also will not engage in the lively debates about goth or the gothic as a genre. Instead, my purpose is to use the term "goth" to show how aesthetics, concepts, and forms can be loosely held together through an analysis of the fleeting but identifiable structures that make up all multi-cellular organisms. In order to achieve this, I've broken the following investigation into three parts: an exploration of how timbre is used in goth music to create dramatic tension, a look at recent findings in cancer research to suggest that our bodies need unresolved tension to evolve, and then a final section where I contrast these lessons with other recent ways of thinking about bodies. Much like what we were calling a physiological view of death in the introduction above, this new view of biology gives us a more philosophically capacious and ultimately aesthetically richer perspective to think about life and living things.

timbre: goth music

As the Gilda Williams quote above testifies, goth informs and entertains by drawing together unlikely things. This act of drawing together is as important as the elements that it gathers. What emerges is a field of relationships, instead of a highly structured causality or the emergence of a new property. In goth music especially, these disparate musical elements are allowed to haunt each other, creating what Eve Kosofsky Sedgwick called a "semiotics of instability" in her discussion of gothic literature, where a vertiginous feeling of dread is created by resisting the collapse of experiences into their normative categories (53). I would argue that the most endearing types of goth music come from their penchant to resist the synthesis of different elements into seamless musical experiences by embracing internal tensions, allowing them to haunt and inform each other.

This type of dramatic tension is especially good at evoking complex feelings about life, death, loss, and alienation. Why is this the case? It would be easy, too easy really, to say the un-synthesizable elements create a complex set of relationships where outcomes can't be specifically known. Although this is sometimes the case, in this article, I am more interested in the haunting that occurs by having these elements persist in an un-synthesizable relationship. This haunting allows for the feeling of incompleteness or alienation to reverberate. This then heightens the realization that one doesn't have enough knowledge to predict an assured outcome, or deepens the sense of loneliness that comes from alienation.

As the musicologist Isabella van Elferen has suggested, holding contradictory musical elements together can lead to the dissociation of space and time that lends much of goth music its feelings of alienation and dis-ease. For van Elferen, this is expressed in how the musical timbres of goth music create its own recognizable aesthetic. As van Elferen writes, "Timbre takes listeners into an unknown outside" and goth "is a specially poignant case of timbral aesthetics. With its penchant for shadows and veils, beyond and outsides, this genre had developed a sophisticated timbral aesthetic as its main musical vehicle" (38). One simple example of how goth music creates tension through the dissociation of musical time is by combining instruments from different periods of Western history into a single song or performance. The combination of a synthesizer and a harp, for instance, simultaneously evokes two different types of musical experiences, such as listening to religious music and listening to post-punk rock. Performers must be careful, however, and make sure these tensions aren't too easily resolved into a new convention, as then these tendencies quickly collapse into new normative categories and musical clichés. Here is how Siouxsie Sioux, from the proto-goth band Siouxsie and the Banshees, describes it:

> I've always thought that one of our greatest strengths was our ability to craft tension in music and subject matter. Juju [the 1981 fourth album of Siouxsie and the Banshees] had a strong identity, which the goth bands that came in our wake tried to mimic, but they simply ended up diluting it. They were using horror as the basis for stupid rock n roll pantomime. There was no sense of tension in their music. Anyway, Juju wasn't all about darkness. (Roberts)

This passage is instructive as Siouxsie rejects a popular way of thinking about goth music, as an existential state that is preoccupied with death and darkness, in favor of a musical view of goth music, as a form of music that "crafts" tension through subject matter. Holding incongruous elements in tension allows for a deepened experience of goth music and, as I will argue, a more nuanced view of how our bodies operate.

Closely listening to how timbre is used to disassociate a sense of musical time and space in a specific goth song is especially instructive. The song that I will briefly analyze is "Other Voices" from The Cure's 1981 album, *Faith* (the second of their recognized "goth period"), as it wonderfully problematizes the temporal relationship between voice and music. The song begins by featuring the rhythm section of the band, with a strongly resonant bass line and drumming that lacks fills, rolls, snares, or the use of cymbals. When the guitar is added it plays mostly ringing textures, creating a series of whirling motifs carefully layered over the rhythm. The overall effect of the song's introduction is drone-like, lending it a sense of timelessness. This feeling of timelessness is further heightened by having a very long instrumental introduction, a compositional device frequently used in other Cure songs from this period, where some introductions take up half of the song's length. When Robert Smith's vocals are introduced, they begin with a shriek before settling into the song lyrics as sung through an echo box. These effects lend the song the qualities of drones and plainchants, which create a sense of timelessness by eschewing the typical pop formulas of the period of catchy lyrics, melodic development, or a prominent instrumental solo. The sound was described at the time in terms such as "brooding, ominous, skeletal." One reviewer even wrote of The Cure's previous album, *Seventeen Seconds*, that it sounded like "sad Cure, sitting in cold rooms, watching clocks" (Westwood).

eternal sickness – the evolution of cancer

Now we are ready to ask how recognizing goth elements within organisms changes how we view biology. What we find is that the body is most definitely goth in how it holds together dissociated (even conflicting) tendencies, but since we see these elements through a value system that prioritizes ideal normal bodies, we tend to view these elements as pathologies instead of inherently constitutive.

How bodies hold together disparate elements is something I've called a "composite" or "non-synthetic" biological self in my book, *Biology in the Grid*, and I argue that it is best understood by concatenating different types of instrumental views of bodies.

> What we call "life" isn't a single metaphysical principle that death negates, it is a teeming collectivity that warps and changes its regulations through its interactions across vastly different scales of time, space, materials, and forms. Explaining life, then, requires skills in very different types of "compositing" to appreciate and understand the variety of ways the world is collected. And this is what we see in how biology is practiced today – the use of a variety of tools for envisioning how living things exist. (Thurtle 212)

I use the term "composite" in the sense that film special effects and animation use it: to suggest how an image can be composed by placing different elements together to create a new image. Think, for instance, of the painted background of a movie scene with live actors moving in front of it. These two elements, the actors and the scenery, combine to create a new image for the viewer. Of even more interest than the term "compositing" are the modifiers that frequently accompany the term. Animations that utilize "closed compositing," for instance, attempt to create seamless images where no source of the composited elements exist; they wish to synthesize their parts into a seamless organic whole. "Open compositing," however, brings together picture elements in a way that preserves differences between the elements in the final image. Imagine the use of a poorly painted scenic backdrop in the scene of a movie. The viewer is never really able to fully synthesize this image into a single coherent ontology as the background signals its constructed nature. In goth terms, the background continues to haunt the final image. Consequently, goth biology can be viewed as an extension of my arguments in *Biology in the Grid*. I remain convinced that thinkers need to find ways to traverse, but not synthesize, non-synthetic biological elements when thinking about living things. Biological knowledge is not a type of knowledge that should always be straightened. Organisms need their curves, bifurcations, junkware, and discontinuities of scales. As it is often in biology's intricacy, its twists and turns, its dramatic tensions, and its seemingly frivolous repetitions, that we find the greatest insights. For goth biology, the devil is always found in the details.

An appropriate and specific physiological example of un-synthesizable biological elements comes from recent work on the evolutionary history of cancer. As psychologist Athena Aktipis and her co-author, physician and evolutionary theorist Randolph Nesse, have recently claimed: "Our understanding of cancer is in the midst of a major transition" (144). We often think of cancer as a monolithic pathology, a problem of cell division run amuck, and often as the consequence of industrialized environments. This view is slowly being replaced by a view that pays greater attention to the evolutionary history of different cancers and the dynamic micro-environments in which they evolve. As cytologist Peter C. Nowell observed in 1976 (the year The Cure was formed!), cancerous cells are often selected for within the body. Nowell used his skills in cytology to demonstrate that cancers can begin with a small number of chromosomal alterations that increase in heterogeneity as the tumor grows. Nowell then theorized that this increasingly heterogenous cell mass would harbor some cell populations that would confer an evolutionary advantage for tumor growth over other cellular populations. Cancer cells are selected for by the internal micro-environments within our bodies, much like organisms are selected for in environments.

The insight that cells are evolving in the body at the same time that bodies are evolving in environments changes how we think about cancer and bodies. The tendency at the level of the cell will be to generate genotypic and phenotypic diversity in tumors. This explains why cancer is such a heterogenous disease that radically differs in its responses to treatment. As Maley et al. claim in a 2017 article, "Neoplasms evolve. This evolution explains the processes of both carcinogenesis and acquired therapeutic resistance. The evolution of neoplasms is shaped by the selective pressures of their microenvironmental ecology" (605). We can best account for the diversity of cancers and their responses to treatment by thinking of the body as a collection of micro-environments selecting for tumors with different types of traits.

In the literature on the evolutionary origins of cancer, goth biology would focus on the antagonistic tensions that make cancer prevalent in the first place. It would suggest that cancer is less pathology than a type of cellular diversity acting at an evolutionary level, a product of an internal ecology which we are only now beginning to understand. Thus, cancer is a consequence of how loosely bound some parts of an organism are in that they are not as tightly tethered to the biological goals of the organism as many might have assumed. Recognizing that the body provides its own selective micro-environments requires us to loosen a supposition of organicism in bodies, where the whole body is supposed to dictate the behavior of the parts. It is the unresolved tension between the evolution of tumor cells and the evolution of immune responses to these cells that marks the qualities and durations, the tensions, of twenty-first-century human lives.

An especially important allied observation that Aktipis and others have noted is that neoplastic growths, such as you would find in a cancerous tumor, are found in many different types of organisms, including invertebrates, plants, and fungi. Cancer also appears to be evolutionarily old as well, as the femur from a 240-million-year-old turtle, known as *Pappochelys rosinae*, was recently diagnosed to have bone cancer (Haridy et al.). This is not an isolated case. Russian scientists have identified a neoplasm in the skull of an early Triassic amphibian (Gubin et al.), and a group led by Bruce Rothschild in the Department of Medicine at Northeast Medical University found twenty-nine occurrences of tumors in the duck-billed Hadrosaurs from only ninety-seven individuals (see Fig. 1) (Haridy et al. 425). Cancer has haunted many forms of life for millions of years.

Recognizing the selective value of cellular neoplasms brings home the lesson that cancer is not so much a de facto pathology, but an expression of a tension that is always occurring within the body anyway. The body of every complex organism possesses a tension between cellular proliferation, or the ability of the cells to reproduce, and cellular specialization, or the ability of the cells to form specific organs with unique functions. A theorist can concentrate on only one of these properties, such as the importance of cellular specialization, but she does so only by ignoring how these two tendencies continue to exist in tension with each other. Recognizing how this tension is

Fig. 1. An illustration of the location of a tumor on a Hadrosaur. See the protruding mass at the right on the bottom jaw (Dumbravă et al. 2).

constitutive and not just cause for pathology shifts the theoretical focus from the idealized perspective of the successful biological subject to a goth perspective that understands how pathology and health exist together as shadow and light. As the gender nonconforming goth music artist *Anna-Varney Cantodea*, the creative artist behind the project Sopor Æternus & the Ensemble of Shadows, recognizes "Humans are sick by default" (Baldovin). I would like to transpose this observation from its intended existential focus on despair and pessimism to goth biology's perspective of a body as composed of loosely held biological tendencies. To be eternally sick is to suggest that sickness is not just a disfunction of an organism, but a consequence of un-synthesized elements within that organism. As Isabella van Elferen and Jeffrey Andrew Weinstock remind us, "Unsurprisingly, goth melodies hardly ever move upward" (42).

from teleology to aesthetics

The goth view of the organism as a compendium of tensions is at odds, or better, in counterpoint with other recent views of life that trace their theoretical imperatives back to German Idealism and Romanticism. Key among these is the philosophy of organicism. Although possessing a complex genealogy, a simple formulation of organicism is that the total organization of an organism, instead of its constituent parts, determines the behaviors of living processes. Organicism was especially popular in the mid-twentieth century amongst many biologists. Some of this popularity can be attributed to the process philosophy of Alfred North Whitehead, some to the desire to establish a non-mechanist philosophy that wasn't vitalistic, and some to the continuing tradition of holism in some forms of developmental biology (Needham; Peterson; Emmeche). Recently, some thinkers have identified a return to organicism with the rise of second-order systems theoretical approaches in biology. This perspective has especially thrived in the continental philosophy of biology, probably because it offers a non-reductive and anti-genetic view on the development and regulation of life often ignored by late twenty-first-century mainstream experimental biology. The question remains, however, how exactly does goth biology differ from holism? I think a brief investigation into Immanuel Kant's *Critique of the Power of Judgment* provides a very solid perspective to see how goth biology can add to recent discussions on the role of organicism in biology.

In the "Introduction" to his third critique, Kant argues that he will use the concept of "judgment" to provide a conceptual bridge between the idea of casual determination of the first *Critique* and the development of moral reason provided in the second *Critique*. Kant begins by defining judgment as the faculty "for thinking the particular as contained under the universal." The third *Critique* is divided into two main parts: an investigation into the role of aesthetic judgment, and an investigation into the role of judgments in nature, or teleological judgment. Key to the importance of the third *Critique* is the role of "reflective judgments," which Kant sets against "determinative judgments." Determinative judgments are important as they allow us to ascertain whether something falls under a general rule (A132/B171). A reflective judgment, on the other hand, is a judgment based on feeling and allows one to see the possibility of a general rule by reflecting on something specific. Kant then proceeds to develop judgments of taste and teleological judgments as different types of reflective judgments.

Judgments of taste are interesting for Kant in that they identify universal principles from observations. They do this through their purposiveness, which puts into harmony the faculties of free imagination and understanding. Purposiveness, however, needs to be seen in distinction to the purposeful. Purposiveness allows one to see how things may be possible without giving them a specific purpose or end, allowing for an understanding of the properties in which a purpose could be identified without seeing the purpose "as the cause of the object" (Kant 5: 220, §10). In other words, one can reflect on the composition of an organism or the beauty of an object without assigning it an ultimate purpose, although one would assume that this judgment would operate as if it would apply in all cases.

Teleological judgment is different from aesthetic judgment in that an end is suggested. Thus, reflection is no longer just a reflection on form without a determining concept; teleological judgment consists of the concept of the object as well. This makes the object both the cause and effect of itself. For Kant then, teleological judgment sets up a special relationship between the parts of an organism and the regulative capacity that brings these parts together into a functioning whole (5: 422, §81). Thus, the form and function of an organism are envisioned to work together as coordinated through teleological judgment.

Kant's theories of judgment have long been a touchstone for discussions of life, purpose, and evolutionary change. Central to my claims in this article is Davide Tarizzo's book *Life: A Modern Invention*. Tarizzo argues that a form of teleological judgment can be traced through much of the history of biology as a principle of individuation, where the organism is engaged in a never complete struggle to liberate itself as an individual subject in relationship to its environment. For Tarizzo, Kant's conception of "the organism remains alive precisely to the degree it manifests such a self-shaping force, precisely to the extent that it continues to *form itself and to organize itself*" (51). Tarizzo finds this will to individuate expressed as an evolutionary principle in writers such as Darwin and beyond. For my purposes, the value of Tarizzo's analysis is that his careful genealogy of well-known biological thinkers allows him to draw a conceptual continuity between the Kantian "will to will" and the biological "will to life." It also allows him to implicate system self-organization into this conceptual framework of life by showing how teleological judgment still operates as regulative force for an organism's "will to individuate" that is never complete.

The more I study biology and the history of biology, however, the less enthusiastic I am about coming up with a single analytical principle to express bodily organization, regulation, and change. The problem isn't that this type of behavior doesn't occur in biology; the problem is that once found, it is used as a measuring stick for all types of biological behaviors. For instance, although systems theoretical models can explain many biological processes, they do so by homogenizing an incredible complexity of biological elements into a few simple imperatives such as closure, reproduction, and self and other. Consequently, they tend to privilege the analysis of the biological phenomenon that fits best with those models. In the recent history of biology this has been an evolutionary perspective reliant on the organicist assumption of a higher synthesis of the parts, whether this synthesis is straightforwardly dialectical (Levins and Lewontin) or through self-reference and the reproduction of the self (Maturana and Varela).

What gets lost in this emphasis are the numerous tendencies of living things that don't lead to individuation or evolutionary success. These tendencies are often ignored, viewed as a mistake, diagnosed as a pathology, or simply deemed unimportant for life. Instead, goth biology views organisms as a motley collection of different processes, some of which are determined, some of which are regulated through teleological processes, and some of which are very loosely coordinated, if at all. In order to come to this more capacious understanding of organisms, one needs to be able to traverse multiple instrumental and disciplinary studies of life while eschewing these disciplines' penchant for identifying single explanatory frameworks (think about the incredibly different views of life that a mathematician, a chemist, a creative writer, a visual artist, a historian, or musician might offer). The point of goth biology is to disrupt without negating a view of organisms as tightly coordinating and coordinated. Life is just so much more than that.

Interestingly, severing the link between process and end in Kant's view of natural judgments not only darkens an easy path to teleological judgment, it opens up another path to the purposiveness of aesthetic judgment (Adam J. Nocek, personal communication). And this, in turn, brings us back to the gothic and the function of timbre in creating musical moods. Goth lives, with their loose collectivity of tendencies, are haunted lives. This not only means that death permeates life on a daily basis but that our existences are always haunted by times and spaces from elsewhere than our sense of self. It also means that goth lives don't find their strength through unity but through the heterogeneity of molecular pathways, cells, and tissues that compose bodies. Not all conflicting tendencies within organisms need to be resolved in a higher synthesis of success; rather, some elements are best left alienated and estranged. And more personally, not all pathologies need to or should be cured – especially if health is defined as return to an ideal state of holism. Frankly, I'm much more interested in the goth medical tactic of finding the best coping strategy than returning to an ideal of health my body never ever really possessed in the first place (Siebers). Finally, it also suggests that what gathers these seemingly contradictory tendencies should be amenable to an aesthetic as well as a purely scientific analysis. Our lives are collections, textures, and swirling patterns created by muddy echoes of rhythms in the micro-environments of our bodies. It's about time we scientifically studied them as such.

This call for a goth biology is a call for a biology that includes shadows as well as light. It is a science that especially focuses on alienated and ambivalent lives as an accompaniment to a dominant biology fixated on health and evolutionary success. Goth biology is a biology that recognizes the difference between biological and molecular scales but remains cautious about the Romantic tendency to synthesize these tendencies into a greater whole. Goth biology also rejects the subtle teleology of identifying an encompassing will to life. It does this through its inherent suspicion of closure and necessity. As Anna-Varney Cantodea pithily recognizes "I have long given up on any goals I might have had" but this doesn't keep me from being inspired by and responding to everything around me (Baldovin).

acknowledgment

Parts of the discussion of Kant are from Phillip Thurtle, *Biology in the Grid: Graphic Design and the Envisioning of Life* (Minneapolis: U of Minnesota P, 2018) 41–43.

disclosure statement

No potential conflict of interest was reported by the author.

bibliography

Ackerman, A. Bernard, and Marcella Malmusi. *A Critical Review of Apoptosis in Historical Perspective*. Philadelphia: Ardor Scribendi, 1999. Print.

Aktipis, C. Athena, and Randolph M. Nesse. "Evolutionary Foundations for Cancer Biology." *Evolutionary Applications* 6.1 (2013): 144–59. Print.

Baldovin, Nicolae. "Like a Whisper in the Dark. Interview with Anna-Varney Cantodea (Sopor Æternus & the Ensemble of Shadows)." *CVLTartes* 19 Apr. 2016. Web. <http://cultartes.com/like-whisper-dark-interview-anna-varney-cantodea-sopor-aeternus-ensemble-shadows/>.

BioChemWeb.net. "Apoptosis." *The Virtual Library of Biochemistry, Molecular Biology and Cell Biology* 7 Sept. 2017. Web. <http://www.biochemweb.net/apoptosis.shtml>.

Carey, James. "Biology of Death." *Evolution and Medicine Review* 4 July 2008. Web. <https://evmedreview.com/biology-of-death-2/>.

Dumbravă, Mihai D., et al., "A Dinosaurian Facial Deformity and the First Occurrence of Ameloblastoma in the Fossil Record." *Scientific Reports* 6.1 (2016): 1–7. Print.

van Elferen, Isabella. "Dark Timbre: The Aesthetic of Tone Color in Goth Music." *Popular Music* 37.1 (2018): 22–39. Print.

van Elferen, Isabella, and Jeffrey Andrew Weinstock. *Goth Music from Sound to Subculture*. New York: Routledge, 2015. Print.

Emmeche, Claus. "Organicism and Qualitative Aspects of Self-Organization." *Revue Internationale de Philosophie* 228.2 (2004): 205–17. Print.

Gayon, Jean. "Leukemia and Apoptosis: History of Modern Biological Concepts of Death and Disease." *Isis: International Review Devoted to the History of Science and its Cultural Influences* 93.4 (2002): 650–54. Print.

Gould, Stephen Jay. "Introduction." *Dance of the Tiger: A Novel of the Ice Age*. By Björn Kurtén. New York: Random, 1980. Print.

Gubin, Iu M., et al. "[Cranial Bone Neoplasm in Early Triassic Amphibia]." *Voprosy Onkologii* 47.4 (2001): 449–55. Print.

Haridy, Yara, et al. "Triassic Cancer – Osteosarcoma in a 240-Million-Year-Old Stem-Turtle." *JAMA Oncology* 5.3 (2019): 425–26. Print.

Kant, Immanuel. *Critique of the Power of Judgment*. Ed. Paul Guyer. Trans. Paul Guyer and Eric Matthews. Cambridge: Cambridge UP, 2000. Print.

Levins, Richard, and Richard Lewontin. *The Dialectical Biologist*. Cambridge, MA: Harvard UP, 1987. Print.

Maley, Carlo C., et al. "Classifying the Evolutionary and Ecological Features of Neoplasms." *Nature Reviews Cancer* 17.10 (2017): 605–19. Print.

Maturana, Humberto J., and Francisco J. Varela. *Autopoiesis and Cognition: The Realization of the Living*. Dordrecht: Reidel, 1980. Print.

Morange, Michel. "Apoptosis and Programmed Cell Death: When Biological Categories are Blurred." *Journal of Biosciences* 35.2 (2010): 177–81. Print.

Needham, Joseph. "Organicism in Biology." *Journal of Philosophical Studies* 3.9 (1928): 29–40. Print.

Nowell, P.C. "The Clonal Evolution of Tumor Cell Populations." *Science* 194.4260 (1976): 23–28. Print.

Peterson, Erik L. *The Life Organic: The Theoretical Biology Club and the Roots of Epigenetics*. Pittsburgh: U of Pittsburgh P, 2016. Print.

Roberts, Chris. "Siouxsie and the Banshees: How we Made JuJu." *Louder* 20 Apr. 2018. Web. <https://www.loudersound.com/features/siouxsie-and-the-banshees-how-we-made-juju>.

Sedgwick, Eve Kosofsky. *The Coherence of Gothic Conventions*. New York: Routledge, 1986. Print.

Siebers, Tobin. *Disability Theory*. Ann Arbor: U of Michigan P, 1995. Print.

Tarizzo, Davide. *Life: A Modern Invention.* Trans. Mark William Epstein. Minneapolis: U of Minnesota P, 2017. Print.

Thurtle, Phillip. *Biology in the Grid: Graphic Design and the Envisioning of Life.* Minneapolis: U of Minnesota P, 2018. Print.

Westwood, Chris. "Oblique Soundtracks [Seventeen Seconds – Review]." *Record Mirror* 26 Apr. 1980. Print.

Williams, Gilda. "Introduction." *Documents of Contemporary Art: The Gothic.* Ed. Gilda Williams. Cambridge, MA: MIT P, 2002. Print.

Phillip Thurtle

introduction

In 1797, Francisco Goya produced one of his signature prints, *El Sueño de la Razón Produce Monstruos/The Sleep of Reason Produces Monsters*, which implied an antisymmetry between the rational and the monstrous (Fig. 1). However, two centuries later, the decades of World Wars saw the definitive refutation of the inverse: not only is it false that reason excludes monsters, the very operation of rational, quotidian procedures can produce monsters: beings against nature. The operations that produce beings outside nature can themselves be quite ordinary, quotidian, even rational. We can extend our world by amalgamating "monsters" – beings against and therefore outside nature – not by taming them or by exhibiting them in cages, but by enlarging our social, technical, political, epistemic practices to include them. By natural, I will mean that which corresponds to the conceptual understanding scaffolding a suite of common practices about what are the putative entities and substances of the world, and how they interact, an understanding which is sedimented in turn across the experience of structuring, posing, manipulating, and operating with those entities.

My proposition is that politics and ethics, being heterogeneously and contingently dynamic, demand not a fixed conceptual category (metaphysics) or methods, but practices non-reductively accommodating that which is not recognized. Rather than making categorial distinctions, surveys or arguments, I will consider the processes by which monsters emerge and by which the monster becomes part of quotidian practice. This chapter focuses on specific practices in twentieth- and twenty-first-century

sha xin wei

THE SQUARE ROOT OF NEGATIVE ONE IS IMAGINARY

mathematics of articulating, barring, taming, and operating with what mathematicians widely call mathematical monsters (Wagner; Kucharski; Feferman; Cooper; Poincaré). We can regard these practices as examples of what can more generically be called *problematization*, a powerful mode of propositional thought shared by mathematicians and speculative philosophers. In an essay on Bachelard and the problematic, Patrice Maniglier cited Deleuze's critique of representation:

> Problems cannot take the form of an inquiry about the essence of things ("what is matter?," "what is life?," "what is X?"); instead they constitute that which makes it important, relevant, critical, to know about

Fig. 1. Francisco Goya, *El Sueño de la Razón Produce Monstruos*, 1797. El Caprichos 43. Google Art Project, Google Cultural Institute. n.d. Web. 11 Feb. 2020.

X [...] if we problematize the world, it is [...] [not] because our theories offer different alternative routes of empirical verification, but because our own thought proceeds as a process that structures a set of propositions. The structure is neither given in advance, nor constructed: it is all in the making. (23)

In that spirit, I outline the structuration of mathematics accommodating monsters in quotidian, intra-disciplinary practices. I will rehearse how over centuries, the quotidian procedures of even the epitome of rational practice – mathematics – have produced monsters, beings outside the purified categories of theorems and proofs. However, mathematical monsters stand in a different relation to their makers than socio-economic and moral monsters, being in productive tension with mathematicians' collective practice and sedimented intuition.

Different from the governors of madness studied by Foucault in his *History of Madness* (2006), or the students of sexual deviancy described by Arnold Davidson, mathematicians have made much more plural and productive accommodation with their monsters. Although some mathematicians have been persuaded by their logicians and "foundationalists" to bar monsters from the temple of mathematics by simply forbidding the operations that gave rise to those beings against nature, most mathematicians have tamed monsters by extending axioms, definitions, theorems, and methods of proving theorems, or simply cohabiting with monsters as a part of quotidian practice.

I will start the discussion of mathematical monsters with a genealogy of "imaginary" numbers, defined as scalar multiples of the square root of negative one: $\sqrt{-1}$. In order to ply their craft, mathematicians have extended the ontology of number to include rationals,[1] irrationals, and then so-called transcendental numbers, calling their union the *reals*. But say one is interested in solving for $x^2 + 1 = 0$ which can be rewritten $x^2 = -1$. The "solution," following standard algebraic method, is therefore $\sqrt{-1}$. However, the square root of a negative number has no value as long as we are constrained by the ontology of real numbers.

Against that we have the lure of a theorem we would *like* to be true: we can always solve a quadratic equation for *x*. In order to *make* that statement true, one *adjoins* to the field of real numbers entities whose square is negative. No real numbers have that property, yet we can *systematically* extend the operations that real numbers enjoy to include these so-called *imaginary* numbers in an enlarged ontology. I sketch this history in order to make my point as clearly as possible: we can systematically incorporate monsters into our world using *not extraordinary or novel but normalized quotidian procedures* in order to make desired states of affairs the case.

These parables prototype the construction of entities at individual, collective, and institutional scales in a heterodox process of (1) producing beings that appear to be outside or against nature; (2) systematically extending the ontology to incorporate monsters *and their modes of inter-operating in non-exceptional ways with other entities*; and (3) rendering aspirational statements about what we would *like* to be the case for the world, true. This art of extending ontology to incorporate the monstrous into ordinary practice is a most powerful faculty of abductive, problematizing process, which goes beyond the domain of mathematics.[2]

Regardless, the emergence and quotidianization of mathematical monsters, to draw from Deleuze and Guattari, provides a rich set of dynamical practices over centuries and peoples, of processes of *deterritorialization, flight*, and *reterritorialization* that may offer some insight when compared against others such as in the emergence and treatment of legal or social monsters. This essay constructs an *abstract machine* problematizing problematic as a generative process. Criticizing linguists (and indirectly other practitioners of the "major" sciences) for creating theories that "far from being too abstract" are "not abstract enough," Deleuze and Guattari write:

A true abstract machine has no way of making a distinction within itself between a plane of expression and a plane of content because it draws a single plane of consistency, which in turn formalizes contents and expressions according to strata and reterritorializations. The abstract machine in itself is destratified, deterritorialized; it has no form of its own (much less substance) and makes no distinction within itself between content and expression, even though outside itself it presides over that distinction and distributes it in strata, domains, and territories. An abstract machine in itself is not physical or corporeal, any more than it is semiotic; it is diagrammatic (it knows nothing of the distinction between the artificial and the natural either). It operates by matter, not by substance; by function, not by form. Substances and forms are of expression "or" of content. But functions are not yet "semiotically" formed, and matters are not yet "physically" formed. (141)

Mathematics can be regarded in just this way. Experimental physicists make material-energetic instruments to measure (pre-given) entities and processes "in nature" while their theoretical colleagues devise explanatory accounts using mathematical descriptions. Mathematicians however develop mathematical "machinery" to manipulate mathematical entities or to enact mathematical processes and give accounts in mathematical language. Rather than merely observing facts as data, mathematicians invent and prove them as carefully and intentionally constructed webs of definitions, axioms, lemmas, theorems, corollaries. Unlike the natural sciences, mathematics blends what would be quite different strata of beings. Unlike other fictive practices, literature, arts and music, mathematics furnishes its expressions with proofs. In Deleuze and Guattari's sense, mathematics knows nothing of the difference between the artificial and the natural; it works diagrammatically, and its matters are not yet physically formed. This essay introduces some of the entities that emerge from the flux of not yet physically or semiotically formed "matter" called mathematics, in which the stuff of notation as articulation, concepts, and expressions and proofs make *sense* as *movement of thought*.

what is a number?

The field of numbers that we learn in grade school, the natural numbers 1, 2, 3, 4, the "rationals" – fractions p/q where p and q are integers, irrationals like π, or e, did not all spring full-formed from the brow of Pythagoras.

Roi Wagner masterfully works with medieval and Renaissance sources in his book, *Making and Breaking Mathematical Sense* (2017), to argue that the extension to irrational numbers came about as a heterogeneous hybrid of calculations addressed to practical concerns as well as to mathematical ontology. Practically, "abacist" mathematicians solving problems from empirical-economic life such as the division of property, or proportioning of values of currency or goods in the face of fluctuating relative values, found it extremely useful to embed the terms for the varying or the unknown (variables) into the stream of the known (constants and operations).

The rules for manipulating algebraic expressions, in particular binomials,[3] yielded the ontological proliferation of species of entities beyond natural numbers: roots, roots of binomials $A - \sqrt{B}$, and later of negative quantities – *meno* – expressed as binomials of the form 0 less a (positive) number. One could regard the manipulation of symbols as a formal exercise with signifiers that stand in for things ("cosa," abbreviated to "c"). But we can also see the acts of writing as *constituting* entities. For example, algebraic operations born as graphical shorthand for operations that one would follow in order to derive some quantities solving particular problems *generate* entities that heretofore had no representation.[4]

I emphasize that the material substrate makes a difference: operations with abacus vs. knotted rope vs. brush on (indelible) ink vs. stylus on (erasable) sand, make quite different conceptual as well as corporeal demands on the reasoning body. Wagner writes:

> We begin with one species of quantity in abacus mathematics: the binomial – namely, the sum or difference of a number and a root. Belonging to a distinct species, binomials required their own rules, including multiplication rules of terms such as (a – $\sqrt{b}$)(c – $\sqrt{d}$). The discussion of the multiplication of the two subtracted roots (referred to as *meno*, literally "less") in a product of such binomials was extracted from this context, giving rise to independent rules for *meno* numbers, including the famous "minus times minus is plus." Extracted from binomials, *meno* became a new species of number, carrying with it the rules derived from the rules governing Maestro Dardi's mid-fourteenth-century algebra.
>
> Next, without any fanfare or ado, we have the following ground-breaking paragraph, possibly the first in Europe to thematize a negative or debited solution independently of an explicit economic context. (49–50)

Wagner provides a translation of Dardi's fourteenth-century text:

> Know that when you get C [*cosa*, thing] and numbers on one side equal to nothing (as some equations can be in many of the cases that we've discussed, many of which involve a difference or other things), you have to subtract the numbers from both sides, and you'll get C equal nothing *meno* number, in which case you have to divide the number which is *meno* by the quantity of the C. Whatever comes from this is the C *debita*. Suppose that you get 5C and 15 n[umbers] equal to nothing. Divide the 15 by 5, there comes 3, and such will be *debita* the unknown [*cosa*].[5]

Taking the roots of expressions involving integers introduce irrationals, numbers that cannot be expressed as ratios of integers, and thus cannot be constructed by classical mathematical procedures of proportions. We emphasize that these procedures are constituted from corporeal manipulations with physical

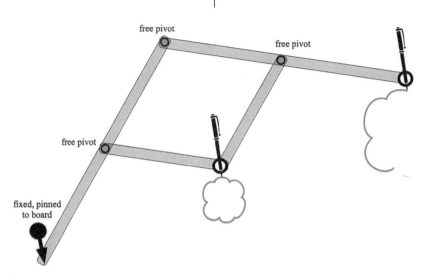

Fig. 2. A pantograph, with one point pinned to a substrate but the rest of the rigid rods on pivots can slide freely across the drawing surface. The proportions of the distances from pens to the ends of their respective rods is the magnification ratio. Hero of Alexandria (c. AD 10–85) described a version of the pantograph.

instruments on physical material substrates like chalk on slate or ink on papyrus (Fig. 2).

the imaginary number *i*

Even the simplest radical, the square root, generated a deeper crisis. Every number, when multiplied by itself, i.e., squared, must be nonnegative. This axiom of the real numbers, which in fact is closed under the basic operations of + (addition) and × (multiplication) with units and inverses, is what was necessary to make consistent the handling of binomials.[6]

However, algebraic procedures yielded monsters in the course of ordinary manipulation. To illustrate this, we reach a few centuries downstream to Descartes. The great innovation of Rene Descartes' analytic geometry is to identify graphical with algebraic entities (Fig. 3). Thus, if a curve is associated with polynomial $p(x)$, the zeros (or roots) of the polynomial – numbers x_0 such that $p(x_0) = 0$ – are also the zero-crossings of the curve – points $<x_0, 0>$ in the plane where that associate curve crosses the *x*-axis. However, this identification introduces a geometric prejudice: reality is that which can be represented on the Cartesian diagram. One would like to affirm that the geometric object and the curve associated with an algebraic polynomial $p(x)$ are the same object, merely shifted.

In other words, one would like to be able to affirm that inessential transformations of the graphical aspect should not change the "algebraic" qualities of the associate polynomial. In fact, the most general theorem that the algebraists would like to be true is that a polynomial of degree n has n roots, no matter what its particulars.

However, this is not the case. As Figure 3 shows graphically, adding a constant to a cubic polynomial whose associate curve crosses the *x*-axis in three points, can shift it to curve crossing the *x*-axis in only one point. In other words, this shifted polynomial has lost two of its intersections. Yet the algebraic formulas discovered by Ferro, Tartaglia, and Cardano in the sixteenth century that yield the zeros of any cubic $ax^3 + bx + c$ are derived and expressed *indifferently* in terms of its coefficients a, b, c. In principle, *any* constant number can be substituted into those algebraic expressions. Descartes wrote:

> Au reste tant les vrayes racines que les fausses ne sont pas tousjours reelles; mais quelquefois seulement imaginaires; c'est a dire qu'on peut bien tousjours en imaginer

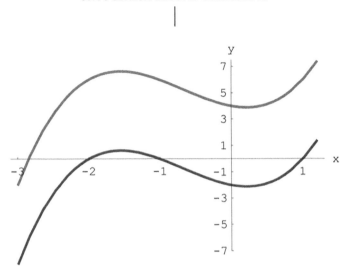

Fig. 3. The curve associated to cubic polynomial p(x) with three intersections (roots) can be shifted up to curve with only a single intersection, associated with the polynomial p(x) + some constant.

autant que jay dit en chasque Equation; mais qu'il n'y a quelquefois aucune quantité, qui corresponde a celles qu'on imagine, comme encore qu'on en puisse imaginer trois en celle cy, x³ − 6xx + 13x − 10 = 0, il n'y en a toutefois qu'une reelle, qui est 2, & pour les deux autres, quoy qu'on les augmente, ou diminue, ou multiplie en la façon que je viens d'expliquer, on ne sçauroit les rendre autres qu'imaginaires. (380)

Moreover, the true roots as well as the false [roots] are not always real; but sometimes only imaginary [quantities]; that is to say, one can always imagine as many of them in each equation as I said; but there is sometimes no quantity that corresponds to what one imagines, just as although one can imagine three of them in this [equation], x³ − 6xx + 13x − 10 = 0, only one of them however is real, which is 2, and regarding the other two, although one increase, or decrease, or multiply them in the manner that I just explained, one would not be able to make them other than imaginary [quantities].[7]

In Descartes' example, the polynomial $p(x)$ is $x^3 - 6x^2 + 13x - 10 = 0$, can also be written as $(x - 2)(x^2 - 4x + 5) = 0$. One solution is the real value 2. The other two solutions can only be constructed as expressions involving the square root of a negative number. This forces the consideration of numbers that, when multiplied by themselves, yield a negative number, *but there is no real number that multiplied by itself yields a negative number!* Imagine a garden A meters by A meters square, with a total area of $A \times A = A^2$. If A were such a quantity involving the square root of a *negative* quantity, lengthening side of length A would yield *less* area, not more. The mechanical application of a standardized algebraic procedure meant to simply find a solution to an abstract equation contradicts our physical spatial experience and classical geometric interpretation. Small wonder that Descartes called these entities *imaginary*.

Yet, a geometric understanding of imaginary numbers is possible in an enlarged mathematical ontology. Adjoining the square root of negative one, $\sqrt{-1}$, written as i, to the real numbers, lifts the algebraic operations from the one dimension of the real numbers to the two-dimensional field of what mathematicians call *complex* numbers. This is a *structural* operation that extends the universe of entities and makes the Fundamental Theorem of Algebra: *every polynomial of degree n has exactly n roots* – not true in the domain of real numbers – true in the extended domain of complex numbers.

Intricately extending the mathematical ontology in order to render true a theorem is one of the creative motors of mathematical ontogenesis. Moreover, whole universes of new properties, techniques, and theorems in what later became the mathematical field of complex analysis open up that have no analogs in the prior domain of the functions on the "reals" $\mathbb{R}$. Indeed, proving the Fundamental Theorem of Algebra took three centuries of progressively richer mathematics, most of which lay outside the domain of algebra itself.[8] The key evolution in mathematical intent was to shift from constructing explicit solutions (in radicals) given explicit coefficients for particular problems, to the study of *conditions* of existence of zeros and the structures (later formalized as algebraic *fields*) in which such zeros existed, in what Deleuze called a "dialectic" subsumption of problem, a *problematizing* move.

do they bite? ...

Wagner points out that the identification of some entities as ontological monsters is also an artifact of the exclusiveness and small number of institutionally recognized professional mathematicians among all users of mathematics.

> But even in classical Greece, practical people went on with the daily business of mixing geometry and arithmetic [...] It was only a small elite that practiced pure geometry. This elite constituted a distributed network of players writing in a practically secret language – not in the sense of a cipher, but in the sense of a highly codified lexicon, syntax, and logic that could not be imitated without proper initiation. (Wagner 28–29)

In practice, mathematicians, by which we include all people who engaged in geometrical or arithmetic reasoning whether for practical or intrinsic mathematical interests, have responded quite diversely to novel entities:

> We see here that plural practical mathematics, which lives with monsters, and codified scholarly mathematics, which seeks to bar monsters, have a third alternative. We'll call it monster taming: the translation of new and suspect entities into the language of an established foundation. The tension between the three strategies is one that mathematics continued to engage with throughout its future. (Wagner 30)

But the kind of monstrousness has become radically more challenging over the 130 years, since Weierstrass and Poincaré. Indeed, the radicality of the monsters' monstrousness has grown hand in hand with the heightening of logical rigor and formalization of mathematical statements in predicate calculus and set theory. It is as if the steelier the gaze and the brighter the light of reason, the more ferocious the monsters made visible and produced by rational regard.

A different order of monster was introduced during the formation of quantum mechanics in the beginning of the twentieth century, the notion of *distributions*. A function is defined as a mapping f from one set X to another set Y, such that for every z in X, there is at most one value $f(z)$ in Y (see Fig. 4). Borrowing the classical terminology of action, implicitly mathematicians regard the argument z as being the patient to the agent f which acts or operates on z.

A particularly wild function is the Dirichlet indicator function on the set of rationals

$d(x) = 1$ if x is a ratio of integers, 0 if x is irrational

which is radically disjointed, in fact it is everywhere discontinuous.[9] Given the infinite density of the rational numbers and irrational numbers – between any two rational numbers there are uncountably many irrational numbers *and* pairs of rational numbers can be arbitrarily close – it is impossible to legibly plot $d(x)$ (see Fig. 5 for a graph of the derived "popcorn" function).

Paul Dirac introduced the delta function $\delta(x)$ (Fig. 6) to model bodies as extensionless points. (In gravitational physics, material bodies interact equivalently to bodies with all their mass concentrated at their center of mass, an extensionless point.) $\delta(x)$ is not to be understood as a function like p with a determinate value $p(x)$ for every value of x. Rather, $\delta(x)$ is a prototype whose behavior is defined in terms of how it interacts with other functions. Intuitively, $\delta(x)$ is thought of as a smooth differentiable function that is zero everywhere except at $x = 0$,

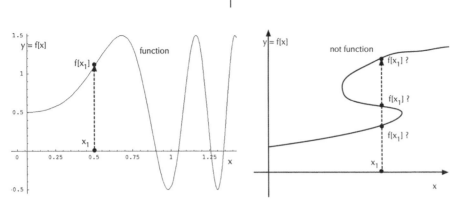

Fig. 4. The graph on the left is a function with a unique well-defined value f[x] for each x. In the graph on the right, f[x₁] has three possible values at x₁, so it is not well defined at x₁.

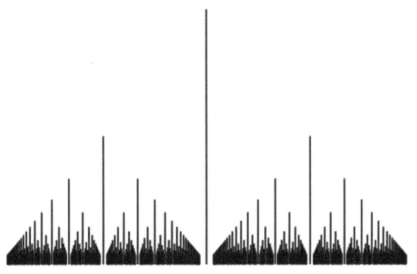

Fig. 5. Thomae's "popcorn" function T(x), a modification of the Dirichlet indicator function where T(x) equals 0 for irrational x, and equal to 1/q for x = p/q in reduced form. Whereas the indicator function is everywhere discontinuous, the popcorn function T is continuous at every irrational x, and discontinuous at every rational x.

undefined at $x = 0$, yet has integral 1:

$$\int_{\mathbb{R}} \delta(x)dx = 1.$$

$\delta(x)$ therefore has the paradoxical property of being zero everywhere except at a point where it is undefined, yet *has a nonzero area under the curve of 1*. This odd behavior depends on the common understanding of the Riemann integral as the area under the curve $f(x)$ over an interval $[a, b]$.

To say that $\delta(x)$ is an almost entirely zero-valued curve with area 1 may not seem very intuitive or useful. Yet, because of the mathematical properties of integrals, the delta function is granted a remarkable power: for arbitrary integrable function $f(x)$,

$$\int_{\mathbb{R}} \delta(x)dx = f(0).$$

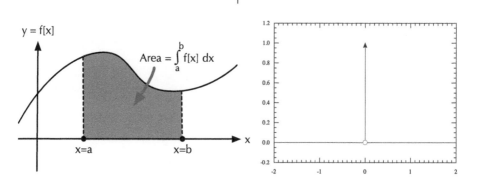

Fig. 6. The integral of classical f(x) can be interpreted as the area under the curve y = f(x). The Dirac delta informally thought of as a "function" that is zero everywhere except at x = 0, has no "area" under its profile, and should have integral 0. But it is *posited* to have integral 1, with generative implications.

It is as if the $\delta(x)$ were a lens that, applied to any other function f, captures the value of that function at 0, in other words $f(0)$.

Heuristically engineers and physicists work with these "generalized functions" *as if* they were functions. Later, mathematicians constructed axiomatic, proof-based theories in which generalized functions could be rigorously understood as entities in their own right *not* as functions, but as limit objects whose existence and qualities could only indirectly be inferred by *convolution* against well-behaved functions.[10]

Let us loosen the attachment of the symbolic operation to the specific field of interpretation and focus on two conceptual operations – *diagrams* of thought – in the problematization of mathematical function, synonymously, transform or mapping. The first conceptual operation or diagram of thought is the idea of characterizing a putative entity not in its own right, but by how it "projects" against known entities. Under such an operation of *convolution* it is as if objects cast light onto one another. Thus, each object serves as an instrument that casts shadows of their peers through their ambience.

A second, related conceptual operation is reversing the agent–patient relation between a function f and an argument x taken its domain (e.g., numbers). Instead of fixing a function and seeing how it acts on elements taken from a domain, we can take a specific element x' (e.g., 0), and consider x' not as a number but as an *operator on the set of all functions*, that acts on a function g by assigning to g the value $g(x')$.

An example from a non-mathematical domain of practice would be applying a law L to person p, in situation s, symbolically written: $L(p, s)$. Note that this may be presumed to be *not* a numerical function and *not* subject to algorithmic implementation, so in principle cannot be represented in any Turing-equivalent computing machine. Instead of taking the perspective of applying a specific law L to the set of "all" people, we can consider a specific person p, and how she "acts" on laws by having them applied to her. In other words, a person p, in a situation s, can be considered an *operator* on a set of laws by mapping a given law L to the effect $L(p, s)$, for "all" laws L. This reversal from operand to operator is quite a general and powerful conceptual move.[11] To these two conceptual operations, we will add progressively more radical abstract machines of problematization in the register of Deleuze and Guattari.

geometric monsters as limits of infinite processes

Suppose we wish to characterize the form of a collective in the twenty-first century general (Bataillean) economy that is optimal for, say, social equity, use of know-how, and dynamic resilience of the ambient biosemiotic ecology. One could try to do statistics on sets of particular structures' accidental features but given the boundless richness of possible worlds, it would be unreasonable to try to extrapolate from a

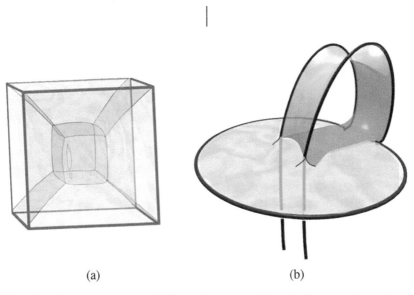

Fig. 7. Minimal surfaces spanning non-trivial boundary curves: (a) a wire frame as a boundary; (b) a non-closed boundary.

few empirical observations, or a probabilistic analysis absent a priori knowledge of the distribution. One might, however, derive theorems such as how power is distributed throughout the collective under the condition that its structure is static, or dynamic.

One could try to prove that there exists an optimal form according to those criteria. Even if some conditions seem "natural," existence must be established, not assumed. Even if a series of ever more "optimal" entities can be constructed, a "smooth," i.e., non-monstrous, limit may not exist! We will see that even in the more well-defined situations of differential geometry (called for by Deleuze in *Difference and Repetition*, and more explicitly invoked in Deleuze and Guattari's *A Thousand Plateaus*), monsters can arise. We can compare this to the question of evolving locally according to some measure (any measure!), and see how an evolutionary process can yield ever more baroque entities. Therefore, whether optimality according to given criteria implies or is implied by flat, hierarchical, or distributed (network) structures cannot be a formal (in particular a computational) problem; it becomes a philosophical, politico-economic, and ethico-aesthetic problematic.

Turning to geometrical and infinite processes with an effective interpretation of limit, we consider the mathematical problem of finding a shape of minimal area spanning a given boundary.[12] The problem has two parts: (1) for a given bounding curve, does a spanning surface even exist? This in turn raises the question: what is a surface? (2) Is that least-area surface regular (smoothly differentiable) aside from some well-defined set of singularities? (Fig. 7).

One way to approach this is to find a necessary condition that any such area-minimizing object must satisfy. *Rather than attempting to directly describe or parametrize the putative entity whose existence and nature is unknown, it is common to first establish conditions for existence of such a family of entities.* In the case of law, when interests of material social collectives are at stake, the opposite approach may be taken: given a putative entity such as the corporation as a legal person, elevate its status by finding metaphysical principles and arguments that make that entity seem durable and inevitable. In this case, the condition arises as the form of a nonlinear partial differential equation. Then consider the infinite, indeed continuous, plenum of all objects that span the boundary and whose area is bounded. In this plenum, if one could find a sequence of surfaces $S_1, S_2, S_3, \ldots$ whose areas are decreasing, we might expect

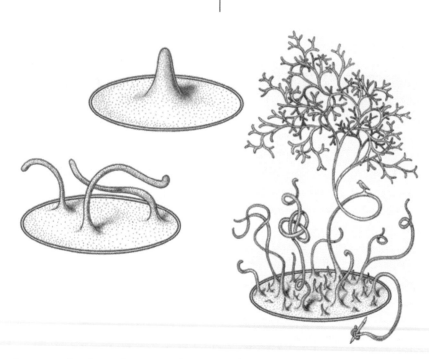

Fig. 8. Sequence of surfaces whose areas decrease to the minimum, but whose topological complexity grows ever wilder.

that this sequence should, in the limit, approach an at least locally optimal spanning surface. But consider Figure 8: even if an area-minimizing limit object were to exist, it is not at all obvious that that "optimal" object is regular – a smooth surface without singularities.[13] Monstrous sets can appear literally out of thin air under even the simplest infinite processes, as discovered by students of geometry, measure theory, and topology in the early twentieth century (Sha, *Poiesis*).

Somewhat like the example of interpreting $x = 0$ not as a number but as an *operator* to be applied to functions, such examples of pathological subsets, to use an adjective from mathematicians' parlance, impelled the characterization of those subsets indirectly not as smooth surfaces a priori, but as *operators* on *fields*.

interior exterior boundary monster

One of the most basic topological qualities of a domain is whether it resembles a "solid chunk" of space, with no holes in it, which we call simply connected. We can formalize the property of *simply-connectedness* (Sha, "Topology and Morphogenesis" 239). The test for a domain U to be simply connected is simple: a loop in U can be contracted to a point without passing outside of U. For example, the *complement* of a torus in R^3 is not simply connected because a "bracelet" around the torus cannot be slid and shrunk to a point without cutting into the torus (and thus passing outside its complement). An ordinary closed loop in the plane R^2 cuts the plane into two components each of which is simply connected. One would expect that a sphere would in general dimensions have an inside and an outside that are simply connected, but this is false in higher dimensions given the example of Alexander's Horned Sphere (Fig. 9): a two-dimensional surface which is homeomorphic to the ordinary round sphere in R^3, but is constituted as a limit of an infinite, convergent process which partitions the ambient space in a surprising way.[14] A bracelet looped around a branch of the Horned Sphere can never be slipped off without

Fig. 9. Alexander's Horned Sphere.

cutting through some branch in its infinitely dense tangle of iteratively constructed protuberances. Therefore, the outside of the Horned Sphere is not simply connected.

Such objects as the Horned Sphere or the Sierpinski spoke or "space-filling" curves and surfaces, which as defined as limit objects in terms of infinite, yet non-divergent series of finite procedures, were called "pathological" by mathematicians when they were constructed, mostly as limits of infinite processes. They constitute a new kind of non-anthropocentric partial object, "objectiles," to use Deleuze's notion (from Bernard Cache),

> The new status of the object no longer refers its condition to a spatial mold – in other words, to a relation of form-matter – but to a temporal modulation that implies as much the beginnings of a continuous variation of matter as a continuous development of form.
> [...] perspectivism, [...] does not mean a dependence in respect to a pregiven or defined subject; to the contrary, a subject will be what comes to the point of view, or rather what remains in the point of view. That is why the transformation of the object refers to a correlative transformation of the subject: the subject is not a subject but, as Whitehead says, a "superject." Just as the object becomes objectile, the subject becomes a superject. (Deleuze, *The Fold* 19–20)

Consider the law as a set of decision processes, code, and professional practices that partitions social space into the legal or illegal, public or private, citizen or non-citizen, corporate person or individual person. In other words, think of "the law" acting as a *boundary* between regions of juridical ontology (Sha, *Poiesis* 152–53). Just as there are topological techniques, machinery, theorems, articulating the relative topology of how a closed surface partitions its complement according to how it is embedded, we can think of how the law's endless and boundless proliferation and *infinite* crenellation partitions social space non-trivially.[15] Just as topological problematizing thought yields provable theorems without metrical data, legal problematizing thought can yield insight without data or surveys. To be clear, I do not propose to simply apply the same instruments and theorems to social legal entities and processes! Instead, I propose to problematize the thought of boundary, interior and exterior via an *abstraction*, but not an application, of topological problematic.

Mathematicians find such surprising *counter-examples* to conjectures that seem intuitively true, extremely productive because they sharpen the coordinated construction of definitions and axioms, statements of conjectures, proof methods, and proofs together with sedimentation into shared intuition what to expect to be true about this class of entities. One cannot over-emphasize this point: we do not have to pre-state the entity in terms of all of its characteristics, or pre-establish the instruments for observing or measuring it, or pre-decide the methods for proving theorems (facts) about those entities. Indeed, what entities come to foreground can be functions of the frames of aspired theorems – what we would *like* to be the case.

We will revisit this question of intuition with Solomon Feferman's discussion of entities that are monstrous in much more fundamental ways, due not to a proof procedure or a mathematical operation like taking a limit of generalized surfaces.

purifying rules of thought – banach–tarski paradox and gödel incompleteness theorems

In 1924, Stefan Banach and Alfred Tarski proved a monstrous offspring of the recent combination of the most rigorous techniques for articulating and proving theorems about mathematical entities. The foundational element from which we derive this last derivation of a mathematical monster is the transfinite Axiom of Choice (AC). Intuitively, the AC is the assumption that for every family of subsets of a set, one can choose one element out of each. Slightly more formally, for every countable family of subsets $\{U_i\}_{i=1,2,3...}$ of a set X, there is a subset K of X comprising of exactly one element from each set U_i.[16]

To generalize the notion of area to arbitrary sets of some set X, we define what mathematicians call a measure: a mapping from subsets of X to the real numbers $\mathbb{R}$.

A measure μ is *finitely additive*, if

(i) A and B are disjoint then $\mu(A \cup B) = \mu(A) + \mu(B)$,
(ii) μ is isometry-invariant, i.e., if A is transformed into A' by a rigid motion then $\mu(A) = \mu(A')$, and
(iii) μ normalizes the unit "cube" C in R^n, i.e., $\mu(C) = 1$.

We define a set A to be *paradoxical* if it is equivalent by finite decomposition to the union of two disjoint copies A' and A'' of itself.

In 1924, Stefan Banach and Alfred Tarski proved the surprising result that: for each $n \geq 3$ the unit ball in R^n is paradoxical. Moreover, they proved that any two bounded subsets of R^n each with non-empty interior are equivalent by *finite* decomposition. This Banach–Tarski Paradox implied that the unit ball could be partitioned into disjoint pieces that could be slid apart, each of which would be equivalent to a sphere with μ-measure equal to the original sphere – a measure-theoretic version of the miracle of loaves and fishes.

Something has broken, or rather the combination of several intuitions put together has broken – the intuitions of "part" of a geometric object, of how an object can be partitioned (e.g., the notion of "choice"), of volume. As Feferman points out, the Banach–Tarski monster is a different order of monster from earlier ones in that it is the very proof procedure itself that is called into doubt: can one or can one not appeal to the AC – carefully refined from ordinary operation and intuition of selecting representatives from subsets, in the same practice that also appeals to sets "in general" – carefully refined from our ordinary experience working with assemblages. Feferman writes:

> Here, rather, the proof is put in question (at least by some), and it is the necessary use of AC [Axiom of Choice] that makes it

questionable; so, the monster is "avoided" by simply barring the use of AC from proofs. But one can reasonably take the opposite position that the monster has not ceased to exist thereby, only that one has somehow hidden from it in this way. (325)

Note the radical quality of such a scorched earth approach to purifying the rules of thought. Disallowing legal arguments referring to distinctions based on gender or ethnicity, and so forth renders sexist or racist acts invisible to the law. Feferman concludes on a pragmatic basis that may seem too mild to those of more formal temperament:

> reliability of intuition undermine its uses in its everyday roles in research, teaching and the development of mathematics? I have argued that intuition is essential for all of these, but that intuition is not enough. In the end, to be sure, everything must be defined carefully and statements must be proved [...] But if the proofs themselves produce such monsters, then the significance of what is proved requires closer attention, and that has to be dealt with on a case-by-case basis. (328)

Perhaps the most fundamental challenge in this regard – of what can be established by the formalizable concurrent development of intuitions (about mathematical entities), axioms and definitions, techniques of proof, and systems of theorems and proofs, all conditioned by the emergence and accommodation of monsters to be tamed, barred, or lived with – is Kurt Gödel's incompleteness theorems. Roughly, in any mathematical theory (based on axiom, definition, predicate calculus, proof) incorporating the integers, one can construct a statement that has no proof inside that formal system. In particular, in any mathematical theory containing the integers, there is no algorithm that can decide (prove) all statements.

But disagreeing with Turing, Wittgenstein had a sanguine assessment of the practical implications of Gödel's incompleteness theorems:

> If you based something on this system [a mathematical theory incorporating the integers and thus necessarily containing inconsistency], I don't see that it would necessarily be detrimental if there were a contradiction in it, as long as this contradiction is just not used as a thoroughfare or circus [thus allowing to derive any statement whatsoever] [...] The only point would be: how to avoid going through the contradiction unawares. (227)

Wittgenstein's logical plurality of mathematical practice stands next to ethical plurality due to the non-simultaneity of the material-causal world.[17] It is an eminently pragmatic attitude. Roi Wagner echoes this pragmatic attitude in his summary of how mathematicians variously deal with their monsters:

> We see here that plural practical mathematics, which lives with monsters, and codified scholarly mathematics, which seeks to bar monsters, have a third alternative. We'll call it *monster taming*: the translation of new and suspect entities into the language of an established foundation. The tension between the three strategies is one that mathematics continued to engage with throughout its future. (30)

Indeed, it is the ability to make conjectures, play propositionally, learn from the emergence and generative constructions with monsters, and even prove theorems on yet to be completely tamed or comprehended bestiaries, that enables the evolution of fresh mathematics. Wagner writes:

> [M]onsters will continue to permeate mathematics. These monsters live at the level of interpretation. It's not that we have to hold on to all relevant interpretations all of the time. But our reconstruction, superposition, and deferral of interpretations are monstrous in their own way.
>
> [...]
>
> In contemporary mathematics, when these interpretation strategies generate conflicts and mathematical monsters, we can count on the arbitration of formal languages to keep mathematical claims in line. In the past, the later resolution of ambiguity did not apply in quite this way, and led to some

substantial debates over the legitimacy of some well-reasoned mathematical entities and claims. But either way, mathematicians did and still do use ambiguities productively. Monsters are a mathematician's friends. (98)

With Wittgenstein, Feferman, and Wagner, we see a living mathematics that ranges far from the Descartes' "dialectic," with a prolific "effective genesis" that generates and accommodates monsters.[18] At the same time, it is the case that never before has there been such consistency and agreement – invariant across generations and sociocultural condition – in mathematics as in the twentieth and twenty-first centuries. This consensus seems to be more consistent in mathematics than any other knowledge practice. As Wagner argues, this is the result of the incorporation of several major methods and practices into contemporary mathematics, notably: the *predicate calculus* which provided a formal way to clearly express all mathematical statements, axiomatic method, the adoption of the *working* formal ground of set theory to underlie all structures, all families of entities.[19] Perhaps equally important is the training of mathematicians since the late nineteenth century to be able to settle disputes on demand by partial formalization to the degree necessary to achieve agreement among mathematicians. Rather than argue that this transindividual, trans-generational, trans-cultural consensus indicates that mathematics points to a higher truth, Wagner notes that this kind of formalizability redefined what constituted mathematical inquiry. He writes that the consensus achievable in modern mathematics is "so successful that any question or argument that could not be submitted to this arbitration mechanism became a nonmathematical question, and was exported to other branches of knowledge" (Wagner 69).

production of novel entities

To recapitulate, we have seen in the course of more or less quotidian activity in mathematics how novel entities and structured spaces of entities co-articulate together with novel practices and theories of those entities. The relations that structure the extended domains of entities themselves emerge out of what can be done by and to those entities. This is an important point. On the one hand, there is no transcendental category or principle prior to the proposition of the entities to which lawyers and judges, or mathematicians appeal. On the other, what emerges in quotidian practice introduces opportunities for establishing through practice and even proof, what practitioners would *like* to be the case.

In the *Mode of Existence of Technical Objects* (2016), Simondon's examples of the steam/diesel engine, the vacuum tube/cathode ray screen, and the clay brick with its mold neatly and naturally partition their world into the material-energetic technical object, the technical individual, and the immaterial fields of individually incorporated and institutionally structured technique. Simondon elaborates in great detail how these technical ensembles, individuals and their milieu co-articulate one another. In this section we launch an analogous program but with a shift in the constitutive material, in this case, mathematical entities, and with a focus on their particular processes of ontogenesis.

Recall the characterization of the form of mathematical problematization which is the co-articulation of four mutually enabling strands of thought: (1) developing intuitions about putative entities and condensing them into definitions and axioms; (2) effectively operating with or relating these entities; (3) making conjectures – speculated or aspired truths – and condensing them into theorems and counterexamples; and (4) creating proofs and modes or techniques of proof.[20] Counterexamples to conjectured, would-be theorems are mathematical constructions, entities, or processes that satisfy the hypotheses, but contradict the claim, showing that the conjecture is not true. Counterexamples play a constitutive role in proliferating mathematics, sharpening both definitions and proofs.

Characterizing putative entities by their consequences – their effects, by how they act in the world is a pragmatist procedure. For example: measurable but pathologically non-differentiable sets – in terms of how they behave under integration against test functions such as indicator functions on balls.[21] An example in law would be integrating how a right-and-duty-bearing corporate entity acts in the world – if it engages in contracts with other persons, and if it takes responsibility at the same time that it assumes rights to property.

Another example is the *operator*. Consider a school, whose mandated operation is to educate any child who walks in through its doors, helping the child grow into the ambient society. One could pick one school and see how it performs with its students. Or one could take a child of immigrants and see how the child *operates on* the schools that she or he may encounter. In other words, rather than being an "input" to a fixed school, we can reverse the attention, and think of a given child as "acting" on an arbitrary school by being enrolled in it.

A final example is the method of proof – of thought comprising the seeking conditions of existence. For example, one asks what are the conditions under which an entity exists, in counterpoint with the discussion of what characteristics it would enjoy, or how it would operate, were it to exist, as in the discussion above of minimal surfaces.

When mathematicians extend their mathematical ontology, they do much more than set theoretic inclusion. And it is not enough to simply argue that the inconsistency is a function of contingency, of historical "rupture." A host of extensions of operations are invented, recognized, or deployed. For example, in order to accommodate the square root of negative one, mathematicians were led by logical argument to extend the one-dimensional set of real numbers (the grade school "number line") to the *two-dimensional field* of real + what mathematicians technically called "imaginary" numbers. Historians of mathematics have shown that mathematics develops no less contingently than other fields of practice, yet mathematical practices have developed in an effectively objective and uniquely durable consensus enriched by ever more mathematical monsters roaming both tamed and free.[22]

disclosure statement

No potential conflict of interest was reported by the author.

notes

I thank colleagues in the Ontogenetics Process Group, in particular Giuseppe Longo, Adam Nocek, Gaymon Bennett, Stuart Kauffman, Cary Wolfe, Mike Epperson, and Phil Thurtle for gamely responding to my piecemeal thoughts. I thank Niklas Damiris and Helga Wild for extensive conversations over the years, and Gabriele Carotti-Sha for careful feedback.

1 What may seem to be colorful language is actually historically justified, as "rational" derives from the notion of "ratio" in Latin, for numbers that can be written as an integer divided by another integer: such as 5/2 whose decimal form is 2.5, or 355/113 whose decimal form is close to 3.141592. Irrational numbers are numbers that cannot be written as ratios of integers except by approximation, such as the number $\pi = 3.141592653589\ldots$ Now one can think of a ratio say 5/2, as a solution to a very simple equation $x = 5/2$, which can be rewritten as $2x - 5 = 0$, so every rational number is the solution to a polynomial equation with integer coefficients, familiar to ancient Greek, Arab, and Chinese mathematicians. However, one can also start with a polynomial equation in the form $p[x] = p_n x^n + p_{n-1} x^{n-1} + \ldots + p_1 x + p_0$, where the coefficients p_i are integers, and ask for the x that yields $p[x] = 0$.

2 In *Capitalist Sorcery* (2011), Philippe Pignarre and Isabelle Stengers identify what they call *infernal choices*. For making healthcare a scarce resource and then demanding the public or boards of experts to prioritize access, when in fact that scarcity is an artifact of vectoring healthcare through private insurance companies whose interest is orthogonal to caring for people's health, but to maximize profit and minimize cost due to "risk." In other words, conflating healthcare with *insurance*. Another canonical example would be nations in which electoral systems present candidates and parties from such a narrow spectrum of political programs that: (1) the majority of people's interests are not represented by formal parties; and (2) noise effects can determine the balance of power. (Such a system can come

about when parties try to win elections with programs constructed not on principle or argument or even history but purely to maximize statistical appeal. This leads to platforms that converge to the mean, yielding parties whose platforms do not provide strong distinctions.)

I underline that my purpose is not to address specific faults in present-day political economic systems, but to address the sorcery of presenting social, technical, affective appearance as if it were the only possible world. We can propose the amalgamation of incommensurate worlds as an alchemical alternative to rational or transcendental politics, as well as a politics of recurrent negation.

3 These are operations that one would follow in order to derive some quantities solving numeric or geometric problems.

4 See Sha Xin Wei, "Differential Geometrical Performance" and *Differential Geometric Performance*.

5 From Dardi (1344 (2001): 297) quoted by Roi Wagner (50).

6 Rather than simply repeat what we learn by rote, let's rehearse a bit of algebraic reasoning that evolved over centuries of mathematical practice between Rome and the Crusades. Applying the notion of proportioning and debt, a minus times a plus yields a minus. (If you owe a debt of 2 to each of 20 people, you have a total debt of 40.) The question is how to interpret the product of two negative numbers.
Let
$P := (a + b)$.
Algebraists already had available the ordinary operation of multiplying two binomials together, yielding:
$P^2 = (a + b) \times (a + b) = a^2 + 2a \times b + b^2$.
Applying that with $a = 10, b = -2$, on the one hand as ordinary integers:
$(10 - 2) \times (10 - 2) = 8 \times 8 = 64$
but as binomials, we have:
$(10 - 2) \times (10 - 2) = 10^2 + 2 \times (10) \times (-2) + (-2)^2$.
So the terms become:
$100 - 40 + (-2) \times (-2) = 60 + (-2) \times (-2)$.
This implies that the consistent way to interpret how to multiply two negative quantities together is via the rule: minus times minus is a plus.

7 Translation from <https://en.wikipedia.org/wiki/Imaginary_number#cite_note-9>.

8 See an efficient summary of proofs of the Fundamental Theorem of Algebra in <https://en.wikipedia.org/wiki/Fundamental_theorem_of_algebra#Proofs>.

9 The indicator function $f(x)$ is defined by $f(x) = 1$ if x is rational, of the form p/q where p and q are integers, 0 otherwise. <http://mathworld.wolfram.com/images/eps-gif/DirichletFunction_1000.gif>.

10 Using mathematical measure theory which generalizes the notion of area to arbitrary sets, such "generalized functions" are understood consistently as measures concentrated at a point. This is different from the colloquial sense of the term. See Tao.

11 One can carry this far in the domain of functional analysis, to consider the algebraic structure of the spaces of functions and the spaces of what they act on. See Rudin.

12 One of the richest areas of mathematics over the past 250 years sprang from Plateau's problem – the problem of finding the surface of least area among all surfaces spanning a given closed curve. First posed by Lagrange in 1760, Plateau's problem in its classical formulation withstood attack till 1930, and was solved independently by Douglas and Radó. See Almgren, and Harrison and Pugh.

13 A lot of the work requires subtly considering what is meant by "spanning" a boundary, defining notions of regularity ("smoothness") that make provable sense even for entities that cannot be presumed to exist a priori as classically pointwise-defined functions. Even more profoundly, one needs to extend the notion of "area" when we cannot assume almost no information about entities whose existence has yet to be proven. We would for example need to prove that some a priori arbitrary set of points in fact has the local structure of a k-dimensional surface.

14 In this case, the Horned Sphere is itself defined as the limit of an infinitely iterated process: start with a fairly homogeneously shaped closed surface that is topologically a sphere. (We are describing a topological surface, in which case we do not care about particular metrical shape, only that this starting point can be deformed from a round sphere.) Imagine your body's skin as the initial topological sphere. Imagine your two arms as the first-generation "protuberances" from the surface of your skin. Then bring your fists close

to each other, and pop open your index fingers and thumbs. Arrange them so that they are close but not touching. Now zoom in so that your field of attention is filled by the tips of the index finger and thumb of one hand, and interpret them as the second-generation pair of protuberances. The process actually splits into two sub-processes, one for each hand.

15 That the law crenulates is a matter of observation. Why or how the law proliferates boundlessly is another matter; see, for example, Agamben's argument about the juridical as a state of exception.

16 The transfinite Axiom of Choice says the same is true even if we consider uncountably many subsets $\{U_\alpha\}$. In the countable case, one can imagine some iterative process in which one can mutter, "1, 2, 3 ..." as one is picking out an element from each set. The process takes an infinite time, but at least in any finite duration, one can imagine iterating through some process of selection. However, the transfinite case is more unimaginable, because even in principle one cannot iterate through a discrete series of decisions. One of the most powerful aspects of elementary topological methods is that one can prove limits without resorting to series. For example, a basic theorem is that a continuous function on a closed and bounded domain achieves its maximum and minimum in that domain.

17 In mathematical physics, non-simultaneity is a consequence of the finite speed of propagation of material effect. One could argue that mortality or finitude imply that some relations must be ethical because they cannot be causal, thus not determined. See Sha, *Poiesis* 9.

18 Deleuze, *Difference and Repetition* 162.

19 Lian, "Fundamentals of Zermelo–Fraenkel Set Theory," 23 Aug. 2011. <https://www.math.uchicago.edu/~may/VIGRE/VIGRE2011/REUPapers/Lian.pdf>.

20 Such as approximations to the identity in distribution theory.

21 An example would be the area and co-area formulas in geometric measure theory (Simon).

22 For exemplary work on comparative histories of mathematics and science, see Hart, *Chinese Roots* and *Imagined Civilizations*.

bibliography

Almgren, Frederick J. *Plateau's Problem: An Invitation to Varifold Geometry*. Providence: American Mathematical Society, 2001. Print.

Cardano, Girolamo. *Ars Magna, or, The Rules of Algebra*. Trans. Richard Witmore. New York: Dover, 1968. Print.

Cooper, J.L.B. "Mathematical Monsters." *The Mathematical Gazette* 28.326 (1954): 258–65. Web. 3 June 2018.

Davidson, Arnold. "The Horror of Monsters." *The Boundaries of Humanity: Humans, Animals, Machines*. Ed. James J. Sheehan and Morton Sosna. Berkeley: U of California P, 1991. 36–67. Print.

Deleuze, Gilles. *Difference and Repetition*. London: Continuum, 2004. Print.

Deleuze, Gilles. *The Fold: Leibniz and the Baroque*. London: Continuum, 2006. Print.

Deleuze, Gilles, and Felix Guattari. *A Thousand Plateaus: Capitalism and Schizophrenia*. Minneapolis: U of Minnesota P, 1987. Print.

Descartes, René. *Discours de la méthode, troisième livre: la geométrie*. Leiden: Jan Maire, 1637. Print.

Douglas, Jesse. "Solution of the Problem of Plateau." *Transactions of the American Mathematical Society* 33.1 (1931): 263–321. Print.

Feferman, Solomon. "Mathematical Intuition vs. Mathematical Monsters." *Synthese* 125 (2000): 317–32. Print.

Foucault, Michel. *History of Madness*. Trans. Jean Khalfa. New York: Routledge, 2006. Print.

Harrison, Jenny, and Harrison Pugh. "Plateau's Problem: What's Next." *arXiv* 3 May 2016. Web. 22 Aug. 2018. <https://arxiv.org/pdf/1509.03797.pdf>.

Hart, Roger. *The Chinese Roots of Linear Algebra*. Baltimore: Johns Hopkins, 2010. Print.

Hart, Roger. *Imagined Civilizations: China, the West, and their First Encounter*. Baltimore: Johns Hopkins, 2013. Print.

Kucharski, Adam. "Math's Beautiful Monsters." *Nautilus* 3 Apr. 2014. Web. 11 Feb. 2020. <http://nautil.us/issue/11/light/maths-beautiful-monsters>.

Lian, Tony. "Fundamentals of Zermelo–Fraenkel Set Theory." 23 Aug. 2011. Web. 11 Feb. 2020.

Maniglier, Patrice. "What Is a Problematic?" *Radical Philosophy* May/June 2012. Web. 2 Apr. 2020.

Pignarre, Philippe, and Isabelle Stengers. *Capitalist Sorcery: Breaking the Spell.* New York: Palgrave Macmillan, 2011. Print.

Poincaré, Henri. *The Foundations of Science.* Trans. G.B. Halstead. New York: Science P, 1913. Print.

Radó, Tibor. "On Plateau's Problem." *Annals of Mathematics* 31.3 (1930): 457–69. Print.

Rudin, Walter. *Functional Analysis.* 2nd ed. New York: McGraw-Hill, 1991. Print.

Sha, Xin Wei. "Differential Geometrical Performance and Poiesis." *Configurations* 12.1 (2005): 133–60. Print.

Sha, Xin Wei. *Differential Geometric Performance and the Technologies of Writing.* Ph.D. Diss. Stanford U, 2001. Print.

Sha, Xin Wei. *Poiesis and Enchantment in Topological Matter.* Cambridge, MA: MIT P, 2013. Print.

Sha, Xin Wei. "Topology and Morphogenesis." *Theory, Culture and Society* 29.4–5 (2012): 220–46. Print.

Simon, Leon. *Lectures on Geometric Measure Theory.* Canberra: Australian National U, 1984. Print.

Simondon, Gilbert. *On the Mode of Existence of Technical Objects.* Trans. Cecile Malaspina and John Rogove. Minneapolis: Univocal, 2016. Print.

Tao, Terence. *An Introduction to Measure Theory.* Providence: American Mathematical Society, 2011. Print.

Wagner, Roi. *Making and Breaking Mathematical Sense: Histories and Philosophies of Mathematical Practice.* Princeton: Princeton UP, 2017. Print.

Wittgenstein, Ludwig. *Lectures on the Foundations of Mathematics, Cambridge.* Chicago: U of Chicago P, 1976. Print.

Sha Xin Wei

helga c. wild

THE SINGULARITY HAS COME AND GONE
the beginning of organization

1 introduction

My title alludes to present-day claims, by Kurzweil and others, that we are about to witness a singularity – namely the moment in history when Artificial Intelligence and robotics will overtake the collective intelligence of the human. I appropriate their term to call out an earlier but equally momentous event: the moment when organization begins to dominate the drives of the individual and subjects them to its ordering principles.

Human beings have relationships, but organization provides the structure to their agency, with levels of hierarchy and subject positions linked by explicit and implicit rules, to which human actors submit in order to coordinate their work and gain its benefits (Bourdieu ch. 3, 53ff.). Individual actions so constrained enact then a stable order, which once established is not further questioned. "Order is a kind of repetition-compulsion by which it is ordained once for all when, where and how a thing shall be done so that on every similar occasion doubt and hesitation shall be avoided" (Freud 55).

How organization has begun to give rise to such coordinated activity is an open question. Theories of organization assume coherence to describe the phenomena unfolding within it; they do not derive it. The power exerted by the whole on its parts, though experienced, is inadequately explained by either the elements or the relations among them.[1]

I use the work of three different authors to present different ways to imagine the beginning. My first vignette deals with Vico's history of society in *New Science*. The second vignette is based on Michel Serres' work on the institution of Geometry, which imagines beginning as an emergent process. The third vignette uses the essays of Paolo Virno to describe beginning as the creation of new practice from within existing practice. In the end I will try to gather what insights into the making of organization these vignettes have provided.

Why is the beginning of organization problematic? Organizations seem intent to hide their origins and present themselves as having always existed. This covers up a larger problem at their foundation: it is not clear who has authority to create order and demand compliance. Answering that this is the role of the state or the government merely passes the problem on. The state is itself in need of foundations: its authority has to come from somewhere. If it derives from an agreement of the people – established by voting or consensus, how can such a procedure be agreed upon before the state is in place? This makes for a necessary, but not necessarily vicious, circularity at the heart of organizations, one that has to be solved performatively: one must act and posit its efficacy of the founding act.

A similar and related regress resides in the logic of rules and rule following. Schmitt and Wittgenstein criticize a school of thought which insists that an organization is created simply by the creation of rules. If human behavior takes the form it takes, they claim, it is because there are rules to guide and constrain it. It follows that if one wants to change behavior, all it takes is a change of the rules. Wittgenstein counters that every rule requires supporting rules to specify when and how it is to be applied, and these need further rules for their application, and so on to infinity. So rules cannot be founded on rules, nor can rules create behavior.

An action becomes a political and social act consequently not by recourse to a rule, but in relation to the practices sanctioned by a specific organization at a certain period in time. If the meaning of an instruction is simply what one does in response to it, then the task of the organization must be to instill the desired forms of behavior in its members without help from rules. How to instill and change behavior must then be part of its recipe – and part of our concern with understanding its beginning (Wittgenstein §206).

The time in which beginning in general and the beginning of organization in particular can be thought cannot be the empty temporal dimension of science. Only a temporality that is rich enough to carry change forward in a substantive way can also contain beginnings. This means a time in which change and development are driven by forces within it, and show irreversibility and path-dependency. Michel Serres likens historical temporality to a complex flow capable of different speeds and different density: sometimes it trickles; sometimes it turns in on itself and circles in a stagnant pool; sometimes currents move alongside one another with the slower current providing a bed for the faster one. While scientists only retain those things that pass the truth criterion and discard all else, historians hang on to everything, he claims, including rejected and forgotten ideas, phrases, and arguments. Only the historian is thus able to relate the emergence of a new idea to the components re-assembled from the heap of discarded historical material (Wild 58).

2 vico on the beginning of organization as divine intervention

Obviously, we can have no record of the first organization. But one can acquire insight into its beginning retroactively by looking at the way it is enacted again and again in every new organization: as an ever-present origin. It is not an accident that the person who first suggests the study of human organization is also the father of historiography: Giambattista Vico proposes to study human organizations and to trace in their design the "design of an ideal eternal history traversed in time by the histories of all nations" (6).

According to Vico we can understand social organizations and institutions precisely because we made them ourselves – unlike nature, which is God's work. Hence his saying: "[v]erum quia factum" or "verum ipsum factum" (Truth is the made. We can recognize as true what we made ourselves). Drawing on this principle he argues against Descartes' reduction of all facts to the ostensibly paradigmatic form of mathematical knowledge (*Stanford Encycl. Philosophy. Entry on Vico*) and for a genetic view. Full knowledge of a thing means discovering *how* it came to be. Phenomena can only be understood via their origins, *per caussas* (through their causes). "The nature of an institution is identical with its *nascence* at a certain time and in a certain manner" (Vico 81) and "The inherent properties of things are produced by the mode or manner in which they arise. Such properties therefore allow us to verify an institution's exact nature and nascence" (81).

This makes for a reflexive, if not recursive, interdependence of method and subject matter.

> Given that *verum ipsum factum principle* the *New Science* both sets knowledge per caussas as its task and as the method for attaining it; or, expressed in other terms, the content of *scienza* is identical with the development of that *scienza* itself. (*Stanford Encycl. Philosophy*. Entry on Vico)

nature contra nature

When it comes to locating the beginning of organization and resolving the paradox of how we can make something, which yet has the power to control us, Vico invokes divine intervention. Following Hobbes, he believes that men in their self-interest "would live in solitude like beasts." But, he adds, "God has ordered and arranged human institutions so that this same self-interest led people, even through these different and contrary ways, to live with justice like *human beings* and to remain in society" (Vico 2; emphasis in original) and with this he makes room for a genuine *social* organization as opposed to laws of nature, which emerge from the individual desire for self-preservation.

If humans do not seek the company of others, they cannot form society. The origin of society, of organization of any kind, must consequently lie without man's nature. And yet the way Vico describes the development of civilization makes it clear that it operates from within mankind in virtue of an inclination to socialize. This addition by divine intervention, which is responsible for man's *social nature* and enables the development of society and civilizations, must result in an ongoing tug of war between man's solitary and social nature. It is a tension that lies in all human institutions and can explain (at least in part) the irrationality occasionally found embedded in organizations.

At the same time the laws and the compulsion to follow them derive from God, which must be granted the state of exemption by definition. With the Providence of God in the background, Vico can explain the emergence of a law-governed society and also anchor it in a dynamic temporality. Vico shows a neat way to overcome the apparent contradiction between social and solitary dispositions by wrapping the beginning of society in an infinite loop (Fig. 1).

god's providence – man's projection

Calling this adding of social nature an act of Providence gives us an important clue. Vico distinguishes acts of grace from acts of Providence, so Providence is not just every divine intervention; it is a special kind. *Providence* comes from Latin "Pro Videre," meaning "to look ahead." Providence is *foresight*. What God foresees by looking ahead is the need to amend human nature so as to enable society and the development of culture and institutions that flow from it. Flatly put, God looks to the future and then does what is needed to bring it about. One could dismiss the argument as faulty logic, since it seems to invert the order of cause and effect: causes should precede effects, not the other way around. Or one might grant it the status of a teleological argument, which argues from the end result backwards to the beginning. In any case the action invokes the future in order to justify what it does in the present.

A similar logic is at work in a form of organization, which starts around 1700 in England, the *joint stock company*, and is described by Daniel Defoe in his *Essay Upon Projects* (1697). He gives the name *projecting*[2] to a mysterious new practice and organization, that consists in joining a project which promises vast returns, and throwing one's money into it. A project is defined by Defoe as a "vast undertaking, too big to be managed and therefore likely enough to come to nothing" (1). What makes for a good project is determined simply by the outcome, not on moral grounds: if it succeeds, it was good, if not, then "it simply miscarried, or else it would have succeeded" (2). Joint stock companies inspire a frenzy of investment and launch all kinds of ventures from bringing spices from the East, starting settlements in the Americas, or looking for sunken treasure. Some projects succeed, some fail, but the

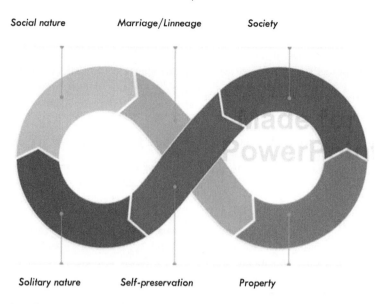

Fig. 1. An infinite loop ties irreconcilable elements into a dynamic genetic constellation (author's image).

thrill of investing is as addictive to the *projectors* as betting on horses. Defoe's own state of wealth fluctuated up and down depending on the success of his ventures.

Given the proliferation of these organizations one would expect that the way they got started was well documented. But this is not so. Researchers who tried to document the origin of the Bank of England could not identify the moment at which the bank "began" to exist or the people acting at its inception. There are conversations in coffeehouses, there is a call to raise capital, and then suddenly there is the company complete with officers, while the identity of the founders remains shrouded in fog.

> So all of these figures [projectors, officers of the Bank] may endorse "it," shape "it," take a stake in "it," but the Bank is produced by none of them. It is as if the Bank finds itself in the throwing forth of these projections and then is assumed to have always been there, a project awaiting projection, an office waiting to be occupied. It is as if the Bank invents itself. (Hamilton and Parker 110)

The term "projecting" appropriately describes the action that this form of organization makes possible: to "throw ahead" (pro-jacere) as in throwing resources and expectations into or at the future. It produces an irreversible direction in time – the project is framed in time and success lies in the future – and a reverse causality similar to God's Providence: the act of projecting is justified by the promise of a state of the future that accords with their projection, and this state can only come about through the act of projecting. The success of a project is the measure of its worth. Circularity again.

Of course, there are significant differences between God's Providence and man's projection, but they have this much in common *the action at the present time is justified by a future state made possible by that very action.* The action frames the time of the project with a beginning and a projected end point and then claims as its end point an identifiable and potentially favorable state of the world. This future state of the world motivates the action that brings it about. The logic is circular, but generative. Once that identifiable state of the future is posited by the act of projecting – it does not exist beforehand – the projector can calculate probabilities of risk and returns.

Pascal's wager can be seen as just such a construction: if the possible outcome of the wager were desirable, one would do well to invest in it, even if probabilities are not in one's favor. One has everything to gain and nothing to lose – at least that was true for Pascal with respect to the existence of God. For the projectors that put their money into a risky enterprise there is, of course, something at stake; but then again, if one had the money to invest, how much better to have chances of significant returns rather than letting it sit idly in one's coffers.

One does not bet on a random event: that would be gambling. Instead one's investment in the future first creates the possibility of gaining and losing, a possibility which the future would not hold were it not for the act of projection.[3] The framing action posits a specific state of the future as a *state* and then calculates the possible ways it can come about. This colonizing of the future in terms of project I consider crucial to the beginning of organization.

One might object that since projects are finite, the end of a project would seem to impose an end to the organization that carries it. This was the expectation placed on corporations by government in former days. But the restriction is easily overcome – and has been overcome – by the strategy of adopting the next project, potentially ad infinitum. An excellent example of such a strategy is adopted by the Bank of England, which was created as a privately held organization in 1694[4] to provide the English king with a large loan. The original loan was never repaid, but the interests were paid regularly by a tax levied for that purpose. The anonymous financiers had no inclination to have their capital returned to them, which would mean that their profitable project came to an end.

marriage and burial: family as first organization

Mere social nature is not enough. For Vico, writing at the dawn of civilization, the issue is to construct the minimal set of principles that will set the machinery of territorialization in motion, because the space framed by the first organization is literally the earth occupied and cultivated. The process of civilization takes off only once people have become sedentary, when they have property and work the land. (Vico heaps scorn on nomadic people, who share their possessions, including their women. They become the lower classes, once they attached themselves to the first group and joined their settlements for protection.)

His principles are "(1) divine Providence; (2) solemn matrimony; and the universal belief in the immortality of the soul, which originated with burial rites" (Vico 9). The choice of marriage and burial as primary is a smart one: they connect to core biological facts and yet are already symbolically distanced from the biological sphere. Intercourse and procreation can be considered biological nature, but monogamy is not. It introduces a symbolic and legal differentiation: only the children of the elected partner are legitimate and can claim the name and the property of their parents. This draws a line around monogamous couples and their legitimate children, and hence the family is instituted. Instead of going forth and multiplying regardless, as the Bible recommends, marriage channels the natural feelings of care for one's offspring into care for the legitimate ones: these form the next generation of this specific couple.

Burial operates in the inverse direction, establishing the concern of the future generation for their forefathers and instituting the "immortality of the soul." Children provide the burial service for their parents, thereby acknowledging their indebtedness and affirming the legitimacy of their birth. The burial site of one's forefathers becomes sacred ground and as their decomposing bodies become humus, the care for the burial site anchors the claim of the family to the land as their own (Harrison xi). The land on which the family settles and where they bury their forefathers becomes their property, to be handed down the chain of generations of legitimate offspring. The institutions of marriage and burial stand at the beginning of history. As they connect the generations into a chain of descent and form the first lineages, they also give rise to settlement and private property. The first aristocratic families are those that are first to settle and work the land; and they become the first leaders and founders of states: "Through protracted settlement and the burial of their ancestors they came to found and divide the first dominions of the earth" (Vico 9).

3 michel serres on geometry: beginning as unintended consequences

This is the state of civilization which Michel Serres assumes for his investigation into the beginning of geometry: a sedentary society that cultivates its land is precondition for the emergence of geometry. Geometry begins by building on, and being abstracted from, the territory and practices established in such a society. Serres calls it an institution, because despite the changes and critiques brought on in the intervening centuries, this branch of geometry operates in much the same way today as when Euclid wrote down his elements – proof of its power to order experience, and proof that it remains tied to the physical ground.

Serres looks for an immanent beginning, one that does not require divine intervention, since the classical origin stories get into trouble when they attempt to explain how something can come from nothing. The immanent story of beginnings has the inverse problem to solve: it has to show how something new can arise from fullness, from within an already sated *Umwelt*, in a world that has no room or need for change. There is no vacuum in nature. Equally, there is no lack in a functioning society: it covers every relevant aspect of being – though always relative to one specific conception of the good life. Where there is no lack, there is neither the impulse nor the room for change or newness. It is only after a new thing has emerged that one can view the time before in terms of lack. Serres must show how a new institution can arise in a world that is complete in both its natural and social aspects.

Serres speaks of historical time as a rich and complex flow. In a like manner he imagines beginning as the confluence of different currents – conditions, factors, ideas, which grow and/or enhance one another until a threshold is reached and a new something emerges into the world.[5] The new entity cannot be new in terms of material; it can arise only as a new form. If geometry is such a new form, what are the factors that give rise to the abstract elements of geometry?

Serres starts by unpacking the word "geometry" = measuring the earth. This practice of using the etymology of a word as a clue to its historical development was already suggested by Vico (and perfected by Heidegger). In executing it, Serres finds first, the meaning of "Gea" (= Earth) as *surface and* second, the act of *measuring*. The meaning of earth as surface owes more to the practice of agriculture than the contemplation of the stars. Before the idea of measuring can arise, one must remove the empirical features of the surface and conceive the idea of an undifferentiated isotropic plane. Such a conception might arise over time through travel and mapmaking, which bring the gradually expanding knowledge of the world into a single abstract representation. But closer to home, Serres claims, is the practice of working the earth, of regularly clearing, smoothing, plowing, planting, and harvesting, which provides a most insistent experience of the earth as a continuous and planar surface. So, the analysis of the word "Gea" moves Serres to discover the beginning of geometry in the organization of agriculture, which moves the problem of beginning back a notch: how did agriculture begin?

acts of evacuation

The usual story of the beginning of agriculture tells that men cut down the forest in order to create fields. This is a logical impossibility, since it assumes the very thing it is supposed to explain. Serres proposes instead that agriculture, or indeed anything new, starts as the *unintended consequence of an already existing practice*. The existing practice prepares the ground by creating an opening in the fullness of the world, but without a conscious thought of making anything. In the case of agriculture, the opening – a clearing in the literal sense – would come about through the practice of sacrificing. The clearing in the forest caused by the fire or the altar of the sacrifice then gives fast-growing grasses the chance to move in and become the first grain monoculture.

As Serres sees it, "*[t]he religious act of the first fury turned, by chance, into agricultural action*" (xii). The clearing could have other causes; for instance, it could have been the consequence of a natural catastrophe – say, a flood – which would explain the emergence of agriculture in the river valleys of the earth. Whichever way the clearing comes about, it is the key to any beginning. Evacuation gives rise to the empty slate, the white page, the empty land, which leads to an eruption of new possibilities. History is, according to him, the evolutionary path that results from acts of clearing followed by spontaneous colonization. "*Our history follows the white blanks from which bifurcating geysers shoot forth*" (Serres xlvi).

Can we say that a path exists before it is taken? Not really. We construe retroactively the image of a multiplicity of paths as if tracing an abstract landscape. Can we then say that we understand the geography in which the paths unfold? Serres declares that the contours of space itself shift as part of the development: for instance, from a centralized, highly differentiated sacred topography to a more planar profane social landscape. The abstract plane, however, is already an idea of geometry, and we are faced, with Vico, with the necessity to reflect on our own concepts, on our *making*, as part of the subject matter.

If the new organization – whether agriculture or geometry – requires an act of evacuation, then this beginning is not a virgin birth, but the inevitable bursting forth of existing forces. In this case one must accord evacuation the most significant and active role. What *making* is involved in it is first and foremost a negative and destructive one: the "violence of religious fury" as Serres called it, acts without a concern for, or knowledge of, the consequences – and side effects – of its action.

abstracted from the earth: the boundary

In envisioning the emergence of the geometric elements, Serres imagines a linked chain of such evacuating events. From the sacred *place* of sacrifice (the *Templum*) arises through evacuation the first plots of grain; these lead to the settling on and cultivating of the field (the *Campus*) and over time establish the fully developed, propertified and circumscribed *Pagus* or *Polis*, which names both the settled and cultivated land and the community. At this stage the abstraction from the earth's material condition and a rendering of earth in symbolic terms becomes possible.

The next step arrives with the introduction of boundaries and boundary markers. Fields are screened off against uncultivated nature, separated by their different functions – for crops, for grazing. Within the sedentary society the cultivated earth becomes property. Cultivated land *is co-extensive with* community, community *means* land under cultivation: it is the definition and form of social organization of the time. This calls for boundaries to separate different fields and different properties to signal their belonging to families and communities. "Pagus," the Roman word for a measured area of land, also means settlement, community. It relates to the English word "peg," meaning to fasten, and can be translated as "a boundary staked out on the ground." Similarly, *polis* comes from the Greek word for stake and refers to the demarcation of land as well as to the community that owns it.[6]

With the determination of function and ownership, the boundary comes into prominence: not just the visible one between nature and field, but an invisible one between the land of different owners. Boundary markers, wooden pegs or stones, are set to demarcate the end of one field, of one property, and the beginning of another. They operate in a symbolic capacity: behind the boundary marker, the demarcated space turns into an abstraction emptied of character and only characterized by its extension. The surface of the earth recedes behind the marker: the empty plane is characterized as "having been staked out" (see note 6 on "pagus").

The marker is abstract itself – abstracted from the material, shape, and size that makes it. Its function is bound up with its position on the surface, but it is best kept as immaterial as possible, since the boundary it marks and the place it occupies belong to no one and should be kept to a minimum, ideally extensionless, so as not to lose valuable soil. The ideal boundary marker is the extensionless point, the ideal boundary an infinitely fine line stretching from point to point, from marker to marker, and the ideal land flat, homogeneous surface. When markers get moved or washed away, as they do regularly in the floods of the Nile for instance, they have to be restored and the space measured and demarcated anew. This work is a ritualistic practice in ancient Egypt carried out by a special profession of priests – the "harpedonaptai" or rope-stretchers. As the name implies, they use knotted ropes to lay down the boundaries and establish markers again.[7] Thus, one can imagine Euclid's geometry and elements – the point, the line, and the plane – emerging from the practices of an agricultural society.

The story is fictitious, to be sure, but even if it is not true, it is plausible that the geometric elements laid down by Euclid emerged as abstract concepts before him and they could have arisen as abstractions from prior practices in such or a similar way. What does it teach us about beginnings in general? First, the story implies a degree of play in the form and function of human practices and selective engagement with material forces – enough to have side effects and unintended consequences. The source of this play is less clearly defined than by Vico's tension between man's solitary nature and the propensity to form society, but it does similar work: it opens up the space for movement and change.

Serres cunningly returns to *creatio ex nihilo* and subsumes it under his form of beginning as a mere phase. The point zero, the empty space, the *nihilo*, from which creation is said to begin, is turned into a moment of passage in a process, not an absolute emptiness, which a divine power fills with being.

Still, for all its brilliance, his use of evacuation (once it is not seen as a single event, but characteristic of all origins) produces a sense of dissonance: how is the act of evacuation to be reconciled with the principle of flow Serres invoked before? A flow can be more or less, slow or fast, but there is no flow without something that flows and the act of evacuation cannot be translated into flow of any kind. The tension sits between Serres' historical time flowing in law-like and path-dependent ways from natural conditions and an act of evacuation, which acts on the flow, intentional or otherwise. So despite his best efforts to make beginning into a natural emergence in which physical and human factors mingle, this act of evacuation can be read as a symbolic intervention into the existing human practice. Because only as an act of rejection of existing conditions can it be recognized as meaningful for human praxis and the source of a departure.

Negation, as Paolo Virno stated, is the one uniquely human symbolic act that separates one from existing conditions without removing the ability to see them. "Verbal language distinguishes itself from other communicative codes, as well as from cognitive prelinguistic performance, because it is able to *negate* any semantic content" (Virno, *Multitude* 176; emphasis in original). Negation makes a different making possible: a state of questioning of what is given, of looking at what is with different eyes, of un-accepting the habitual.

4 paolo virno: doing new things with words

Paolo Virno looks at organization first as linguistic exercise: it operates a phrase regimen (Lyotard) in parallel with its quasi-spatial structure to give sense and meaning to habitually occurring contexts and situations. He is concerned to show that human actors not only navigate the linguistic space of organization successfully – by reading signs, communicating, and responding correctly – but also change the way the organization operates through the creative reuse of phrases to the point of making new situations and new responses possible.

In contradistinction to the sweeping historical processes of Vico and Serres, he focuses on the lowest, most commonplace and everyday way in which organization shapes human: he carries out a micro-analysis of how we are making or are being made in and by language. It is nevertheless still related to beginnings. If language has unique power to shape how humans read a situation – a power, which every organization exploits – it also furnishes a mechanism to change what is given or expected of human behavior.[8]

The function of language within organization is to present situations in terms of social norms. We saw in the arguments of Schmitt and Wittgenstein why this is problematic. If rules acted directly on behavior, one would have to be able to decide when someone is following a rule, and equally, when a person is transgressing it, by no other means than recourse to the rule itself. This cannot be done, because "[n]o application ever agrees with the rule" (Virno, *Multitude* 119).

The issue is best explained with the help of an example: imagine that you take a walk and happen to pass a lake along the way. There you see a sign that says, "Swimming is not allowed." Since you are not swimming at the lake, can one conclude that you are following the rule? Not really: since you never intended to swim, the rule did not enter into your decision at all. Alternatively, if you were to wade into the lake to retrieve your hat, would you be in violation of the rule? Maybe, maybe not. This is merely to make obvious what we are well aware of in any concrete situation, but which we forget, when we think about rules in the abstract: namely, that every situation brings a unique set of conditions into being that informs one's decision. It is neither the sign nor the rule expressed on the sign that act upon us. It is only when the rule is reinforced, by an executive instance other than the rule, that it acquires the power to help or hinder one's actions.

What does that tell us about behavior? First, says Virno, that it is ungrounded: the norms we invoke to explain behavior have merely the status of an explanatory shortcut. The actual power lies in an established practice. "To obey a rule, to make a report, to give an order, to play a game of chess, are customs, uses, institutions" (Wittgenstein 81). A specific form of life has no foundation in logic or in anything else. This means, secondly, that customs can change and that habits can become fluid again.

Even though the behaviors within a form of life are regular, repeated, and expected to repeat, there is nothing that makes or guarantees this regularity. This groundlessness is vital to the operation of the joke and the ruse: they work with the play that exists in the different ways in which rules are seen to be applied and behavior seen as compliant with them. They thereby reveal the ungroundedness of habitual behavior and propose different and unexpected ways to behave in a given situation, which are nevertheless reconcilable – with some eccentricity, of course – with a given rule. Virno takes the analysis further: the failure to find the ground for the norm or rule is the moment when "the warp of human life gains unexpected prominence" (*Multitude* 116) – because when the norm has become suspended, what shows up behind it is "the normality of processes, customs, relationships, inclinations, conflict" (ibid.).

innovative action or "how to do new things with words" (Virno, Multitude 77)

It is by operating on this ground that linguistic acts can produce new practices, new meanings. The joke is such an act in minimal form. It looks like logic misapplied: *paralogic*, as Aristotle called it, when he classified logical fallacies to unmask the sophists' arsenal of tricks.[9] The joke, of course, uses paralogic not to persuade someone to accept an erroneous conclusion, but instead to uncover a larger truth about rules: that the rule that seems to be violated in the joke has no power to reinforce the expected meaning, it is nothing but a hardening of a behavioral regularity, an expectation based on established habits. And thereby it offers linguistic means to escape from the expected, to change the meaning of a situation, and in the case of a new unprecedented situation it offers the means to create a new rule or a new application to use.

Austin pointed out that the speech act, even though "merely" linguistic, is performing an action with decisive and often irreversible social and legal consequences. Equally consequential is an organization's phrase regimen,[10] which frames everyday situations linguistically and offers publicly accepted ways to act within them.

As long as the linguistic framing lets participants identify with their position and gives them traction with the situation, the rule instantiated thereby is not challenged. What happens, however, when one encounters a situation which the existing arsenal cannot handle, or, alternatively, when the existing frame places a person in an unacceptable or disadvantaged position? Then *innovative action* of the kind modeled by the joke comes into play as logical ones do not avail themselves or cannot be accepted. Virno identifies two classes of innovative responses based on the analysis of jokes: one creates a new application through combining existing elements in new ways. This is the entrepreneurial innovation as described by Schumpeter. The second form of innovative action is more radical and produces a departure from the phrase regimen: it bypasses existing choices altogether and comes up with a new option. An example of the second kind would be Alexander's response to the Gordian knot: instead of accepting the options on offer – to try to untangle it and succeed or fail or not to engage, he created a new option by hacking through the knot. In the process he destroyed (literally) the previous options. Destruction, though not always of such an obvious kind, inevitably follows both types of innovation: by stepping outside the existing frame, one not only creates a new one, but also destroys, deforms or evacuates the action space that preceded the intervention, because one cannot avoid considering the new option when confronting the same situation the next time.

Now we can understand why Virno saw the joke as a "*diagram* of innovative action" (*Multitude* 73): it represents in minimal form – like a map or a mathematical equation – the essential elements and proportions of a certain phenomenon. By undermining the claims to necessity and inevitability from the given universe of rules it opens up the legitimate possibility for new behavior, creates variation in a form of life. By placing a new and different linguistic action into the opening, the innovation engages the same ontological ground (of a form of life), in a new way: this is *genesis* of an ontological kind. It becomes historical over time by coupling to existing conditions and seeding new developments, maybe even new regimens.

This form of making should remind us of the social making Vico advocated in his "verum ipsum factum" in that it produces its own truth criteria. It creates both the conditions for its existence and the evidence that establishes their truth in fact, turning expectations, actions, and confirmations into a self-perpetuating whole. Every new fact compels a new use of language. Read in the opposite direction, one can also say that every new use of language generates a new fact. Neither is a deed one can produce at will, as practitioners of either domain will attest. Both new fact and new language use shift the social space irreversibly.

5 lessons learned: fichte's *tathandlung* and ontological genesis

We have arrived a long way from the stories of beginning we contemplated above. The flow of historical movements has given way to a micro-analysis of linguistic action. Historical genesis has been replaced or better, sublated, by linguistic innovation. The position of the aloof historian and observer shifts to that of a participant that innovates from within the organization. And yet, there is some continuity: we have invoked the role of the symbolic several times, identified an apparently necessary departure from logic and linear causation. And repeatedly we find a circularity and self-referentiality of the account: what looked like a flaw in Vico's method – contradictory elements in human nature, the mirroring of method and content – turns out to be a stable feature of the genetic process. So apparently is the projection of something unknowable into the future. Last, but not least – at least to my thinking – an intentional act is required for beginning. A purely hands-off material emergence will not satisfy the requirements.

Strange as it may seem, it is Johann Gottlieb Fichte, a lesser-known German philosopher and precursor to Hegel and Husserl, whose *Wissenschaftslehre* (science "novo methodo," translated as *"science of knowing"*) may offer a unifying conceptual ground for these observations. He claims to have found a genetic method by which one can establish new and secure (i.e., synthetic a priori) knowledge modeled after Euclid's geometry and the Spinozist tradition.[11] What follows is a brief rendering of some key points to demonstrate why his science of knowing is relevant for thinking beginnings.

Fichte starts from the *oneness of being and thought* as a not-further-decomposable primary intuition in/of consciousness. He takes this oneness or unity, sometimes abbreviated as "I = I" to be more foundational than logic ("I = I is philosophy," says Fichte, "A = A is logic" (Wood 147). It cannot be in the form of an already achieved separation of subject and object, but achieves a differentiation of any subject matter through performing acts of positing and constructing. "I is not a 'substance,' a 'reality' or an entity previous to my act. 'I' is an act I perform and not some fact I would be" (Stolzenberg and Rudolph 420). This genetic process operates dialectically and recursively: it ascends step by step the rungs of a ladder consisting of philosophical expressions of a state of mind and of knowing, which it proceeds to overcome and supersede, and thereby arrives gradually at more and more clearly intuited and less contingent statements.

The final insight is secured by the careful and thoughtful enactment of the genetic sequence of steps. In this sense Fichte's claim is similar to Vico's, namely that the understanding of a thing is given through its causes; but in Fichte's case the causation is the performative enactment of the philosophical process, not reflection on a historical one. One posits a first statement as an accepted starting point and a first position of personal investment. Careful evaluation of the assumptions that go into this statement produce dialectically opposed statements with equal validity, which force one to refine the prior statement and raise the position to a more sophisticated level, which then is mirrored in the more refined critique from the opposing position. This process sheds gradually all dependence upon empirical content: turning back from the higher plane and equipped with more general insights one can revisit the lower level and restate it in more secure, a priori terms. In this way one moves from level to level to generate more universal insights of the synthetic a priori kind like those of mathematics. The description of this process, published in several versions around 1800, forms the content of Fichte's *Wissenschaftslehre*.

The method by which this is achieved is linguistic and performative. To merely read his description of the process is not productive of genuine knowing. Each person must carry out the genesis herself in "living thought," must posit ("setzen") for herself each statement, question its assumptions and enact the steps of this ascending ladder of insights. "Fichte's distinctive characteristic, like Austin's, is to determine thinking as acting and acting as thinking. For both to think is to act" (Stolzenberg and Rudolph 420).

A speech act is an expression of acting, not the observation of a fact, and this is the central proposition in Fichte's philosophy.

> The identity of the posing and the posed is an act we're performing. It is an originary act, with neither cause nor necessity, which is by the very fact that it is effected, performed and accomplished. The freedom of the first principle is the starting point and should also be the point of arrival. In any of our concepts and productions, we must realize this identity. This means that, in one single act, *we must think contradictory determinations* (such as the posing of freedom and the knowledge of freedom). Realizing this circumstance amounts to an effectuation of the sublime process. It does not lead to a

failure but to the creation of new, intermediate concepts that all express reflexive identity. (Stolzenberg and Rudolph 424–25; my emphasis)

Tathandlung – translatable as "performed/enacted deed" – is the term Fichte gives to this profound action, which creates by enacting what it posits and brings out both the intentional subjective and the generative objective aspect of the event. The *Tathandlung* creates the stepping stone, which propels the actor in an irreversible direction, since every such positing achieved in living thought encounters a changed world of facts and positions. Thought as act is successful because the I is part of that world and by giving itself a principle it turns itself into the complement of a reconfigured world.

If we attempt to apply the oneness of being and thought to our examples, it would appear that none of the theories of beginning would count as complete in Fichte's view. The objective material and temporal accounts of genesis have to be accompanied by an account of the subjective activation of structure, its enactment in practice or in the case of a past, as an active remembering.

Genetic is both the process Fichte demonstrates, since every one of us has to enact it for ourselves, and the result of the process, the entity thus created, in that it retains the connection to the process of its origination. The fact that one can discard the ladder once one has climbed up onto the higher ground indicates that the result is not a change in form, but an entirely new entity. This fact marks the difference between a morphogenetic account and an ontogenetic account, and separates the naturalistic account of Serres from the genuine genetic accounts of Virno and Vico; both of them in their own way acknowledge the radical discontinuity of social forms inherent in the new and the dependence of genesis on prior social forms, both as jump-off point and material for transformation. "Ontogenesis, by definition, denotes the creation or birth (genesis) of the social being (*on*), where collective ideational creativity manifests itself, [...], in the transformation, alteration, and diversification of material and organizational settings,

that is, of social structures and institutions" (Bouzanis 591). And it

> intends to show that the idea of the context/concept/activity-dependence of social forms implies that: (1) the persistence and the orderliness of social relations do not mean that they (i.e., social relations) are necessary, since they do not signify a natural emergent phenomenon, but a socio-cultural product; (2) we can only theorize, act upon, and transform these forms as long as we intersubjectively share a cultural context of imaginary schemes; and (3) novelty in the social domain stems from the elaboration of the ideational level. (Bouzanis 586)

Being as enduring and selfsame, which many philosophers take as the necessary and irreplaceable ground of knowledge, is dead matter for Fichte as long as it is not enacted in living thought. It is a byproduct of the genetic process at some level, produced by the negation of ongoing genesis. That should demonstrate the dramatic departure Fichte effects from classical idealist and contemporary realist philosophies. In this manner Fichte arrives at the recognition that the human gives itself its own ground by acts of *selbst-prinzipiieren* (= by giving oneself a principle). In other words, one posits and adheres to the principle of one's own making by projecting oneself into a new existence through creating a new social entity from the existing context. This creating is outside of temporality, of transcendental origin, though only in the act, not in the specific principle thus formulated. The principle is a sociocultural product and so are the social institutions that flow from it, as Bouzanis said above, and open to change.

disclosure statement

No potential conflict of interest was reported by the author.

notes

1 In most of the organizational literature organization and system are treated as synonyms and a

system requires the observer to delimit its boundary. See Coase, "The economic system works itself" (34), Penrose 15, Drucker 130, Ramos 102.

2 "[A]bout the year 1680 began the art and mystery of projecting to creep into the world" (Defoe 3).

3 Compare also projective in the geometric sense: it similarly determines a (generative) *method*, which creates a range of similar – similar since generated by specified transformations – figures. "From the beginning we do not consider the metrical and projective relations in the manner in which they are embodied in any particular figure, but take them with a certain breadth and indefiniteness, which gives them room for development" (Poncelet qtd in Cassirer 81).

4 Bank of England Act 1694 (c.20) p. 1. <http://www.statuelaw.gov.ukcontent.aspn?legType=All-Primary&page Number=1>.

5 Emergence has a naturalistic flavor, which is how Serres prefers to cast the issue. He is the detached observer, who notes, but does not participate in the making.

6 Pāgus, the Roman word for field, derives from the Latin root pāg-, a lengthened grade of Indo-European *pag-, a verbal root, "fasten" (English peg), which in the word may be translated as "boundary staked out on the ground."[2] In semantics, *pag- used in pāgus is a stative verb with an unmarked lexical aspect of state resulting from completed action: "it is having been staked out" [...] In classical Latin, pagus referred to a country district or to a community within a larger polity. <https://encyclopedia.thefreedictionary.com/pagus>.

7 In ancient Egypt, a rope-stretcher (or harpedonaptai) was a surveyor who measured real property demarcations and foundations using knotted cords, stretched so the rope did not sag. The practice is depicted in tomb paintings of the Theban Necropolis. <https://en.wikipedia.org/wiki/>.

8 The mechanism is revealed in the analysis of jokes. The joke is the "black box of innovative action," says Virno (*Multitude* 124). It goes behind or beneath habitual praxis to enable and enact "alternative combinations and deviated trajectories" (Virno, *Multitude* 139) and teaches how new behavior comes into being.

9 Some examples of the logical principles deliberately violated in jokes:

> *Ambiguity*: "Did you take a bath today?" – Answer: "Why? Has one gone missing?"
> *Ignorance of the law of the excluded middle*: "I never borrowed your pot, and it had no hole, when I returned it" (Lyotard 15).
> *Making a contingent feature into an essential one*: "You recognize the snark by its habit of getting up late!" (*The Hunting of the Snark*, Carroll).

10 Lyotard's *phrase regimen* also considers the possibility that people are being placed at a disadvantage by it (28).

11 "Fichte taking geometrical intuition as the model of a pure (non-sensible) intuition" (Wood 269).

bibliography

Bourdieu, Pierre. *The Logic of Practice*. Originally published 1980 by Les Editions de Minuit as *Le sense pratique*. Trans. Richard Nice. Stanford, CA: Stanford UP, 1990. Print.

Bouzanis, Christoforos. "Ontogenesis Versus Morphogenesis. Towards an Anti-realist Model of the Constitution of Society." *Human Studies* 39 (2016): 569–99. doi:10.1007/s10746-015-9376-y. Print.

Cassirer, Ernst. *Substance and Function. And Einstein's Theory of Relativity*. 1923. London: Classic Reprint Series, Forgotten Books, 2012. Print.

Coase, Ronald. *The Firm, the Market and the Law*. Chicago: U of Chicago P, 1988. Paperback ed. 1990. Print.

Defoe, Daniel. *An Essay Upon Projects*. 1697. Web. <https://freeditorial.com/en/books/an-essay-upon-projects/>.

Drucker, Peter F. *Concept of the Corporation. With a New Introduction by the Author*. New Brunswick: Transaction. 2nd Printing 1995. New material 1993. Print.

Fichte, Johann Gottlieb. *The Science of Knowing. J.G. Fichte's 1804 Lectures on the Wissenschaftslehre*. Trans. Walter E. Wright. New York: SUNY P, 2004. Print.

Freud, Sigmund. *Society and its Discontents*. Web. <https://bradleymurray.ca/texts/sigmund-freud-civilization-and-its-discontents-pdf>.

Hamilton, Valerie, and Martin Parker. *Daniel Defoe and the Bank of England. The Dark Arts of Projectors*. Winchester: Zero, 2016. Print.

Harrison, Robert Pogue. *The Dominion of the Dead*. Chicago: U of Chicago P, 2003. Print.

Lyotard, Jean-Francois. *The Differend. Phrases in Dispute*. Minneapolis: U of Minnesota P, 1988. Print.

Penrose, Edith. *The Theory of the Growth of the Firm*. New York: Oxford UP, 1995. Print.

Ramos, Alberto Guerreiro. *The New Science of the Organization*. Toronto: U of Toronto P, 1981. Print.

Serres, Michel. *Geometry. Third Book on Foundations*. English Trans. Randolph Burks. London: Bloomsbury, 2017. Print.

Stanford Encycl. Philosophy. Web. <https://plato.stanford.edu/>.

Stolzenberg, Juergen, and Oliver-Pierre Rudolph (Herausgeber). Fichte-Studien. Band 35. Bd 1. *Wissen, Freiheit, Geschichte. Die Philosophie Fichte's im 19th und 20. Jahrhundert. Beitraege des sechsten internationalen Kongresses der Johann-Gottlieb-Fichte Gesellschaft in Halle 3.–7. Oktober 2006*. Amsterdam: Rodopi, 2010. *Fichte and Austin*. Cited article by Isabelle Thomas-Fogiel. 417ff.

Vico, Giambattista. *New Science. Principles of the New Science Concerning the Common Nature of Nations. Third Edition Thoroughly Revised, Corrected and Expanded by the Author*. Trans. David Marsh. Introduction Anthony Grafton. Harmondsworth: Penguin Classics, 1999.

Virno, Paolo. *Déjà Vu and the End of History*. Trans. David Broder. London: Verso Futures. English ed. 2015. Print.

Virno, Paolo. *Multitude. Between Innovation and Negation*. Los Angeles: Semiotext(e), 2008. Print.

Wild, Helga. "The Making of Stakeholder Ethnography." *Methodological Innovations Online* 7.1 (2012): 46–60. Web.

Wittgenstein, Ludwig. *Logical Investigations I*. Web. <https://www.docdroid.net/FmkyBAp/ludwigwittgenstein-philosophicalinvestigations.pdf>.

Wood, David D. "Mathesis of the Mind." *A Study of Fichte's Wissenschaftslehre and Geometry*. Fichte Studien Supplementa Bd 29. Amsterdam: Rodopi, 2012. Print.

Helga C. Wild

introduction

Even in an age of omnipresent artificial light, we rely on the geophysical realities of the earth to divide our days. We spin around the earth's axis, rising with light, resting in dark. Within that daily framework we measure our moments in relation to the *meridiem*, or midday point. Anything that happens before the meridiem, *ante-meridiem*, or a.m., moves out of darkness while *post-meridiem*, or p.m., ushers us back into the black. This binary system of oscillating twelve-hour intervals – indebted in form to the sundial – links very closely to the pan-species evolution of an internal, biological clock.

Time-sensing is essential to our generational, cultural, and species' identities. In 1900, Georg Simmel tied relational time to the accelerated movement of money and the pace of city life. Yet our role as time-based beings goes beyond capitalism and urbanism. As Rebecca Solnit describes it in her 2003 article (later book), "The Annihilation of Time and Space," a multitude of mechanics shifted our timekeeping habits and species' positionality around the turn of the last century:

> Before the new technologies and ideas, time was a river in which human beings were immersed, moving steadily on the current, never faster than the speeds of nature – of currents, of wind, of muscles [...] Work was done according to task and available light, and tasks varied from season to season [...] Time itself had been of a different texture, a different pace [...] It had not yet become a scarce commodity to be measured out in ever smaller increments as clocks acquired hands, as watches became more affordable mass-market commodities, as exacting schedules began to intrude [...] (11)

And as first suggested more than a century ago by Ricciotto Canudo, representations of time became even more diverse as cinema, the "seventh art," burgeoned.

Amid these perceived shifts in temporality, we have continued to rely on the classic twelve-hour clock as icon and compass. The European city clock (Big Ben, for example); the Deira Clock Tower in Dubai; or the fictionalized skyscraping timepiece constructed for a clinging Harold Lloyd in *Safety Last!* (1923). Analog watches, alarm clocks, school clocks, factory clocks, grandfather clocks. These

erin espelie

IN-KIND DISRUPTIONS
circadian rhythms and necessary jolts in eco-cinema

twelve-hour timepieces are linguistically ascribed with anthropoid features: a flat face, two hands, occasionally feet, and even a waist. In one anthropomorphic rendering, the photographer Philippe Halsman collaborated with Salvador Dalí in 1953 to create a literal chiron of clockface and man ("Dali Clock Face, From 'Halsman/Dali' Portfolio"). In the close-up portrait, Dalí dons clock numbers on his face, with the 12 upon his forehead and the 6 upon his jutted chin. Most jauntily, his left-hand mustache end points up to the 3 and his right-hand one greasily drapes down between 7 and 8. We are our own timepieces, replete with internal body clocks.

Timekeeping on an epochal scale has become a way of tracking the existence and fate of our species. In 1947, the *Bulletin of the Atomic Scientists* set up the Doomsday Clock as a response to global nuclear threats, inspired by a cover designed by the artist Martyl Langsdorf (Benedict). Her rendering, in the hopes of conveying urgency, set the time to seven minutes until midnight: seven minutes until catastrophic, apocalyptic destruction and self-annihilation of the human species. Until 2007, the rhetoric of the clock was dominated by war, weaponry, and the global nuclear arms race. More recently, other threats have intervened, including social media, though nothing as forcefully as "unchecked climate change" or "nearly inexorable climate disruptions." On 23 January 2020, the new position was announced as 100 seconds until midnight – the closest yet ("Current Time"). The clock functions as a warning: do not let us move ourselves, by our own hands, so to speak, any closer to midnight.

12:00 p.m.: all hands point up

The middle of the day, solar noon, high noon, the showdown.
Hands up.
The time with the shortest shadows.
Lunchbreak for the natural-light (cinema)photographer.

All photosensitive lifeforms organize their lives by light, both in the biological and ontological sense. Moreover, being situated on a planet with a twenty-four-hour sun cycle, most photosensitive species have evolved, in turn, to become time-based creatures that operate on a twenty-four-hour schedule of cellular organization. This geophysical link between our environment and our bodies is only recently being investigated in genetic detail.

Light sensitivity pervades four kingdoms of life, from archea to fungi, indicating a clear genetic advantage to being linked to light. Cyanobacteria likely gained the skill of telling time with their bodies first, 2.5 billion years ago, synchronizing to the dark–light cycles of the rotating earth (Bass and Lazar). Darkness was a time set aside for DNA repair. Daylight was a time for feeding, nourishment, and energy replenishment. So, too, nearly every human cell functions as a clock, with genes oscillating on and off based on exposure to light. The main body clock sits in the hypothalamus, in the suprachiasmatic nucleus, which connects to the optic nerve. In a 2016 review of new data, *Science* published the following summary of transcriptional clocks in humans:

> The circadian system is organized hierarchically with master pacemaker neurons in the central nervous system entrained to light each day, in turn conducting a distributed network of local clocks expressed in most peripheral cells and tissues. Within the brain, the clock plays a role not only in maintaining the timing of sleep/wake cycle relative to light but also in many behaviors, including learning, reward, and neurogenesis. Peripheral tissue clocks are entrained to the brain clock, although feeding and temperature are dominant in some physiological settings. Peripheral clocks may also become uncoupled and desynchronized from the central pacemaker during aging, shiftwork, jet travel, overnutrition, obesity, or cancer. Circadian disruption and associated impairment in sleep contributes to the molecular pathogenesis of disorders such as metabolic syndrome, obesity, diabetes, autoimmunity, and cancer. (Bass and Lazar)

1:00 p.m.: cinema clock

In my film *A Net to Catch the Light* (2017), I look at the unraveling of the human circadian cycle due to the pervasiveness of blue light, notably between 440 and 450 nanometers. Light-emitting diodes backlight our computer and phone screens and they operate largely in the blue-light spectrum. Our retinal cells respond to this light by cueing the brain to stay awake. This kind of light, rather than nutritive, can be toxic and even increase aging of the retina. Synchrony of cells can be lost when bathed in such light, leading to some of the pathogenesis listed above. *A Net to Catch the Light* creates a chorus of Macintosh computer startup sounds – or "chimes" as Apple refers to them – from the 1980s to 2016. The sound mix also reverberates with the voice of Steve Jobs speaking in 1983 about entering an age when our predominant form of media was in the process of becoming the computer, replacing television and "even the book" ("The 'Lost' Steve Jobs Speech from 1983"). The film draws attention to the material and physiological effects of being in a new world of motion-picture viewing that relies primarily on emitted rather than projected light.

Viennese filmmaker Peter Kubelka eschews the digital and, if anything, has sought to lay analog filmmaking as bare as possible. In 2012, he insisted upon the importance of the astronomical connection to celluloid film projectors and film viewing:

> [Cinema] consists of two main parts, one is the domesticated sun, the light; there is this strong light, which is of course a domesticated sun. It's not too hot; it inhabits this space and it's always burning like the sun, always giving light. The projector in front of this sun has this so called "shutter" which is a circle, turning on an axis, and which is half covered by black metal, and half is empty. So when it turns, in front of the static light, it alternates light and darkness. In general language, it creates day and night, and it turns in a speed, which makes it create day and night twenty-four times a second [...] Just very fast, day and night. (Budd)

All celluloid film projection recapitulates day/night cycles for Kubelka. Still, he probes the possibilities for extremism in three of his works of art – *Arnulf Rainer* (1960), *Antiphon* (2012), and *Monument Film* (2012). In all three, the film strips consist only of black and clear leader, organized in metrical form. The light–dark oscillation creates its own sound and silence through presence and absence on the optical track. A *New York Times* review suggested that the aforementioned work has "a minutely calibrated, filmic heartbeat" stemming from its "frame-by-frame artisanship" (Rapold).

Other filmmakers have attempted to break time down in formal, metric fashion on screen. The *Continuous Quantities* series by David Gatten derives its structure from a mathematical concept by Leonardo da Vinci, who yearned for a way to divide the hour "into 3,000 parts" (Blackburn 139). Gatten calculated that to be twenty-nine frames per second and has completed two films in the cycle, *Shrimp Boat Log* (2006/2010), with 300 shots, and *Journal & Remarks* (2009), with 700 shots. As described by Johnny Lavant after the 47th New York Film Festival, "[H]is steady sense of meter and bar [give] this piece its percussion [...] the Platonic form becomes reality; art gives way to life and stillness to movement."

In 2009, the Dutch artist Maarten Baas created a sweeping clock: a twelve-hour performance of two humans literally sweeping trash into two lines on a beach in Italy. The two lines of trash become real-time moving hands of a clock, as the performers take exactly one minute to move the minute-hand to its next position. Baas has created other iterations of what he calls the "Real Time" series. Perhaps most widely viewed is his projection at Amsterdam's Schiphol Airport, which launched in 2016 (Baas). In it, a man appears to be working behind a translucent clock face, painting the hands in real time. The man uses a rag to squeegee off the minute hand of the clock, then uses a mini paint-roller brush to apply the next minute hand. The illusion is perpetrated by a pre-recorded video that runs, of course, exactly twelve-hours in length.

No discussion of cinema as clock would be complete without Christian Marclay, who premiered his twenty-four-hour work of art, *The Clock*, in 2010. Like Baas' work, it functions as a literal clock. Rather than mirror the shape of a twelve-hour clock, the video operates in digital and figurative fashion, composed as it is of roughly 12,000 unique moments from films. By using film history to pace our experience of time in the present, *The Clock* suggests that we cannot use cinema as an escape from time, even though we might look to Marclay's piece as a full day's respite from our own lives. Indeed, *The Clock* reminds us that we are in lockstep with the genre-conforming narrative tropes and familiar plots of Western culture that make the hours both monumental and routinized (noon, quitting time, midnight). Freedom comes only in snatches of untethered sound and, occasionally, the more elusive somnambulant dreamtime. Thom Andersen writes for *Cinema Scope* about his experience of *The Clock*:

> We seem to live in an eternal present. Thus our reckless politics and our reckless destruction of nature. *The Clock* literalizes this condition [...] *The Clock* suspends time. Lived time is teleological, that is, directed to some goal, even if it's just eating lunch. Movies mimic this experience of time, and they try to intensify it by placing obstacles in the way of achieving these goals. Before you can go to lunch, you have to escape from an alien spacecraft. It is then a time of anticipation, a time of suspense. The characters who appear in *The Clock* are often obsessed by this vectorized time. Not only must they escape, they must escape within an hour, or ten minutes, or 30 seconds.

Rather than placing blame on the larger human condition, Genevieve Yue, in writing for *Film Comment* magazine, critiques Marclay's mainstream source material:

> The people that populate *The Clock* are yoked to the clock. I would hazard that the obsessive minute-by-minute clock-watching is a function of the kinds of commercial films, along with the stray television show, that Marclay selected. Mixed together in this way, *The Clock* reveals the rhythms of these accumulated genres, with attention to time governing and uniting a fairly predictable set of actions and outcome. (Yue)

In almost every review or account I have read of *The Clock*, writers have been compelled to relate just how much or how little of the twenty-four-hour cycle they witnessed. No one I encountered managed a full day's viewing. If circadian-rhythm studies have established anything, we know that disrupting sleep, sitting, and staring at a screen for twenty-four hours qualifies as unhealthy, if not ruinous, behavior. Thus, the installation itself impairs our internal clocks if watched in full. To experience *The Clock* as Marclay made it, we must disrupt our cells, add stress to our biological systems, and, at the very least, recall our corporeality. Marclay himself identifies *The Clock* as a *momento mori*, and a recent London reviewer extended the reference to the *vanitas* genre of still-life painting (Eisen).

I would venture that the piece, more than any durational film, may actually have the capacity to shorten the lives of any ardent viewers, accelerate the aging of their retinas, and disrupt their sleep. A cinema clock that alters our own internal clocks is mighty indeed in its haptic sway, and all the more powerful for its empty, yet alluring, narrative vectorization. We are not watching for reasons of being, affect, or empathy. Instead, we witness our own unwinding.

2:00 p.m.: cinemetrics

Filmmakers are constantly in search of new timekeeping methods to reflect and respond to current times. For "cinemetric" film scholars, such as Barry Salt, James Cutting, and Kristin Thompson, trends in timing can best be assessed through the analytics of editing. This quantitative data-combing almost always focuses on Hollywood. As Cutting and his co-authors of the book chapter for *Psychocinematics: Exploring Cognition at the Movies*, explain:

[F]or the purposes of this chapter, we will refer specifically to popular, or Hollywood, films in our discussions of film and movies. This sample of films is particularly relevant because, in most cases, popular Hollywood films are made to mimic reality. Movies are projected in a way that movement appears biologically appropriate. The color in modern movies is intended to mimic color stimuli in the real world. From a young age, we learn the nuances of continuity editing, so much so that adults often fail to notice cuts (the junction of two shots) when viewing a movie. (Brunick, Cutting, and DeLong 2)

Mimicking reality and creating biologically appropriate movement are not aspirations for many artists. Still, the selected dataset allowed the authors to conclude that

> there is little question that shot length has been decreasing over time. In an extensive review of over 7,000 films, Salt (1992, 2006) examined shot durations in Hollywood films from 1913 to 2006 and found a steady linear decline in ASD. This finding has been corroborated by Cutting, DeLong, and Nothelfer (2010) in their sample of films from 1935 to 2005. (Brunick, Cutting, and DeLong 3)

The authors proceed to examine patterns of shot duration as a way of varying tempo, rhythm, and general pacing, and yet they end on a note of insecurity, acknowledging that many of their critics believe that quantitative analysis does "a disservice to film studies." Still, they believe readers' perceptions will be enhanced by their statistics.

3:00 p.m.: avoiding parasitism

Virginia Woolf once wrote a scathing critique of how clumsily cinema translated literature. In speculating about cinema's capabilities, she asked, "How would it walk erect?" In short, she believed that cinema was "parasitic" and the only hope for the artform would come if filmmakers embraced abstraction. Only by setting aside the obviousness of reality might filmmakers find a path forward for "the seventh art." Woolf writes:

> [S]ome residue of visual emotion which is of no use either to painter or to poet may still await the cinema. That such symbols will be quite unlike the real objects which we see before us seems highly probable. Something abstract, something which moves with controlled and conscious art, something which calls for the very slightest help from words or music to make itself intelligible, yet justly uses them subserviently – of such movements and abstractions the films may, in time to come, be composed. Then, indeed, when some new symbol for expressing thought is found, the film-maker has enormous riches at his command. The exactitude of reality and its surprising power of suggestion are to be had for the asking. (Woolf)

In light of Woolf's comments, I want to suggest that there is a need today for film to play a role in providing shifts in tempo and scale. Our sense of time must be altered in connection with our species' dystopian prospects. We need works that can adequately alter our sense of time, but not just as a warp-speed, ever-shortening series of shots. Nor is the allure of metrics enough.

As the effects of climate disaster play out over generations, how might the boundedness of discrete media reckon with such a timescale? Moreover, the inequity of those climatic effects upon disparate communities forces an even more complex cinematic reckoning. Such considerations stand in contrast to the plethora of post-apocalyptic optics currently offered in scholarly debates and the popular realm, which perpetuate the reductive and violent outlook of an erased, tabula rasa landscape.[1] How might artists, who have historically been tasked with the challenge of representing the ineffable, complicate this picture and add texture to it? Perhaps that which cannot be directly stated might be more fully expressed if sung or intoned or painted or danced. Stacy Alaimo, for instance, outlines the need for greater ecological consideration within the arts, in this way:

> [P]erforming exposure as an ethical and political act means to reckon with – rather than disavow – such horrific events and to grapple

with the particular entanglements of vulnerability and complicity that radiate from disasters and their terribly disjunctive connection to everyday life in the industrialized world. (7)

Some attempts to make manifest the abstract and entangled idea of environmental disruption have been quite literal. In 2008, for example, a Parisian-based duo, Helen Evans and Heiko Hansen, known together as HeHe, went to the Salmisaari coal-burning power plant located in a residential district of Helsinki, Finland, and "drew" a green-laser outline of a cloud, a "Nuage Vert," on the actual plume of smoke above the plant, marking in real time over several weeks the amount of electricity locals used ("Nuage Vert"). Brother Nut from China, starting in 2015, vacuumed up "the air" of Beijing to create "smog bricks," by which you can hold, taste, and smell the otherwise seemingly diffuse particulate that we ingest. The potency of these material projects stems from their site specificity, their time-based data visualization, and the equitable public availability of their materials, forming a barometer for real-time environmental impact. I want to extend these ideas fully into how cinema has been approaching environmental crises. Within this ever-morphing context of an anthropogenically degraded environment, the making of moving images, or any of the other arts, demands a consideration of ethics: of the materials we have extracted, modified, and reinserted into landscapes, as well as an understanding of the vulnerabilities of viewers to feeling inundated and ineffectual.

4:00 p.m.: deborah stratman

The free-fall of consumer excess is at the heart of Deborah Stratman's film *O'er the Land* (2009). Guns, massive RVs, fire torches, cameras, and even scientific equipment – all of these objects feature prominently in the fifty-two-minute film. Stratman shows us the glut so many Americans have at their disposal, a glut even of freedom itself, freedom to play with material fodder for purposes of distraction and entertainment. In contending with this surfeit, we must accept what appears to be inescapable loss and waste. In a kind of condensed allegory of this larger problem, one scene in *O'er the Land* takes us into a birdsong laboratory. The affect is particularly subtle in its haunting: a bird is seen in beautiful close-up, singing, then flitting, until the camera reveals the full situation of the enclosure – only a square foot of space. The bird struggles for a foothold and for room to flap its wings. The singing suddenly reads as distress.

In a more recent film, *Illinois Parables* (2016), Stratman pushes into deeper timescales, testing cinema's capacity for prospecting the past. Sonically, she takes us back via the reenacted voices of Enrico Fermi, Ralph Waldo Emerson, Alexis de Tocqueville, and more. Historical texts come into conversation with present-day images, often unsettling ones. One of most indelible scenes is populated by yellow police tape and a sign indicating that deer have been attacking locals who dare to walk down the park's cordoned-off path. The warning is both oddly funny, given our dominant relationship with cervine creatures, and also eerie. It echoes the 2009 novel *Drive Your Plow over the Bones of the Dead*, by Olga Tokarczuk, who imagines the possibilities of deer turning the tables and becoming assassins of targeted human hunters.

Michelle Puetz, at the Cinema, Nature, Ecology Conference at the University of Chicago in 2009, described Stratman's films as follows:

[R]ather than telling stories, [the films] pose a series of problems, and through their at times ambiguous nature, allow for a quite complicated reading of the questions she is asking [...] [They] point to the relationships between physical spaces or environments and the very human struggles for power, ownership/mastery and control that are played out on the land, meanwhile questioning elemental historical narratives about freedom, expansion, security, and the regulation of space. (Stratman)

5:00 p.m.: nikolaus geyrhalter

In *Our Daily Bread* (2005), Austrian filmmaker Nikolaus Geyrhalter takes on similar dialectics. He seeks out some of the most mechanized sites of food production in Europe, from abattoirs to salt mines to fish factories. One of the most surprisingly unsettling is at a poultry farm. Thousands of yellow chicks, only a few days old, are launched into crates by a sorting machine that alternates between two settings. With each flick of the machinery, the chicks are shot projectile-like from a cannon. Although the chicks' fragility seems at odds with the harsh treatment, they rebound quickly and seem almost protoplasmic in their malleability. Another shock comes in the idyllic setting of a nut orchard: a machine rolls up to a massive old tree, embraces its trunk, and proceeds to shake the tree violently until all its nuts fall onto tarps beneath it. The act seems so gratuitous that it reads like a molestation. In a stroke of brilliance, Geyrhalter contrasts these images of food processing with the mild and often drab lunch and coffee breaks had by the food workers at their requisite locations. Cigarettes and meager sandwiches appear to be denuded of nourishment or comfort, let alone the potential for enjoyment. Our bodies become the mundane masticators, while the machines become the shiny objects of aesthetic fetishization by the camera.

Geyrhalter began his career as a still photographer; relying on that expertise, he refrains in his work from moving the camera or changing focus. Not unlike Peter Kubelka, he cuts with mechanical precision, suggesting that his camera is another one of those tools for slicing, piercing, and organizing the organic world around us, making it digestible for human consumption. Notably, in his film *Homo Sapiens* (2016), all shots clock in at exactly thirty seconds. And it is in *Homo Sapiens* that Geyrhalter most apparently establishes a different mode of coping with the current environmental crises. The metronomic quality of the editing quickly establishes a pattern that eases expectations from the viewer, allowing her to settle into a regular rhythm and discover each image in its own right.

In a 2017 interview with Scott MacDonald, Geyrhalter says that he views "subjects and filmmakers" as a team, even if the subjects are landscapes absent of humans. In the making of *Homo Sapiens*, he wanted the film to feel "democratic," allowing the viewer to have more agency.

> [T]he audience is allowed to search for details in the image and to see what they can discover. Usually in film we just make a cut and go closer, telling the audience what detail to focus on – and I wanted to avoid that. (MacDonald 152)

The force of the film, I would venture, comes most of all from the removal of location specificity in the film or the credits, suspending viewers in a speculative future of the planet, hinting at a crossover into fiction and asking us to imagine the minutes and hours and days after the doomsday clock hits midnight.

6:00 p.m.: mikael kristersson

Swedish birdwatcher Mikael Kristersson has a most delicate touch in his depiction of the present. In his film *Ljusår, or Light Year* (2008), Kristersson operates in a lyrical and mythopoetic tradition. Shooting only in his backyard garden over the course of ten years, he condenses those years into four seasons. Although this trope might feel trite at this point in time, what differentiates his approach and establishes its relevance for the current context is the mastery he has over the space, as seen from the vantage of all the garden's inhabitants: wasps, birds, butterflies, spiders, bees, dogs, cats, potatoes, raspberries, chickens. The film is not, however, about showing different points of view or different subjectivities. Rather, I would argue, it is about drawing infinite connections to all forms of matter – living and inorganic. The perspectives or, better, the locations of the non-human (which are not "points of view" per se) seemingly drive the cuts, if not the movements, of the camera.

This is the opposite of what Donna J. Haraway bemoans in her discussion of "crittercams" in *When Species Meet*:

> How could a mentalistic "camera's eye" narrative ever take hold in the face of such immersion in boats, sea spray, waves, immense whales and slippery dugongs, speed and diving, piloting challenges, team interactions, and the materialities of engineering and using the plethora of cameras and other data-collecting devices that are Crittercam? Indeed, the visual structuring of the TV episodes emphasizes bodies, things, parts, substances, sensory experience, timing, emotions – everything that is the thick stuff of Crittercam's lifeworld. The cuts are fast; the visual fields, littered; the size scales of things and critters in relation to the human body, rapidly switched so that the viewer never feels comfortable with the illusion that anything much can be physically taken for granted in relation to oneself. Part bodies of organisms and technologies predominate over whole-body shots. But never is Crittercam's audience allowed to imagine visually or haptically the absence of physicality and crowded presences, no matter what the voice-over says. The word may not be made flesh here, but everything else is. (254–55)

Kristersson has found a way – in an era that's well beyond anthropomorphizing – to mete out a rendering of the world that shows true intersubjectivity, in the Husserlian sense. He manages to achieve this with a host of non-reductionist aesthetic choices made possible by his immersion in his own "lifeworld" setting at home, and by the fact that he was able to shoot over an extended period of time. Parachute filmmaking, traditional ethnographies, and even sensory ethnographic explorations cannot tap into these intricate interconnections that depend on extended temporalities for their depth of portraying a full ecosystem in time and space.

7:00 p.m.: endosymbiotic structures

In 2018, I made a film, *Inside the Shared Life*, which takes its title from a loose and poetic translation of the Mandarin character for *endosymbiosis*. The film uses underwater sounds of marine creatures ranging from snapping shrimp to Weddell seals and blue whales. Yet the closest the images get to the ocean is a Petri dish and a womb. A human voice, namely Lynn Margulis, acts as our narrator, describing how she came to resurrect the idea of endosymbiosis, an idea originated and outlined by Ivan Wallin in 1927 (Margulis). She also insists, "We don't want to name organisms based on the outcome of their relationships […] You will never understand biology unless you look at it as community ecology." The film attempts to mirror that ethic in form – a model of growth, adaptation, and malleability of non-autonomous identities.

As Kayla Anderson expresses it,

> Anthropocene narratives coming from the art world seem to be most potentially destructive when they propose to do something, further reinforcing an attitude of human dominance over the planet […] The ecological problems we face are not going to be solved by eco-art, representations of fake-nature or collections of plastic hybrids from polluted coastlines. (339)

Similarly, Shilyh Warren has forged a definition for eco-experimental documentary filmmaking as, "[engaging] less in a call to action than in the reorganization of perception: to experience time and nature in a new way is to potentially develop a new ethic towards the environment" (103).

8:00 p.m.: chirality

"Chirality" is a term in organic chemistry, coined by Lord Kelvin in his 1893 Oxford University lecture, that identifies an object unable to be superimposed on a physically realized mirror image. The human hand is an often-cited example: the left hand mirrors the right hand, when facing palm-to-palm, but cannot be matched in three dimensions because of its asymmetry. An artwork always fails to match precisely with what it represents, however true to form. As Lukács writes, "Art, the visionary reality of the world made to our measure, has thus become independent: it is no longer a copy, for all the models have gone" (67). Yet art, I would suggest, can have a chiral reality. Rather than being indexical, in the sense of Charles S. Peirce's categories of signs, an artwork that achieves a transportation of place, a control of time, and its unique containment of space moves into a cinematic realm of what I see as chirality.

Tom Gunning writes on the drawbacks of indexicality in analyzing the photographic medium:

> [I]t would be foolish to closely identify the indexical with the photographic; most indexical information is not recorded by photography. Long before digital media were introduced, medical instruments and other instruments of measurement, indexical instruments *par excellence* – such as devices for reading pulse rate, temperature, heart rate, etc., or speedometers, wind gauges, and barometers – all converted their information into numbers. Although a photograph combines both types of signs, the indexical quality of a photograph must not be confused with its iconicity. The fact that rows of numbers do not resemble a photograph, or what the photograph is supposed to represent, does not undermine any indexical claim. (40)

In separating indexicality from iconicity, I suggest here that there is a place for this term chirality, either linking those two ideas or acting as a substitute for how to consider the photographic signifier. In reconciling planetary changes with the representational tools available, there needs to be a greater focus on iconicity as well as an additional means of reference, such as chirality, which I believe can speak to the inversion that occurs in attempts to represent the corporeal as digital and emitted light.

The clock could become chiral, too, I would venture, if we step over the "doomsday" hour of midnight. The clock folds in upon itself if we declare the world to be over, and we enter a different time-sensing. If we declare the end of human time, the end of earth time by our metrics, then we make way for an alternate representation of the time to come.

9:00 p.m.: humankind cannot bear very much reality

"Where is the present?" asks William James in *Principles of Psychology*. "It has melted in our grasp, fled ere we could touch it, gone in the instant of becoming" (608).

10:00 p.m.: entrainment

Here is the moment of compression, when the clock appears to speed up. Our slide into the future appears impossible and the look back through deep time happens in a flash. We must match the hours of the clock.

11:00 p.m.: time signatures as a theory of everything

In order to prevent Woolf's cinematic parasitism, we must activate the further potential of cinematic representation through in-kind perturbations and shifts in temporalities. Cinema – especially experimental eco-documentary – can respond to the new magnitudes of our time. Instead of moving back and forth from the local to the planetary, moving-image artists can suggest a more expansive investigation of space *and* time in order to learn from past and present experiences, to imagine more ethically durable futures. Sometimes that means staying in one place. Sometimes that means duration. Sometimes that means a metric edit.

Clearly there are no catch-alls, only timings.

12:00 a.m.: doomsday. the end of the world. the return

The poet Eleni Sikelianos writes:

> Earth shows us how
> a minute is round, an hour is, a day
> Because it is round we cannot help coming
>   round
> upon ourselves again (41)

In a time when philosophical thinking has shifted into posthumanism, new materialism, and object-oriented ontology, the countdown to the end of the human species might be reconceived as a celebration, a new beginning for the rest of the planet. The doomsday and apocalypse transforms into rebirth. The time signature changes and the planet gets a new start.

All hands point up.

disclosure statement

No potential conflict of interest was reported by the author.

note

1 For this line of inquiry, I owe a debt to my colleagues at the University of Colorado Boulder with whom I'm hosting a Mellon Sawyer Grant in 2020–21: Brianne Cohen, Lori Peek, and Andy Cowell.

bibliography

Alaimo, Stacy. *Exposed: Environmental Politics and Pleasures in Posthuman Times*. Minneapolis: U of Minnesota P, 2016. 7. Print.

Andersen, Thom. "Random Notes on a Projection of The Clock by Christian Marclay at the Los Angeles County Museum of Art, 4:32 pm, July 28, 2011–5:02 pm, July 29, 2011." *Cinema Scope*. Web. <cinema-scope.com/features/random-notes-on-a-projection>.

Anderson, Kayla. "Ethics, Ecology, and the Future: Art and Design Face the Anthropocene." *Leonardo* 48.4 (2015): 338–47. doi:10.1162/leon_a_01087. Print.

Baas, Maarten. *Schiphol Clock*. Web. <http://maartenbaas.com/real-time/schiphol-clock/>.

Bass, Joseph, and Mitchell A. Lazar. "Circadian Time Signatures of Fitness and Disease." *Science* 25 Nov. 2016. Web. <science.sciencemag.org/content/354/6315/994/tab-pdf/>.

Benedict, Kennette. "Science, Art, and the Legacy of Martyl." *Bulletin of the Atomic Scientists* 9 Apr. 2013. Web. <thebulletin.org/2013/04/science-art-and-the-legacy-of-martyl/>.

Blackburn, Bonnie J. "Leonardo and Gaffurio on Harmony and the Pulse of Music." *Essays on Music and Culture in Honor of Herbert Kellman*. Ed. Barbara Haggh. Paris: Minerve, 2001. 128–49. Print.

Brunick, Kaitlin L., James E. Cutting, and Jordan E. DeLong. "Low-Level Features of Film: What They Are and Why We Would Be Lost Without Them." *Psychocinematics: Exploring Cognition at the Movies*. Oxford: Oxford UP, 23 May 2013. *Oxford Scholarship Online*. Web. 13 Jan. 2020. <https://www-oxfordscholarship-com.colorado.idm.oclc.org/view/10.1093/acprof:oso/9780199862139.001.0001/acprof-9780199862139-chapter-7>.

Budd, Amy. "Writer Amy Budd on Universal Film: Peter Kubelka LUX." *LUX* 15 Feb. 2017. Web. <lux.org.uk/writing/universal-film-peter-kubelka>.

"Current Time." *Bulletin of the Atomic Scientists*. Web. <thebulletin.org/doomsday-clock/current-time/>.

"Dali Clock Face, From 'Halsman/Dali' Portfolio." *Museum of Contemporary Photography*. Web. <www.mocp.org/detail.php?type=related&kv=2551&t=objects>.

Eisen, Erica. "Under the Eye of the Clock." *The White Review*. Web. <www.thewhitereview.org/reviews/under-the-eye-of-the-clock>.

Gunning, Tom. "PLENARY SESSION II. Digital Aesthetics. What's the Point of an Index? or, Faking Photographs." *Nordicom Review* 25.1–2 (Jan. 2004): 39–49. doi:10.1515/nor-2017-0268. Print.

Haraway, Donna Jeanne. *When Species Meet*. Minneapolis: U of Minnesota P, 2008. Print.

James, William. *The Principles of Psychology: American Science Series – Advanced Course. In Two Volumes*. New York: Henry Holt, 1890. Print.

Lavant, Johnny. "24 Hours of Avant-Garde: The Good Hours, Part III." *MUBI* 2009. Web. <mubi.com/notebook/posts/24-hours-of-avant-garde-the-good-hours-part-iii>.

"The 'Lost' Steve Jobs Speech from 1983: Foreshadowing Wireless Networking, the iPad, and the App Store." *Life, Liberty, and Technology* 4 Oct. 2012. Web. <lifelibertytech.com/2012/10/02/the-lost-steve-jobs-speech-from-1983-foreshadowing-wireless-networking-the-ipad-and-the-app-store/>.

Lukács György. *The Theory of the Novel: A Historico-Philosophical Essay on the Forms of Great Epic Literature*. London: Merlin P, 1971. 67. Print.

MacDonald, Scott. *The Sublimity of Document: Cinema as Diorama: Avant-Doc 2*. New York: Oxford UP, 2019. Print.

Margulis, Lynn. "Rutgers Interview with Lynn Margulis and Jay A. Tischfield." 2004. Web. <https://www.youtube.com/watch?v=KlhW12dGfFk>.

"Nuage Vert (Green Cloud)." *Curating Cities: A Database of Eco Public Art*. Web. <eco-publicart.org/nuage-vert-green-cloud/>.

Rapold, Nicolas. "A Feminist's Beer Ads and Safaris." *New York Times* 2 May 2013. Web. <https://www.nytimes.com/2013/05/03/movies/fragments-of-kubelka-directed-by-martina-kudlacek.html>.

Sikelianos, Eleni. *Body Clock Poems*. Minneapolis: Coffee House P, 2008. 41. Print.

Simmel, Georg. *Metropolis and Mental Life*. Chicago: Syllabus Division, U of Chicago P, 1961. Print.

Solnit, Rebecca. "The Annihilation of Time and Space." *New England Review (1990–)* 24.1 (2003): 5–19. Web. 11 Jan. 2020. <www.jstor.org/stable/40244205>.

Stratman, Deborah. *PYTHAGORASFILM*. Web. <www.pythagorasfilm.com/oertheland.html>.

Tokarczuk, Olga. *Drive Your Plow over the Bones of the Dead*. New York: Riverhead, 2019. Print.

Warren, Shilyh. "Hum, Buzz, Gurgle: Ecological Soundscapes in Poetic Ecodocs." *Vocal Projections: Voices in Documentary*. Ed. A.H. Roe et al. New York: Bloomsbury Academic, 2019. 101–18. Print.

Woolf, Virginia. "The Movies and Reality." *The New Republic*, 1926. Web.

Yue, Genevieve. "Clocks for Seeing: Christian Marclay's The Clock." *Film Comment* 19 July 2012. Web. <www.filmcomment.com/blog/clocks-for-seeing-christian-marclays-the-clock/>.

Erin Espelie

The term "*ontogenesis*" receives its full sense if, instead of giving it the restricted and derived meaning of the genesis of the individual [...] one uses it to designate the character of *becoming of being*, that by which being becomes, insofar as it is, as being. The opposition between being and becoming can only be valid within a certain doctrine that supposes that the very model of being is a substance. (Gilbert Simondon 5–6)

The actual world is a process, and that process is the becoming of actual entities [...] In the becoming of an actual entity, the *potential* unity of many entities in disjunctive diversity [...] acquires the *real* unity of the one actual entity; so that the actual entity is the real concrescence of many potentials [...] In other words, it belongs to the nature of a "being" that it is a potential for every "becoming." (Alfred North Whitehead, *Process and Reality* 22)

michael epperson

RELATIONAL REALISM AND THE ONTOGENETIC UNIVERSE

subject, object, and ontological process in quantum mechanics

In both Simondon's concept of ontogenesis and the Whiteheadian, relational realist interpretation of quantum mechanics,[1] the term "global" refers to a synthetic process of collective individuation. It is an unfolding totality driven via locally contextualized potential predicative relations wherein every quantum individuation – every quantum unit of relation (i.e., every quantum measurement event) – is properly understood as an actualized potential relation that is at once "subjectively" *contextualized locally* and "objectively" *constitutive globally*. Thus, both Simondon's ontogenetic universe and the relational realist interpretation of quantum mechanics depict the mutual implication of local/subjective and global/objective in terms of locally contextualized *actualized*

facts (Simondon's "individuated" facts) and their globally extensive *potential relations* (his "preindividuated," potential facts). Both frameworks are "ontogenetic" in the sense that the process of individuation – the novel actualization of potential relations – generates novel actual facts that, in turn, lead to novel potential relations, yielding additional novel actual facts, and so on.

Fundamentally, then, the ontogenetic universe entails two mutually implicative ontological categories: "individuated" actualities and "preindividuated" potential actualities in a mutually implicative and mutually synthetic relationship. Each category yields its own distinctive portrait of the world and its own modality of experience; more important, the mutually implicative and mutually synthetic relationship of these categories obviates the possibility of reductively assimilating one portrait to the other. The category of individuated actualities evokes the *individuated-contextual-actual* portrait of ontogenesis – the global as an objective totality of locally contextualized dative facts – namely facts whose local spatiotemporal contextualization allows for their coherent relation both causally and logically. The category of preindividuated potential actualities evokes the *preindividuated-precontextual-potential* portrait of ontogenesis – the domain of pure, precontextualized potential relations among facts – i.e., those aspects of potential relations that exceed local contextualization within the process of individuation.

> Individuation must therefore be considered as a partial and relative resolution that occurs in a system that contains potentials and encloses a certain *incompatibility in relation to itself* – an incompatibility made of forces of tension as well as of the impossibility of an interaction between the extreme terms of the dimensions. (Simondon 5)

Likewise, for Whitehead, the category of "Pure Potentials for the Specific Determination of Fact, or Forms of Definiteness" (*Process and Reality* 22) are always "potentialities *for* actual entities." Every pure potential is "precontextual" in that it "is neutral as to the fact of its physical ingression in any particular actual entity of the temporal world" (44). In quantum mechanics this "pure potentiality" in the category of the *preindividuated-precontextual-potential* is reflected in the fact that the global state vector $|\psi\rangle$ in the equation –

$$|\psi\rangle = \alpha_{ijk} \sum_{i,j,k} |s\rangle_i |d\rangle_j |e\rangle_k$$

where $|s\rangle$ represents a locally contextualized system state, $|d\rangle$ represents the state of the related locally contextualizing measurement basis, and $|e\rangle$ represents the state of the unmeasured environment – can be expressed as the sum of an indefinite number of potential states or "potentialities of definiteness," referent to no specific actualities and potentially referent to all. Many of these potential states are incapable of integration, forming nonsensical, interfering superpositions, reflective of Simondon's characterization of the *preindividuated-precontextual-potential* as enclosing "a certain *incompatibility in relation to itself* – an incompatibility made of forces of tension as well as of the impossibility of an interaction between the extreme terms of the dimensions" (5).

A binocular view of these two portraits together, the *preindividuated-precontextual-potential* and the *individuated-contextual-actual*, yields a third portrait – a view of the global as a unified, nonlocally restricted, relational structure (a "transductive" structure in Simondon's terminology) – the *transductive-transcontextual-relational* portrait of the universe. Together, these three portraits evoke a fundamental depiction of the universe as an ontogenetic network of actualizations of potential relations constitutive of a global process of emergent unfolding.

Each of these three philosophical portraits finds its reflection in the Whiteheadian, relational realist interpretation of quantum mechanics, which mathematically formalizes the connective structure by which the distinctive features of each portrait can be coherently interrelated. For example, the *individuated-contextual-actual* portrait is exemplified quantum mechanically as a *locally contextualized measurement outcome state*, i.e., a locally contextualized evaluation of a physical observable, such that the local contextualization is representable as a Boolean subalgebra. The *preindividuated-precontextual-potential* portrait is exemplified quantum mechanically by the fact that potential relations among observables always exceed the constraints of any *particular* local measurement context/Boolean subalgebra, and more important, even exceed the constraints of the global totality of all particular local contexts together (namely the Kochen–Specker theorem[2]). In quantum mechanics every measurement event – every individuated actualization of a potential quantum state – is locally contextualized via an orthonormal measurement basis/Boolean subalgebra whereby potential measurement outcomes are expressible as mutually exclusive and exhaustive, probability-valued, either-or propositions. Every such locally contextualized measurement is always understood as "non-maximal" because there will always be potential evaluations that exceed not only that particular local contextualization, but the totality of all local contextualizations. There is, in other words, no "global Boolean algebra" in quantum mechanics that can be taken to represent the totality of all locally contextualized potential states. This idea finds its analog in Simondon's concept of ontogenesis:

> It is possible to put forward the hypothesis, which is analogous to that of the quanta in physics and also to that of the relativity of potential energy levels, that individuation *does not exhaust all of the preindividual reality* [...] A certain level of potential remains, and further individuations are still possible. (8)

The phenomenon of nonlocal quantum entanglement in composite quantum systems well exemplifies this idea. In such systems, locally contextualized regions of the composite system are spacelike separated and therefore nonlocal relative to one another (i.e., mutually causally irrelevant). Nevertheless, measurement of such systems reveals a nonlocal "transductive" overlapping of the constituent local measurement contexts, such that correlations between the restricted set of potential measurement outcomes ("individuations") defined by the local contexts individually are exceeded. This nonlocal overlapping is formalized mathematically via a topological overlapping of the Boolean subalgebras representing the local contexts in relation. This is the *transductive-transcontextual-relational* dimension of ontogenesis, evinced quantum mechanically by the fact of nonlocal correlations among locally contextualized measurements – i.e., correlations among measurement outcomes that exceed the spatiotemporal restrictions of their individual local contextualizations. The phenomenon of nonlocal probability conditionalization (an example of Simondon's "transduction") in EPR-type experiments – a signature feature of quantum mechanics which will be discussed in greater detail presently – is perhaps the most conventional exemplification of the transductive-global-relational portrait of ontogenesis in modern physics.

> By transduction we mean an operation – physical, biological, mental, social – by which an activity propagates itself from one element to the next, within a given domain, and founds this propagation on a structuration of the domain that is realized from place to place: each area of the constituted structure serves as the principle and the model for the next area, as a primer for its constitution, to the extent that the modification expands progressively at the same time as the structuring operation. (Simondon 11)

When one considers nonlocal quantum mechanical correlations via either Simondon's concept of transduction or the Whiteheadian, relational realist interpretation of quantum mechanics, one finds these correlations are ultimately grounded in a mutually implicative relationship between local and global. This relationship has only two possible modes, jointly operative in every quantum measurement event (Epperson and Zafiris 54–57, 186–94, 217–18, 229–34):

[1] *Extension of the local to the global*, wherein locally contextualized individuations/actualized measurement outcomes (i.e., the *individuated-contextual-actual* portrait) condition global potentia (i.e., the *preindividuated-precontextual-potential* portrait) via a fundamentally nonlocal, non-metrical, non-spatiotemporally restricted, global relational structure (i.e., the structure of the *transductive-transcontextual-relational* portrait) by which the global unfolds as a synthetic process. This is evinced, as mentioned above, by nonlocal probability conditionalization in quantum mechanics, whereby locally contextualized individuations/

actualized measurement outcomes, when extended relationally to the global state, synthetically *augment* the global state, such that the latter is properly understood not as a static totality, but rather as an emergent, unfolding totality.

[2] *Restriction of the local by the global*, wherein global individuations (actualized quantum states) condition local potentia and their local contextualization. This is evinced, for example via the phenomenon of environmental decoherence in quantum mechanics.

Thus, the bidirectionally conditional mutual implication of local contextuality and global objectivity in quantum mechanics is exemplified by the concurrence of [1] the *extension* of locally contextualized *actual* measurement outcomes *to* the global quantum state, and [2] the *restriction* of local contextualization of *potential* measurement outcomes *by* the global quantum state. In the relational realist interpretation of quantum mechanics, this bidirectional conditioning is formalized mathematically via the category theoretic concept of adjunction (Epperson and Zafiris 229–32, 273–76, 328–30) – a particularly powerful innovation in that it is uniquely suited to the local–global topological relations of quantum measurement contexts discussed above.

The central conceptual challenge, then, for any ontogenetic interpretation of quantum mechanics and its practical, empirical application is not only the problem of measurement (i.e., the problem of actualization of potentia – the problem of the existence of a unique actual measurement outcome when quantum mechanics terminates in a matrix of probability-valuated potential outcomes) – nor is it merely the problem of local subjective measurement contextualization having global objective significance; the central challenge underlying both of these problems, rather, is properly understanding, via a coherent and empirically adequate conceptual scheme, the mutually implicative relationship between local and global in quantum mechanics. This necessarily entails the construction of a formal philosophical and mathematical framework that adequately depicts how the *logical* features of this relationship can be shown to condition the *causal* features in a way that yields the nonlocal, transcontextual correlations ("transductions") discussed above. Further, the framework would need to depict what Simondon calls the "metastability" underlying not only these correlations, but also underlying the process of the actualization of potential measurement outcomes in general.

These desiderata are all central features of the relational realist interpretation of quantum mechanics and the ontogenetic universe it portrays. Its connection with Simondon's concept of ontogenesis is most clearly illustrated by focusing on the relationship between:

[a] the *individuated-contextual-actual* portrait
correlated with
local-metrical-coordinate spacetime
structure

and

[b] the *transductive-transcontextual-relational*
portrait
correlated with
global-mereotopological-genetic
quantum event structure

As introduced above, the *individuated-contextual-actual* portrait of ontogenesis depicts the global as a totality of locally contextualized dative ("individuated") facts – namely quantum events – whose local spatiotemporal contextualization allows for their coherent relation both causally and logically. In the relational realist framework, this causal-logical order has its basis in the Whiteheadian notion of an objective mereological ordering (a mereotopological ordering in the relational realist interpretation) of fundamental relational events (i.e., quantum events as Whiteheadian "actual occasions"). Crucially, this objective global *mereotopological* ordering of quantum events must not be misconstrued as an objective global *spatiotemporal* ordering. While the *individuated-contextual-actual* portrait of ontogenesis is compatible with an ordering structure of linear-sequential time (i.e., local spacetime), in the relational realist interpretation of quantum mechanics, local temporality, and indeed all *metrically* extensive relations, constitute a higher-order reflection of a fundamentally *mereotopological* extensive structure. This structure is grounded in the concept of histories of quantum events,[3] with each event bijectively related to its local contextualization. Here, "local" does not refer to metrically extensive (relativistic) locality, but rather to the idea, introduced earlier, that each quantum measurement context is representable as a particular Boolean algebra. Locality, in other words, is fundamentally defined topologically, not metrically.

Likewise, for Simondon, the spatiotemporal ordering of individuals presupposes the transductive, ordering operation of individuation. Returning to the previous quote:

> By transduction we mean an operation – physical, biological, mental, social – by which an activity propagates itself from one element to the next, within a given domain, and founds this propagation on a structuration of the domain that is realized from place to place: each area of the constituted structure serves as the principle and the model for the next area, as a primer for its constitution, to the extent that the modification expands progressively at the same time as the structuring operation. (Simondon 11)

As an ordering structure, the concept of transduction can be correlated with the Whiteheadian, relational realist concept of a quantum event structure – a mereotopological supersession of *internally related*[4] quantum events that includes, bijectively, a mereotopological supersession of the events' local Boolean measurement contexts. In this way, the serialized internal relation of each locally contextualized quantum event/individuation to its dative global environment can be correlated with the serial-inclusive mereotopological relatedness defining the fundamental extensiveness of the universe, with each concrescent integration of the whole internally related to the totality of logically mereotopologically prior integrations (i.e., prior in sequence, not prior in time).

It should be noted, however, that for Simondon, transductive internal relations of this kind are characteristic of "living individuals" only, not "physical individuals."

> The physical individual, perpetually de-centered, perpetually peripheral to itself, active at the limit of its domain, *does not have a veritable interiority*; the living individual, on the contrary, does have a veritable interiority because individuation carries itself out within the individual; the *interior is also constitutive* in the living individual, whereas in the physical individual, only the limit is constitutive, and *that which is topologically interior is genetically anterior*. The living individual is contemporary to itself in all of its elements, which is not the case for the physical individual, which carries something of the past that is radically past, even when it is still growing. (Simondon 7–8)

If one generalizes the complexity of individuation and transduction in Simondon's category of living systems to his category of physical systems per the Whiteheadian approach, where the more complex internal relations constitutive of higher-order (e.g., "living") systems exhibit the same categorical structure as less complex, lower-order (e.g., merely "physical") systems – thus differing not categorically but only in degree of relational complexity – one finds that in both relational realist quantum mechanics and in Simondon's concept of ontogenesis, individuation and transduction entail a rich and highly complex internal relational structure with both extensive and intensive dimensions. One dimension is the local, relativistically restricted mode of spatiotemporal causal relation of the individuated-contextual-actual portrait of ontogenesis. This spatiotemporal-extensive *coordinate structure of individuals* when extended to transduction, however, presupposes an underlying global logical (mereotopological) *genetic structure of individuations*.

> Transduction corresponds to this existence of relations that are born when the

preindividual being individuates itself; it expresses individuation and allows it to be thought; it is therefore a notion that is both metaphysical and *logical*. It applies to ontogenesis, and is ontogenesis itself. (Simondon 11)

This, again, is the *transductive-transcontextual-relational* dimension of ontogenesis. In relational realist quantum mechanics, the global, logical-mereotopological quantum event structure – the *genetically intensive structure of individuations* – is the basis for the relativistic causal structure – the *coordinately extensive structure of individuals*. And as discussed above, the global mereotopological structure is a fundamentally asymmetrical, serially ordered global structure of internal relations. In relational realist quantum mechanics, in other words, the logical-mereotopological order, not the metrical spatiotemporal order, is the fundamental order of the extensive continuum. In the words of Whitehead:

The extensive continuum is a complex of entities united by the various allied relationships of whole to part, and of overlapping so as to possess common parts, and of contact, and of other relationships derived from these primary relationships [...] *It is the first determination of order* [...] The properties of this continuum are very few and *do not include the relationships of metrical geometry*. (*Process and Reality* 66)

These extensive relationships are more fundamental than their more special spatial and temporal relationships [...] Extension, apart from its spatialization and temporalization, is that general scheme of relationships providing the capacity that many objects can be welded into the real unity of one experience. (*Process and Reality* 67)

Whitehead's conception of the fundamental, non-spatiotemporal, mereological order of the extensive continuum and its unifying role within his cosmological scheme is thus central to the mereotopological order formalized in relational realist quantum mechanics, and the role played by this order in the *transductive-transcontextual-relational* portrait of ontogenesis.

And as has been well-demonstrated in physics, without a single exception to date, any deduction from that fundamental logical-mereotopological order to a more special order, such as the causal order of relativistic spatiotemporal extensiveness, always maintains commitment to the fundamental, internal relational, logical-mereotopological order. But equally well-demonstrated in physics, commitment to this order never entails sheer reduction to it. As discussed earlier, the global, transductive, mereotopological quantum event structure is itself an inherently non-reductive, synthetic structure; it cannot be reduced to a single classical logic – i.e., a global Boolean algebra. Likewise, for Simondon,

Classical logic cannot be used to think the individuation, because it requires that the operation of individuation be thought using concepts and relationships between concepts that only apply to the results of the operation of individuation, considered in a partial manner. From the use of this method, which considers the law of identity and the law of the excluded middle as too restrictive, a new notion emerges that possesses a multitude of aspects and domains of application: that of *transduction*. (Simondon 10–11)

While transduction across multiple individuations cannot be reduced to the classical logical relations defined by the context of any single component individuation – i.e., the laws of identity, excluded middle, and non-contradiction as defined by that individual local context – transduction does entail a transcontextualization *across* these component individuations. Thus, transcontextualization presupposes some degree of compatibility with respect to these contexts.

In relational realist quantum mechanics, the asymmetrical internal relation among local quantum measurement contexts, combined with the presupposition that individual local measurement contexts are always structurally Boolean, together constitute the *compatibility condition for logical causality* in quantum mechanics (Epperson and Zafiris 58–63, 148–56). Here, "logical causality" refers to the necessary presupposition in modern physics of the universal, categorical correlation of [a] the asymmetrical order of material implication and logical consequence with [b] the asymmetrical order of causal relation – i.e., the correlation of *if* → *then* with *cause* → *effect* (Epperson 80–83; Epperson and Zafiris 139–78). Thus, logical causality is fundamentally about the process of relational individuation, not relations of individuals. Likewise, for Simondon,

> If it were true that logic provided statements about being only after individuation, it would be necessary to institute a theory of being that is anterior to any form of logic; this theory could serve as the foundation to logic, because nothing proves in advance that there is only one possible way of individuating being. If multiple types of individuation were to exist, multiple logics would also have to exist, each corresponding to a specific type of individuation. The classification of the ontogeneses would allow us to *pluralize logic* using a valid foundation of plurality. (13)

Relational realist quantum mechanics does precisely this in its own depiction of ontogenesis. The compatibility condition[5] is formalized as a sheaf-theoretic mereotopological description of the local–global relation of Boolean algebras – specifically, as a transition morphism from one local Boolean context to another, generating asymmetrical logical and mereotopological revisions of equivalence classes of local contextual Boolean algebras.

Topologically, these revisions yield partial compatibility on their overlapping regions (e.g., partial Boolean compatibility of coarse-grained position and momentum observables, up to the limit of the Heisenberg uncertainty relations). This "inductive limit" (Epperson and Zafiris 156–58, 207, 226–28, 270–307) by which local compatible families of Boolean algebras can be extended globally, is constructed via the formation of a set of equivalence classes of partially compatible Boolean subalgebras, representing partially compatible Boolean contextualized observables, on *all* possible overlaps. The compatibility condition thus requires as a categorical presupposition that all local measurement contexts are structurally Boolean, and that the asymmetrical Boolean structure of any local context is preserved when extended globally, via internal relation, to other contexts (156).

The compatibility condition is thus built upon two foundational concepts:

[1] *Locally*, every measurement context must be Boolean, such that in the mixed state, Boolean material implication holds – e.g., for any measurement context A it will always be the case that for potential outcomes a_1 and a_2, $a_1 \to \neg a_2$ ("if a_1, then not a_2") and $a_2 \to \neg a_1$. This, of course, is just the law of non-contradiction for an observable a with only two possible eigenstates (i.e., potential outcome states) a_1 and a_2. This number, however, has no upper limit in quantum mechanics.

[2] *Globally* (i.e., when local contexts are brought into nonlocal relation), intra-contextual Boolean material implication (that is, *within* individual local measurement contexts) must be relatable transcontextually, *across* these local contexts (i.e., "globally"). As discussed earlier, the structure of relations among the totality of quantum events is non-Boolean, evinced by both the non-commutativity of quantum observables, and because the laws of non-contradiction and excluded middle cannot be shown to hold globally in quantum mechanics. That is, one can never, even in principle, evaluate the totality of quantum observables as a comprehensive scheme of mutually exclusive and exhaustive true/false propositions.

However, this *can* be done within local Boolean contextualizations of this global structure; that is, local Boolean sectors of the non-Boolean global lattice can be defined. In this sense, the global quantum event structure, even though it cannot be fully embedded within a global Boolean algebra, can be represented via a partial Boolean algebra – again, so long as one categorically presupposes that all local measurement contexts are structurally

Boolean (i.e., representable as a Boolean subalgebra, or as an equivalence class of such subalgebras).

This presupposition is central to the relational realist interpretation of quantum mechanics, which defines the transcontextual structure by which Boolean local–global relations (cf. Simondon's "transductions") can be specified. For even though the totality of facts contained in the global quantum lattice can never be defined completely via deductive analysis, it can be defined approximately via induction from the overlaps of a sufficiently large number of equivalence classes of compatible, or partially compatible, local Boolean subalgebras. It is via this structure that global quantum events can be shown to logically condition local potential measurement contextualization – i.e., *restriction of the local by the global* discussed earlier; likewise, it is via this structure that locally contextualized quantum events can be shown to condition global potentia – i.e., *extension of the local to the global*. Formally, the structure of these overlaps is not fundamentally metrically extensive, and therefore not an implicit feature of the *individuated-contextual-actual* dimension of ontogenesis; rather, it is a *mereotopologically* extensive feature of the *transductive-transcontextual-relational* dimension of ontogenesis.

With respect to relational realism's commitment to a global (but only locally definable) mereotopological order – a crucial question is: do the presupposed topological axioms, definitions, and assumptions given in relational realism (Epperson and Zafiris 261–353) provide sufficient justification for the order they yield? They are first principles of causal relation that correlate, by mutual implication, with the first principles of logical (mereotopological) implication; as first principles, there is thus no deeper principle by which to account for the correlation itself. One could argue that for any physically significant philosophical framework, there must be some additional specified dynamical process that would yield the sought-after correlation in the language of physics. But ultimately this is akin to Plato's exploration of the question, "Why is the universe reasonable?" His own cosmology in the *Timaeus*, like Whitehead's, contains similarly presupposed first principles – along with an insuperable argument in the *Theaetetus* that attempting to apply a physical reductionist argument to account for cosmological first principles will always lead to nothing – literally, to no thing.

As discussed earlier, this correlation of causal relation and logical-mereotopological implication in the *transductive-transcontextual-relational* dimension of ontogenesis is perhaps best exemplified via the phenomenon of quantum nonlocality in measurements of spacelike separated components of a composite quantum system. EPR-type systems[6] are the most widely recognized systems of this kind, where local measurement contexts A and B – i.e., detectors A and B – are spatially well-separated, each measuring a different component of the composite system. Because of their spacelike separation, it is assumed that given the relativistic speed of light limitation, the order of component measurement (A then B, or B then A) should be irrelevant, since any physical causal correlations between components would require a faster-than-light propagation of energy between A and B.

What these experiments reveal is that while there is, indeed, no measurable nonlocal, efficient causal influence between A and B, there *is* a measurable, nonlocal probability conditionalization between A and B that always takes the form of an asymmetrical internal relation. For example, as discussed above, if A registers first, the outcome at B is internally related to the outcome at A, inducing a probability conditionalization of the *potential* (Simondon's "pre-individuated") outcomes at B by the *actual* ("individuated") outcome at A; specifically, the integration of B's contextualized potential outcomes, represented as an equivalence class of Boolean subalgebras, is "revised"[7] by the actual outcome at A. This "transductive" revision, indicative of the asymmetrical internal relation of B's outcome to A's outcome, has been well-demonstrated in countless EPR-type experimental investigations of quantum nonlocality.

While some interpretations resort to exotic explanations such as superluminal propagations of hidden energy or other efficient causal, physical-dynamical mechanisms, the phenomenon of quantum nonlocality can instead be understood intuitively as a logical (mereotopological) conditioning of causal relations – a conditioning implicit in the logical relational structure presupposed by all scientific theories, and rendered explicit in the Whiteheadian, relational realist interpretation of quantum mechanics. Specifically, the mereotopological conditioning of causal relations, defined earlier as the "compatibility condition for logical causality in quantum mechanics," renders explicit the implicit presupposition of: [1] the Boolean internal relational structure of each local context A and B (again, locally Boolean measurement contexts being a necessary presupposition of the scientific method in general); and [2] the logically coherent global relation of locally contextualized measurement outcomes[8] via a fundamentally logical-mereotopological quantum event structure.

From this perspective, in summary of the present example, the equivalence class of Boolean subalgebras representing the integration of potential outcomes at B is "transduced" in Simondon's language – i.e., ontologically revised – by the measurement outcome at A, thus exhibiting B's internal relationship to A, even when A and B are space-like separated. This nonlocal revision entails no propagation of energy of any kind from A to B and is thus not properly understood as an efficient causal influence of the actualized outcome at B by that of A; rather, it is a "logical conditioning" (namely a nonlocal probability conditionalization) of the contextualization of the *potential* ("preindividuated") outcomes at B via the internal relation of these potential outcomes to the *actualized* ("individuated") outcome at A.

The advantage of the topological, category-sheaf theoretic formalism of the relational realist interpretation of quantum mechanics is that it explicitly reveals the formal mereotopological ("transductive") structure by which these nonlocal internal relations are integrated ontogenetically. This type of predication has no classical analog, and no classical analog should be expected in fundamental physics since quantum mechanical potentiality ("preindividual reality") has essentially broadened the concept of a measurement event as an actualized potential outcome state ("individuated actuality").[9]

In this way, writes Simondon, one grasps "ontogenesis in the entire progression of its reality, and [knows] *the individual through the individuation, rather than the individuation through the individual.*"

> The search for the principle of individuation must be reversed, by considering as primordial the operation of individuation from which the individual comes to exist and of which its characteristics reflect the development, the regime and finally the modalities. The individual would then be grasped as a *relative reality*, a certain phase of being that supposes a preindividual reality, and that, even after individuation, does not exist on its own, because individuation does not exhaust with one stroke the potentials of preindividual reality. (Simondon 5)

In further exploration of how the mereotopological-intensive *transductive-transcontextual-relational* structure of "becoming" pertains to the metrical-extensive coordinate structure of *individuated-contextual-actual* "beings" in the relational realist interpretation of quantum mechanics, it is useful to examine Whitehead's theory of extensive connection (*Process and Reality* 283–336) – a description of the mereological, logically governed relations subsumed by the concept of a serial supersession of quantum event actualizations ("concrescences") – i.e., a quantum event history. In Whitehead's Theory of Prehensions each concrescing occasion (each "individuation in process") is internally related to the world-as-history, "*each creature including in itself the whole of history*" (*Process and Reality* 228). In his Theory of Extension, Whitehead precisely describes the meaning of the words "including in itself" in that quote: it is defined as a logically governed, serial-inclusive, internal relational, mereological order of whole to part. This order is intended to give *extensive meaning* to the *intensive notion* of a concrescing occasion, in the process of its own individuation, as internally related to the history of the world.

Likewise, for Simondon, "that which the individuation makes appear is not only the individual, but also the pair individual-environment" (5). Thus, both Simondon's concept of ontogenesis and the Whiteheadian, relational realist interpretation of quantum mechanics entail a relational/relativistic notion of "coming into beingness" in terms of [a] the spatiotemporally extensive local contexts of actual occasions in the process of individuation/concrescence, in relation to [b] the spatiotemporally coordinated global environment defined via these local contexts. But again, as evinced by the phenomenon of quantum nonlocality discussed earlier, this relativistic spatiotemporal extensive structure of individuals in no way trumps the logical-mereotopological-intensive structure of individuation and transduction.

With respect to the quantum mechanical exemplification of Simondon's concept of transduction discussed earlier and its necessary presupposition of the "compatibility condition" at the level of the mereotopological *transductive-transcontextual-relational* structure of ontogenesis, there is an analogous presupposition at the level of the *individuated-contextual-actual* structure of ontogenesis: the a priori congruence definition presupposed by relativistic depictions of spatiotemporal extension (Whitehead, *Process and Reality* 331–32). Whitehead writes, for example, "The transformations into an indefinite variety of coordinates to which the 'tensor theory' refers, *all presuppose one congruence definition*. The invariance of the Einsteinian 'ds' expresses this fact" (*Process and Reality* 98). This congruence definition is ultimately anchored in the constancy of the speed of light – although as I noted in *Quantum Mechanics and the Philosophy of Alfred North Whitehead*,

> it should be emphasized that for Whitehead (and likely as well for Einstein) the critical importance of the constant c had little to do with its relation to the phenomenon of *light per se*; its significance, rather, lay in the derivative invariance of spacetime intervals and the associated possibility of (i) the asymmetrical, logical and causal ordering of events within spacetime reference frames, and (ii) the provision of a congruence relation that allows for the comparison of spatial and temporal extensive coordinations across diverse spacetime reference frames. (Epperson 177)

Whitehead writes:

> The critical velocity c which occurs in these formulae has now no connexion whatever with light or with any other fact of the physical field (in distinction from the extensional structure of events). It simply marks the fact that our congruence determination embraces both times and spaces in one universal system, and therefore if two arbitrary units are chosen, one for all spaces and one for all times, their ratio will be a velocity which is a fundamental property of nature expressing the fact that times and spaces are really comparable. (*The Concept of Nature* 193)

It is thus a cornerstone of both Simondon's concept of ontogenesis and the relational realist interpretation of quantum mechanics that these two structural levels of ontogenesis – the genetic level of mereotopological *transductive-transcontextual-relational* structure, and the coordinate level of *individuated-contextual-actual* structure (namely relativistic spatiotemporal order) – are inherently compatible. Empirical exemplifications of this fact, seen at deeper and deeper levels in the physical sciences, continue to accrue, including explorations of relational realist quantum mechanics and its particular solution to the infamous problem of reconciling quantum theory and general relativity.[10] One of the central implications of these explorations is that the fundamental mereotopological structure of relational realist quantum mechanics provides an empirically sound theoretical framework that accounts for the ad hoc presuppositions and boundary conditions of relativity theory by which the latter's congruence relations are defined. These include the theory's presupposition of set theoretic partial ordering, without which the general theory of relativity would inaccurately portray the universe as a patchwork of causally unrelatable and logically incoherent extensive regions.

In summary, the *transductive-transcontextual-relational* structure of relational realist quantum mechanics depicts the universe as a globally coherent, ontogenetic process of locally contextualized, synthetic, internal relational individuations. In the words of Whitehead:

> The many become one and are increased by one. In their natures, entities are disjunctively "many" in process of passage to conjunctive unity [...] Thus the production of "novel togetherness" is the ultimate notion embodied in the term "concrescence" [cf. "individuation"]. (*Process and Reality* 21)

> The atomic actual entities individually express the genetic unity of the universe. The world expands through recurrent unifications of itself, each by the addition of itself, automatically recreating the multiplicity anew [...] The atomic unity of the world, expressed by a multiplicity of atoms, is now replaced by the solidarity of the extensive continuum. This solidarity embraces not only the coordinate divisions within each atomic actuality, *but also exhibits the coordinate divisions of all atomic actualities from each other in one scheme of relationship.* (*Process and Reality* 286)

Likewise, with respect to Simondon's concept of ontogenesis:

> Individuation in the form of the collective turns the individual into a group individual, linked to the *group* by the preindividual reality that it carries inside itself and that, when united with the preindividual [potential] realities of other individuals, *individuates itself into a collective unity*. (8)

In relational realist quantum mechanics, the key to the coherence of this "one scheme of relationship" and its "individuation into collective unity" described by Whitehead and Simondon in these passages is its mereotopological framework of structure-preserving, ontological internal relations.

> The basis of the collective reality is already partially contained in the individual, in the form of the preindividual reality that remains linked to the individuated reality; that which we generally consider to be a *relation*, because of the mistaken hypothesis of the substantialization of individual reality, is in fact a dimension of the individuation through which the individual becomes. The relation – to the world and to the collective – is a *dimension of individuation* in which the individual participates starting from the *preindividual reality* that individuates itself step by step. (Simondon 8–9)

This dimension of individuation is the *transductive-transcontextual-relational* dimension of universal ontogenesis. Its exemplification in modern physics, formalized via the serial-mereotopological framework of relational realist quantum mechanics, is grounded in the internal relatedness of each quantum event to the perpetually unfolding, synthetic global totality of all quantum events as each is actualized/individuated. It is by this process that

> the oneness of the universe, and the oneness of each element in the universe, repeat themselves to the crack of doom in the creative advance from creature to creature, each creature including in itself the whole of history and exemplifying the self-identity of things and their mutual diversities. (Whitehead, *Process and Reality* 228)

disclosure statement

No potential conflict of interest was reported by the author.

notes

1 See Epperson and Zafiris.

2 See Kochen and Specker 59–87.

3 See, for example, Omnès, "Consistent Interpretations"; *The Interpretation* and Griffiths.

4 See, for example, Moore 40–62; Epperson and Zafiris 52–54, 231–36.

5 The compatibility condition in relational realist quantum mechanics can be thought of as a supplement to the Griffiths "consistency condition" (119–27).

6 See Aspect, Dalibard, and Roger.

7 See Bub, "Quantum Logic"; "The Problem of Properties."

8 See, for example, Omnès, *The Interpretation* 163:

> Rule 4: Any description of the properties of an isolated physical system must consist of propositions belonging together to a *common consistent logic*. Any reasoning to be drawn from the consideration of these properties should be the result of a valid implication or of a chain of implications in this common logic

and his No-Contradiction Theorem (162). See, also, in this same volume, chapter 5: "The Logical Framework of Quantum Mechanics" (144–200).

9 For more on the ontological significance of quantum potential states, and the dipolar relation of actual and potential states in quantum mechanics, see Epperson; Epperson and Zafiris 29–102, 139–78; and Kastner, Kauffman, and Epperson 158–72.

10 See Epperson and Zafiris 376–88; see also Zafiris and Mallios 1–14.

bibliography

Aspect, A., J. Dalibard, and G. Roger. "Experimental Test of Bell's Inequalities using Time-Varying Analyzers." *Physical Review Letters* 49.25 (1982): 1804. Print.

Bub, Jeffrey. "The Problem of Properties in Quantum Mechanics." *Topoi* 10.1 (1991): 27–34. Print.

Bub, Jeffrey. "Quantum Logic, Conditional Probability, and Interference." *Philosophy of Science* 49 (1982): 402–21. Print.

Epperson, Michael. *Quantum Mechanics and the Philosophy of Alfred North Whitehead*. New York: Fordham UP, 2004. Print.

Epperson, Michael, and Elias Zafiris. *Foundations of Relational Realism: A Topological Approach to Quantum Mechanics and the Philosophy of Nature*. Lanham: Lexington, 2013. Print.

Griffiths, R.B. *Consistent Quantum Theory*. Cambridge: Cambridge UP, 2003. Print.

Kastner, R., S. Kauffman, and M. Epperson. "Taking Heisenberg's Potentia Seriously." *International Journal of Quantum Foundations* 4.2 (2018): 158–72. Print.

Kochen, Simon, and Ernst Specker. "The Problem of Hidden Variables in Quantum Mechanics." *Journal of Mathematics and Mechanics* 17 (1967): 59–87. Print.

Moore, G.E. "External and Internal Relations." *Proceedings of the Aristotelian Society* 20 (1919–20): 40–62. Print.

Omnès, Roland. "Consistent Interpretations of Quantum Mechanics." *Reviews of Modern Physics* 64 (1992): 339. Print.

Omnès, Roland. *The Interpretation of Quantum Mechanics*. Princeton: Princeton UP, 1994. Print.

Simondon, Gilbert. "The Position of the Problem of Ontogenesis." Trans. Gregory Flanders. *Parrhesia* 9 (2009): 4–16. Print.

Whitehead, Alfred North. *The Concept of Nature*. Cambridge: Cambridge UP, 1920. Print.

Whitehead, Alfred North. *Process and Reality*. New York: Free P, 1978. Print.

Zafiris, E., and A. Mallios. "The Homological Kähler–De Rham Differential Mechanism Part I: Application in the General Theory of Relativity." *Advances in Mathematical Physics* 2011 (2011): 1–14. Print.

Michael Epperson

1 introduction

More and more often we hear echoes of a new metaphysical tension between ethics and science: on the one hand, transcendence and absolutes of a religious and ethical kind claim to permeate scientific research (the infinite kindness of divine intelligent design, for instance, in theories of evolution), while on the other hand, scientific answers propose yet again a new universality of knowledge, instead of an absolute, and the ethical values thereof. To a great extent, this tension and the problems in resolving it have to do with the new order presented by new dogma holders. Some thinkers propose a counterattack that evidences, with intellectual vigor, the distinct values of anti-dogmatic propositions that too often come with "relativistic" accents. It is this relativism that seems to us inadequate in responding to dogmatic absolutes. We will discuss this in the first part, with the aim of underscoring the difference between universality and the dynamic generality of scientific thought, on the one hand, and the thinking of absolutes on the other. In the second part, we will try to highlight the role of critical reflection, as well as its complex interplay in relation to the universality of concepts and scientific intelligibility, so often motivated by negative results. The "ethics of knowledge" that guides scientific research provides renewed motivations today for the analysis of the foundations of the various sciences, and makes it the point of departure for any thoughtful critique of their constitutive principles, a "relativizing" rather than a "relativistic" one.

Giuseppe Longo
translated by David Gauthier

SCIENTIFIC THOUGHT AND ABSOLUTES
for an image of the sciences, between computing and biology[1]

The interplay between computing and biology will allow us to provide some examples and reflect on the image that a certain "common sense" suggests for the scientific analysis of life.

2 relativism and scientific universals

A first fundamental observation against "relativist slippery slopes," whether they be propositions or accusations, needs to underscore that scientific thought is not relativistic: it would be false to say that "everything is fine" with a few

---

This is an Open Access article distributed under the terms of the Creative Commons Attribution-NonCommercial-NoDerivatives License (http://creativecommons.org/licenses/by-nc-nd/4.0/), which permits non-commercial re-use, distribution, and reproduction in any medium, provided the original work is properly cited, and is not altered, transformed, or built upon in any way.

minor constraints of coherence or efficacy. Religious fundamentalists (comprising those we have been able to moderate with the force of scientific and philosophical thought, if not with the violence of politics, for example) base their accusations on the loss of (absolute) "values" and on "relativism" that, according to them, cover the whole of ethics and the modern sciences. Because of the limits of my own scientific experience, I will only address the second accusation, the question of relativism, and a single yet important aspect of ethics in science, hoping however to arrive at some reflections on the first.

Science of the twentieth century is "relativizing" and not "relativist." Because of this, it can provide a very general example of knowledge construction. Let me explain with particular reference to Einstein's theory of relativity. My goal is to help us understand how scientific thought possesses "bearing axes," some strong knowledge propositions by which we make "choices" and propose "universals," but not absolutes.

The great mathematician of relativity theory, Hermann Weyl, who was very close to Einstein, illustrates quite well the crucial contribution that Einstein's theory makes to epistemology. In a very general manner, relativity teaches us that scientific theorization must be considered "objective knowledge" if it makes explicit the "frame of reference and measure" and the (mathematical) "conceptual invariants," as well as the transformations of the frame of reference, that preserve them; it is from this explicitness that the construction of knowledge takes effect (Weyl). In other words, when doing scientific research, we must try to make explicit where we start, what hypothesis we are making, in which conceptual frame we are evolving, which frame of reference (Cartesian axes or more general, conceptual) we are choosing, and what is stable (invariant) in relation to the transformations of this base (these frames of reference) of knowledge. The expert will recognize the epistemological heart of Einstein's theories, as well as Weyl's "gauge theory," the mathematical theory of "capacity" that relativizes and puts in relation inertial and non-inertial systems. It is in relation to these frames of reference, in the larger sense, that we obtain scientific objectivity, precisely because it is these frames that are subject to an evaluation, a critique and a measure, in terms of not only theoretical coherence and experimental "friction" with the real, but also, and most importantly, the "extension" of knowledge. But let's apply Weyl's discourse to a better-known example: the link between the Ptolemico-thomist epicycle theory and the theory of Copernicus–Kepler (reread in light of modern physics).

Let's first observe that any number of points on an ellipse around the sun can be interpolated by enough epicycles around the earth – it is a question of series summation with a good frame of reference. Therefore, in itself, the system is coherent. At a certain moment in history, some audacious thinkers (the aforementioned two are the most well known and the greatest) dare to say: the criterion of intelligibility (the frame of conceptual reference, the measure) must be "simplicity" or geometric "regularity" of the planetary orbits – as suggested by Greek figures and polyhedrons; in modern terms, this was to be transformed in the principle of optimality, if not of minimization of energetic variations (the principle of least action) – that of which will produce somewhat different orbits.

Far beyond this first approach to optimality as elegance, Newton, Lagrange, and Hamilton would demonstrate that from Newton's equations one can derive Kepler's orbits and more generally the trajectories of bodies in any physical conservative vector field; we will come back to this, since the proofs are based on principles of optimality (geodesic). Their predecessors, Saint Thomas for instance, used different criteria to construct knowledge: God created man, and him only, in his image, and put him on earth; then he sent him his only son in order to complete the history of Redemption. So the earth must be the center of the Universe; what counts is our absolute criterion and referent of knowledge, namely, the divine creation of the Universe. Some dissidents ended up at the stake for not accepting this basic principle of reasoning, which in itself is coherent. Obviously, Copernicus, Kepler, Giordano Bruno, and Galileo did not have the Hamiltonian or Lagrangian approaches in mind, that is, the modern criterion of optimality, the mathematical geodesics – optimal curves – that marked the physics of the last two centuries. However, we can say that they explicitly referenced the "simplicity" of the trajectories, which contradicts Ptolemic epicycle theory's recourse to intricate geometrical tracings to explain the movement of the stars.

In short, it is erroneous to think that in scientific work "everything goes well as long as it is coherent (and that it works)": once the frame of reference, the criterion of judgment and measurement, are made explicit, different intelligibilities must confront each other. In principle, on the basis of the "relativizing" principles of Einstein–Weyl, it is absolutely legitimate to propose the earth as the origin of a frame of reference to analyze the movement of the planets and the sun. With the planetary epicycles, perfectly coherent from a geometrical and logical point of view, we do not, however, understand much of the sudden back and forth, if not the route inversion, the knots, and interlacing of celestial trajectories. The principle of inertia (the conservation of momentum) makes them impossible: neither Galilean nor Einsteinian transformations allow a passage from a Ptolemic system to another (inertial). And, equally important, we are obliged, each time, to add hypotheses and ad hoc corrections, epicycles on epicycles; the researcher can measure the quantity of hypotheses and epicycles that, planet after planet, must be added to the model to make it plausible. With the "geodesic principle" (the criteria of optimality and simplicity), which guides the birth of modern scientific thought and which, progressively over time, was to be fully mathematized as we say (Newton, Maupertuis, Lagrange, Laplace, Hamilton, etc.), we understand in a coherent way a great quantity of the universe's fragments: in particular, by Hamilton's variational method, the geodetic principle could be derived from conservation properties (inertia or momentum conservation and energy conservation). A single grand instrument of intelligibility allows, in a unitary manner, an accounting of phenomena ranging from gravitational movement on the earth (the apple that falls) to the celestial movement of the stars, all the way to thermodynamics. In fact, the latter can also be analyzed in terms of optimal trajectories of gas particles described in statistical physics (to the infinite limit, a mathematical integral). And even in quantum physics, the passage to objectivity is obtained by the "gauge invariants" of Weyl; these are invariants with respect to the passage from one frame of reference or measure to another and are defined on the basis of modern extensions of the great geodesic or conservation principles.

2.1 "relativizing" objectivity

The knot is precisely here: the passage from the absolute-subjective (look at the sky and say: "I am at the centre of the Universe, son and creature of God, the stars are revolving around me") to the relativizing-objective directly implies the choice to make explicit a frame of reference, of measure, and of (mathematical) invariants with the transformations that preserve them (principles of conservation, energy, and momentum, as we said); and before this, the capacity of the observation of nature, curiosity about the world, all of which are foreign to religious fundamentalisms. Having arrived at this point, I can now affirm: the two theories (epicycles vs. the geodesics of Kepler–Hamilton) are not "equivalent"; we cannot put everything in the same boat. The criterion of intelligibility, the power of explication, the type of unity they presuppose, the criterion of measurability (also modifiable, if not falsifiable), tell me the modern theory is clearly better, far more important for the human and her knowledge. It does not resort at any moment, for every planet and every star, to trajectory adjustments, to divine will, to new hypotheses and ad hoc corrections. It is not only – I would even say not at all! – a matter of simple experimental evidence (is it not evident that it is the sun that revolves around the earth?) but rather an audacious proposition, counterintuitive (it is clear that the earth is flat and immobile [...]), but capable of organizing events on the basis of "universal" and not absolute knowledge criteria – criteria that are there for all humans, yet also categories that can be revised, if necessary, a dynamic with a history. Galileo did not believe in the influences and effects of the attraction between the earth and the moon and did not understand tide dynamics; and from Copernicus to Laplace or Einstein, a long journey was to be travelled, but the commonly adopted principles present themselves as objective propositions, to revise, if necessary, in relation to these very same criteria, of relativizing invariance as we said, and thus they are not relativistic ("everything is fine").

2.2 explicitness and universality of theoretical principles

Let's take another example: Buffon, a fervent naturalist, affirmed that the earth and living beings, Nature, have a history, that they were not created all at once the way they are today. Misfortune followed: accusations from theologians, in a majority at the Sorbonne in 1751, humiliating retraction, the burning of books. After him, Lamarck, by meticulously studying mollusks and, thanks to the new liberty of thinking made possible by the French Revolution (which gave rise to a flowering of scientific debates and schools, despite the murderous fervor of the Terror), explicated the "progress" of living species – and that, from the height of one of the twelve chairs created by the Convention in the first public Natural History museum. He was to make a mistake in his criterion of progress (*adaptation*, as he explicitly framed it as a true scientific principle); then, Darwin was to propose a frame of intelligibility of great scope for the evolution of the living, based on reproduction with variation and natural selection. Even today, the selective theories of the immune system (Edelman and Gally) and of the neural system (Changeux; Edelman) confirm the extraordinary generality (universality) of the Darwinian conceptual frame; it renders intelligible phylogenesis, and a part of ontogenesis (at least for neural and immune systems – we are working in this direction to understand ontogenesis in general (Soto, Longo, and Noble)[2]). We can then compare such a theory with absolutist theories (creationism) in relation to the scope of the intelligibility they propose and observe that the former is significantly better. We can also say that our proposition is fed by universal criteria, ready to be revised, modified, updated, as has been the case in the past. However, with the theory of evolution, we have realized the construction of a scientific objectivity, mixed with empirical evidence (Lamarck's shellfish, Darwin's turtles); and precisely because we are analyzing the constitutive principles of such a science, we introduce them into debate and measure their scope of application. Creationist theories require divine intervention case by case: there is no universality of either method or criteria, but only faith in an omnipotent God, who created species and biological functions one by one, each with their own characteristics. Generality is in God, not in the method of knowledge.

We can say the same of the modern version of creationist absolutism: "intelligent design" theory, which is having great success with the American public. Tapping the molecular alphabet on the genetic keyboard, God would program DNA mutations for his own supreme ends.[3] But then, paleontological evidence tells us that approximately 99 percent of species that were formed on earth have disappeared, and that, especially in the five greatest known extinctions, massacres and death have ravaged our planet. That all of this has taken place to conserve us, as well as the 1 percent of species that have survived, does not seem to be very productive, or particularly intelligent. Hence, we invoke the impenetrability of divine design, of the Absolute Programmer, as the face of the tens of millions of deaths caused by the mutation of the flu virus (the "Spanish flu" of 1918 for example). Whenever we see fit, this "intelligent design" becomes impenetrable (unintelligible), the criteria change, and we invoke faith. It was even worse when we added epicycle on epicycle to justify, one by one, the zigzags of the stars in the sky over the immobile earth. Custom-made criteria, a shaky and limited intelligibility: science says no, this is not knowledge construction. We are looking to propose criteria that are dynamic in their generality, revisable with time and with the expansion of the field of applicability, but nonetheless universal, particularly in the sense that they do not need to be modified at birth in their own original field, with pseudo-theoretical and ad hoc adjustments.[4]

For these reasons, it will be difficult to dispense with the great frames of intelligibility that are physics' geodesics and Darwin's theory of evolution. The former is the basis of numerous profound results from the twentieth century and are correlated to conservation phenomena (energy, momentum, etc.), which are themselves linked to symmetries (by Noether Theorems, see Longo and Bailly), the mathematico-philosophical pilasters of Greek geometry. And this correlation passes through equational negotiations, that is, through the distant heritage of the "algebraization" of geometry, the great marriage (cultural "métissage") of the Greek tradition and the Arab algebra, that is Descartes' geometry. Similarly, Darwinian evolution marks a resolute turning point in the intelligibility of the living. It will be difficult, like I said, to remove ourselves from such historical and conceptual depths, but not impossible: it is not a matter of absolutes here. Besides, these two frames are for now far from each other, in physics and in biology, despite the efforts of some in "dynamical evolutionary physics." To link both will perhaps require "reorganizing" them, possibly modifying one or enriching both (we are currently trying to do so with a tentative enriching of the history of evolution in terms of "historicized invariants," a complex interplay between stability and variation (Longo, "How Future Depends")). Here, potential negative results (Longo, "On the Relevance"; "Interfaces of Incompleteness") are equally theoretical and empirical, but also suggest alternate frameworks as deep and vast, helping us modify, partially or totally, these different manners of understanding nature.

This has already happened in part in quantum physics, for which the unity I have indicated with classical optimality is only indirect; it must not be extended to common, everyday bodies and space-times. Observations at the microphysical level forced us to revise the causal structure (the field) of the very nature of physical "objects" and their "trajectories" beyond classical (and relativist) frameworks. We arrived in fact at saying that quanta do not follow trajectories in space-time, and this after 2,500 years of "trajectory" physics – Schrödinger's equation describes the trajectory of a law (amplitude) of probability, not of a quantum. Once again, the scientific universal has its own motivated and gradual dynamic that is recomposed by the discussions and proofs around new axes of thought, new experiences; it is not an absolute.

2.3 science vs. ethics

Can the distinction between *universal* and *absolute* scientific propositions help us say something about ethics or politics? I have in mind the Kantian distinction between science and ethics, and I realize that the search for universals, with all their historical weight, is already complex in a scientific framework, and even more complex in ethics. But if we do not want to leave the latter facing alone the insoluble conflicts of dogmas against dogmas, knowledge paradigms might help us say something about living together (and vice versa).

In *La Nascita della Filosofia*, a book on Greek thought, Giorgio Colli observes:

> how can we explicate, then, the passage from this religious background to the elaboration of abstract, rational, and discursive thought? [...] [W]ith dialectics [...] the art of discussion between two living persons [...] the vision of the Greek world becomes more nuanced [*mite*]. The bitter backdrop of the enigma, the cruelty of the gods fades away, being replaced by a purely human confrontation [*agonismo*] [...] the one who will lose will not lose life, as it happened with Homer.[5] (73–80)

The scientific universal, as we know it, is thus the result of a dialogical process; this is what the Greek heritage consists of. It gave its origin to an *ethics of knowledge*, which demands a continuous reflection on what we mean by *better, just, knowledge,* "critical *thinking*," etc. Today, beyond Kant, a renewed pragmatism proposes the notion of "teleological gesture" as a new frame for an ethics and knowledge of the living: an intentional gesture governs human action, for knowledge as well as for the social (Maddalena).

Once again we must continue to interrogate the principles of knowledge and the conceptual categories through which we make the world intelligible and livable, each time stepping aside to see and evaluate our own work as we progress, always interrogating the reasons for the very principles by which we research, measure, inquire, operate, in science and also in society. Such a process is necessary in order to make choices, while also assuming other responsibilities, by saying: "this theory is better than the other" (even: "there are no teaching positions in physics for a Ptolemist, nor in biology for a creationist, even if there are many publications on both perspectives in *The Watchtower Announcing Jehovah's Kingdom*"[6] or in similar journals). So, the center of scientific thinking, and of each of its *praxes*, must be firm in its choices, and not "relativist." And this, in spite of the immense difficulty of choice, when we know the universal is what potentially concerns everything by reason, even if *it cannot* be imposed, while the absolute *can only* be imposed by subordination to a leader – ("ab-solute," detached from any bonds and Constitutions), as an act of faith or as the result of war or holy war (as there were many in history) – who imposes his own values and principles of absolute repute.

Both the universal *Déclaration des Droits de l'homme et du Citoyen de 1789* [Declaration of the Rights of Man and of the Citizen] of the French Revolution, as well as the United Nations' *Universal Declaration of Human Rights* of 1948, have a similar sense to what I have sketched out here in relation to the opposition *universality/absolute* in the sciences: we determine forms of living together that can be presented as better, the unit of measure being analyzable, criticizable, and always in evolution. Without imposing absolutes, some men *propose to all other men* certain values to share, a common history; such are the bases of a human construction of our societies, of our living together. These propositions are dynamic, subject to justified revisions, just as in the case of scientific work, where great changes make history. They put forth relatively few necessary values, essential but extremely important, in contrast to the modes of living together and the political structures dictated for centuries by the great religions. These propositions are perhaps even based on a single absolute principle, which we absolutely cannot question, a sort of secular dogma of science, that has never featured in the sacred books of any monotheist religion: the possibility to think over everything in order to construct with others – the *absence of dogmas* (except this one).

3 analysis of the foundations and ethics of knowledge, on "dogmas" in biology

We have discussed above an "ethics of knowledge," which always occupies itself with thinking over what was presupposed, the evidence of common sense, and the very principles of any constituted knowledge, even scientific, particularly if those principles are implicit. Too often in science, the researcher lives in the midst of a technicity that loses the sense of its roots and succumbs to the blinding force of mainstream concepts. This can leave the researcher imbued with a "common sense" regarding the critical capacity of her own knowledge, and can make her pass from rational/universal propositions, that will need to be relativized (as we say), to forms of absolutes. For example, I am thinking of the "central dogma in molecular biology," perhaps originally dubbed so with irony and lightness, but which has since become a new absolute of biological intelligibility. And this to such a point that certain dissidents, in recent decades, have been called (I quote) "rascals" or "mad" by their technically competent colleagues who are nonetheless locked in a scientific present influenced by information society and incapable of seizing elements of interest other than the ones of the dominant vision – elements that are even more influential today, unfortunately.

Here is what this dogma says about the heart of the genetic *program*'s functioning:

- *information* (which information? Classic? *À la* Kolmogorof, or following Von Neumann? In the sense of quantum mechanics? Or is it, rather, negentropies of dynamic systems, *à la* Brillouin? (see Longo et al.; Perret and Longo, for an analysis of the confusion around the concept of information that dominates molecular biology, even in articles of reference)). Information, we learn, is:
- *deterministic* (in the strict sense of Laplace, or in the larger sense of Poincaré? Or is it a quantic indetermination, of probability, of classic or quantum statistics? See, in this case, Buiatti and Longo for the phenotypical consequences of quantic effects in the cell; ah, so uncertain is this genetic information in these last cases!) and is:
- *transmitted and elaborated* by replicas, based on enzymes and by mRNA *transcriptions*, messengers that emerge from the nucleus (eukaryote) thanks to exact correspondences (stereospecific: a correspondence of the type, "key-lock"), but sufficiently elaborated so that ribosomes can:
- *read* and *translate* it (again: letters, the alphabet, transcription, a reader, and a book are invoked,[7] but what is the phoneme that produces sense, as when we are reading, how is it alphabetized? Or, where is the operating system or compiler, if we are talking computing?).

And all of this is done in an entirely *unidirectional* manner. As in the Holy Scriptures, the metaphors of everyday life describe the nature of God's action: shape man out of clay, like a Neolithic pot, today with writing and reading, or better, with quotidian computing, the one of common sense. The term "dogma" is thus a good choice here, in the era of information society with its computers; the common usages dictate, without critical analysis, the sense of the words, of the "metaphors" we use, without scientific content. Therefore, as in any dogma proposing an absolute, the present subject places herself at the center of the universe and, enveloped in her topical social affairs with her contingent technologies, she holds them as absolute – that is, intrinsic to a natural process: DNA is a complete program for ontogenesis. And once again, everything would be inscribed in *alphabetico-formal notation*, as Aristotle was saying already of thought and Hilbert of mathematics: the Greek alphabet, or one of a formal language, or the DNA's alphabet, would form the intrinsic or complete signs of thought, complete descriptions of the world, of mathematics, or of hereditary biology and the organism, its functions, if not its behaviors.[8]

Of course, scientific passion can lead to such attitudes, but we must always strive toward secularism in scientific thought and always be ready to listen to the critique of dominant frames, especially if these are imbued with common sense.[9] As we were saying earlier, this implies the engagement of an explicit and motivated theoretical choice, comparative, and sustained by observations and empirical analysis. In this case, critical refection on foundations is at the center of all scientific activity and fosters, might we add, positive scientific propositions that should not be confused with the search of "absolute foundations," which are proper to other foundational approaches, such as logicism and Platonicism. In opposing the latter, the non-logicist mathematician – the one who does not look for foundations in the definitive and pre-human (better: a-human) rules of logic – can in fact view with interest approaches towards knowledge that claim an "absence of foundations." We can say the same of the physicist who appreciates the relativizing analysis of Einsteinian space-time, as well as the construction of knowledge and the very object of knowledge proper to quantum physics, entirely permeated with a relativizing subject–object polarity. In these analyses, and even more in quantum physics, the object is co-constituted, between the "real" and a knowing subject, in experimental and theoretical activity; it is the result of a "friction" between subject and world, whose objectivity needs to be encompassed by making explicit the methods of experimental and theoretical construction – by making explicit the frame of reference and of measurement.

In this optic, the Wittgensteinian school of thought, amongst others, has rightly picked up on a problematic in "the second Wittgenstein" by developing a very stimulating reflection on "knowledge without foundations" (Gargani). This is a true breath of fresh air against the obsessive search for "unshakable certainties" specific to formalism (as Hilbert wrote in a letter to Brouwer), but above all specific to Platonic logicism: the ideal that rules of logic that are external to the world, or that precede the world, would be the norms of mathematics (and of the world). But then, why insist on the problems with "foundations"; why insist on distinctions – like the ones presented in Longo and Bailly's book *Mathematics and the Natural Sciences: The Physical Singularity of Life* – between "principles of construction" and "proof principles," that are at the heart of a foundational proposition in mathematics or in physics?

In the case of this book, the argument is epistemological, not logical: it is above all a search for *épistème*, for historical and conceptual paths, that are constitutive of forms of knowledge. It revisits, as much as possible, the practices of scientific knowledge so as to retrace their dynamics, but more so, their constitutive principles. In other words, the question is finding the *sense* of axiomatic and logical propositions, finding views that are concerned with certain purely empirical practices that mold between each other the different sciences. And this must be done, not to bring to light "unshakable certainties," nor to propose absolute or definitive bases: on the contrary, the goal is almost the inverse. I'll explain.

The individuation of the principles of order or symmetry in mathematics, or the identification of the omnipresent role of the geodesic principle in physics, must be accomplished with the goal of gathering "what lies behind" the theoretical choices, the principles, explicit or not, the constitution of their signification or "origin," usually in more a conceptual sense than a historical one, but historical as well. This is done to *put into discussion* these principles, if necessary, and if this can render intelligible other fragments of the world.

For these reasons, on the one hand, the fact of understanding that, from Euclid to Riemann and Connes, some *common* principles of construction *do* found the geometrical organization of physical space and our relation to it on the basis of access to space and its measure is subtended to the following three great moments of geometry that "found" themselves on *instruments of access*, of measures of space: the rule and compass of Euclid, the rigid bodies of Riemann, and the non-commutative algebra of Heisenberg for quantum measurement employed by Connes. This is at the origin and conveys the sense of each corresponding theory, while taking into account the radical change of views that each of these approaches proposed. Likewise, the fact that the geodesic principle can make intelligible a historical path from Copernicus and Kepler to Schrödinger's equations (derivable from the Hamiltonian, just like Newton's equations) allows us to glimpse the power of the theoretical proposition in modern physics, in its successive stages. On the other hand, the "foundational" operation that also counts for us here is a reflection on the principle of each science: "stepping aside," as we said, to look at them from a perspective, to think them over, especially when considering other scientific domains. That is what we do when we observe in the aforementioned book that the phylogenetic (and in part ontogenetic) "trajectories" of living beings must not be understood anymore as "specific" (geodesic) but as "generic" (possibilities of evolution); it is rather the individual being that is "specific," historical, individuated. Or to put it differently, in physics, the (experimental) object is generic (a grave, a photon, can be replaced by any other) and follows "specific" trajectories (critical, geodesics in a good phase space), contrary to what happens in biology. The latter is thus in a duality with physics that allows a seizing of the necessity of a theory specific to living beings that *enriches* the underlying physical principles – which also participate in the intelligibility of the living. It is a foundational analysis that, once conducted, allows for a highlighting of the force and limits of the theoretical physico-mathematical framework, its non-absolute character, and the boundaries of its universality, particularly when trying to apply it to biology (Longo, "Information and Causality") – a framework that is to be revised entirely, outside its historical domains of construction and the blissful rapport between physics and mathematics.

To conclude, the goal of foundational analysis today is not the same as the one of the founding fathers: the quest for certitudes, understandable in an epoch of great crisis of the foundations – I think especially of the collapsing of the absolute Euclidean space-time of Newton, of the catastrophe of common sense due to the intrinsic indetermination of quantum measurement. This quest for certitude in and by foundations has been rightly questioned by many, including the second Wittgenstein. Our goal today is rather to give a place to the ethics of knowledge I discussed earlier: the duty of each researcher to make explicit the great *organizational or founding principles* of his own knowledge, to reflect critically in order to work better, and above all to turn to other scientific domains in an open manner, where these principles might be insufficient to understanding, or where they can be thought over, even radically rethought, as was the case both in relativity and in quantum physics (which is what I have tried to also do in the passage from physics to biology (see below the volumes with Bailly, Montévil, and Soto)). Here is a possible image of science that is always in construction, that expresses a universal dynamic, the relativizing proper to scientific knowledge, and that is far away from any forms of the absolute and of relativism.

disclosure statement

No potential conflict of interest was reported by the author.

notes

1 Note on the translation(s) – Pensée laïque et absolus: les paradigmes des sciences.

2 We refer to articles listed in the bibliography for a too vast bibliography necessary to this rather quick overview.

3 During a recent colloquium on biology in Paris, I have heard with dread *all* American colleagues, but fortunately only them (for the moment), lost 20 percent of their time and brain power combat intelligent design theory, so much the stakes have become drastically central, even for the financing of research, in this country.

4 To give new ammunitions, even unintentionally, to the absolutes of ad hoc writing and of the unicity of the "center," the genocentered theories of genetic programming come to tell us, in rather prestigious publications, to have identified the gene of "monogamy" (Young et al.). That is how is mingled, in a pre-modern melange, the Protestant idea of predestination and the notion of genetic program: every phenotype would be pre-written in a gene, all the way to behavior. With the aim of inscribing everything in the DNA, the very beautiful discovery of a few regulator genes of genetic expression (Jacob, Monod, Lwoff, Nobel Price of 1965) has been for too long extended to all genes: their expression would always be regulated by other genes, regulator gene on regulator gene, epicycles on epicycles (Longo and Tendero), excluding by principle all epigenetic control (Fox Keller, *The Century of the Gene; A Feeling for the Organism*).

5

[…] come si spiega allora il passaggio da questo sfondo religioso all'elaborazione di un pensiero astratto, razionale, discorsivo? […] con dialettica […] di arte della discussione […] tra due o più persone viventi, […] dialettica interviene quando la visione del mondo del Greco diventa più mite. Lo sfondo aspro dell'enigma, la crudeltà del dio verso l'uomo vanno attenuandosi, vengono sostituiti da un agonismo soltanto umano […] se sarà sconfitto non perderà la vita, come era accaduto invece a Omero. (73–80)

6 In some southern states of the United States, Republican representatives have proposed "democratically balanced" hires in state universities: as many Darwinian teachers as creationists.

7 ["La surprise, c'est que la spécificité génétique soit écrite, non avec des idéogrammes comme en chinois, mais avec un alphabet comme en français [...]"] ("The surprise, is that genetic specificity is written, not with ideograms as in Chinese, but with an alphabet as in French [...]") (Jacob pr. 34).

8 See the interview by Craig Venter, on the human genome's "decoder" in 2001, published in *Die Spiegel* on 29 July 2010: "We Have Learned Nothing from the Genome" (Von Bredow and Grolle) where he gets to call "phonies" his colleagues who iterated, in 2001, the promise of soon understanding everything, in biology of organisms, thanks to DNA decoding. We should also read the severe autocritique of great import, for forty years, of all genetics in cancer biology: in 2014, he recognizes the limits, if not the dramatic errors proper to this approach (Weinberg). No one doubts the extraordinary importance of this incredible physico-chemical trace of evolution: DNA (Longo, "How Future Depends"); we are criticizing here the myths of its descriptive completeness, common image of the biological, that, while being pre-scientific (coded Aristotelian homunculus) and having in turn penetrated common sense, is difficult to exceed, from wherever it comes from.

9

[Nous croyons, en effet, que le progrès scientifique manifeste toujours une rupture, de perpétuelles ruptures, entre connaissance commune et connaissance scientifique, dès qu'on aborde une science évoluée, une science qui, du fait même de ces ruptures, porte la marque de la modernité.] (We believe, in fact, that scientific progress always manifests a rupture, perpetual ruptures, between common knowledge and scientific knowledge, as soon as we tackle an advanced science, a science that, by the very fact of these ruptures, bears the mark of modernity.) (Bachelard 207)

bibliography

Bachelard, Gaston. *Le materialisme rationnel*. Paris: PUF, 1963. Print.

Buiatti, Marcello, and Giuseppe Longo. "Randomness and Multi-level Interactions in Biology." *Theory in Biosciences* 132.3 (2013): 139–58. Print.

Changeux, Jean-Pierre. *L'homme neuronal*. Paris: Fayard, 1986. Print.

Colli, Giorgio. *La Nascita della Filosofia*. Milan: Adelphi, 1975. Print.

Edelman, G.M. *Neural Darwinism: The Theory of Neuronal Group Selection*. New York: Basic, 1987. Print.

Edelman, G.M., and J.A. Gally. "A Model for the 7S Antibody Molecule." *Proceedings of the National Academy of Sciences of the United States of America* 51.5 (1964): 846–53. Print.

Fox Keller, Evelyn. *The Century of the Gene*. Cambridge, MA: Harvard UP, 2001. Print.

Fox Keller, Evelyn. *A Feeling for the Organism, Life and Work of Barbara McClintock*. San Francisco: Freeman, 1983. Print.

Gargani, Aldo G. *Il Sapere Senza Fondamenti*. Turin: Einaudi, 1975. Print.

Jacob, François. *Génétique cellulaire: leçon inaugurale prononcée le vendredi 7 mai 1965*. Paris: Collège de France, 1965. doi:10.4000/books.cdf.1303. Print.

Longo, Giuseppe. "How Future Depends on Past Histories and Rare Events in Systems of Life." *Foundations of Science* 23.3 (2018): 443–74. doi:10.1007/s10699-017-9535-x. Print.

Longo, Giuseppe. "Information and Causality: Mathematical Reflections on Cancer Biology." *Organisms: Journal of Biological Sciences* 2.1 (2018): 83–103. doi:10.13133/2532-5876_3.15. Print.

Longo, Giuseppe. "Interfaces of Incompleteness." *Systemics of Incompleteness and Quasi-systems*. Ed. G. Minati et al. Cham: Springer, 2019. 3–55. doi:2443/10.1007/978-3-030-15277-2_1. Print.

Longo, Giuseppe. "On the Relevance of Negative Results." *InFluxus*, 2012. Web. <influxus.eu/article474.html>.

Longo, Giuseppe, and Francis Bailly. *Mathematics and the Natural Sciences: The Physical Singularity of Life*. London: Imperial College P, 2011. Print.

Longo, Giuseppe, and Maël Montévil. *Perspectives on Organisms: Biological Time, Symmetries and Singularities*. Dordrecht: Springer, 2014. Print.

Longo, Giuseppe, and Pierre-Emmanuel Tendero. "The Differential Method and the Causal Incompleteness of Programming Theory in Molecular Biology." *Foundations of Science* 12.4 (2007): 337–66. doi:10.1007/s10699-007-9111-x. Print.

Longo, Giuseppe, et al. "Is Information a Proper Observable for Biological Organization?" *Progress in Biophysics and Molecular Biology* 109.3 (2012): 108–14. doi:10.1016/j.pbiomolbio.2012.06.004. Print.

Maddalena, Giovanni. *The Philosophy of Gesture*. Montreal: McGill Queen's UP, 2015. Print.

Perret, Nicole, and Giuseppe Longo. "Reductionist Perspectives and the Notion of Information." *From the Century of the Genome to the Century of the Organism: New Theoretical Approaches*. Spec. issue of *Progress in Biophysics and Molecular Biology* 122.1 (2016): 11–15. doi:10.1016/j.pbiomolbio.2016.07.003. Print.

Soto, Ana M., Giuseppe Longo, and Denis Noble, eds. *From the Century of the Genome to the Century of the Organism: New Theoretical Approaches*. Spec. issue of *Progress in Biophysics and Molecular Biology* 122.1 (2016): 1–82. Print.

Von Bredow, Rafaela, and Johann Grolle. "We Have Learned Nothing from the Genome." *SPIEGEL International* 29 July 2010. Web. 14 Jan. 2020. <www.spiegel.de/international/world/spiegel-interview-with-craig-venter-we-have-learned-nothing-from-the-genome-a-709174.html>.

Weinberg, Robert A. "Coming Full Circle – From Endless Complexity to Simplicity and Back Again." *Cell* 157.1 (2014): 267–71. doi:10.1016/j.cell.2014.03.004. Print.

Weyl, Hermann. *Philosophy of Mathematics and of Natural Sciences*. Princeton: Princeton UP, 1949. Print.

Young, Larry J., et al. "Increased Affiliative Response to Vasopressin in Mice Expressing the V_{1a} Receptor from a Monogamous Vole." *Nature* 400.6746 (1999): 766–68. doi:10.1038/23475. Print.

Giuseppe Longo
Centre Cavaillès

School of Medicine
Tufts University
Boston
USA
http://www.di.ens.fr/users/longo

David Gauthier

In my role as founding editor of the *Posthumanities* series at the University of Minnesota Press, I get asked a lot about trends. What's hot now? What's the next big thing? How do you see the future of theory? And so on. One of the things I say in response to such questions is that "the question of the animal" – even as it certainly remains a growth industry in a number of disciplines in the Humanities and interpretive Social Sciences – seems to have been left behind, all too predictably, by the economy of planned obsolescence in academic knowledge production and theory. As Niklas Luhmann pointed out long ago, the autopoiesis of the disciplines within the education system, as with other social systems, depends upon the ceaseless production of novelty (*Reality of the Mass Media* 21, 28). And in that context, "the Animal" needed to be replaced – predictably enough, and as quickly as possible – by Plants, then Plants by Stones, then Stones by the Object more generally, and finally (as part of a more general desire in theoretical discourse over the past decade for the bedrock of the "real") by a more general "materialism" (sometimes styled as "new materialism," so-called) and "realism" (in all its various permutations).

Against this more general background of the drive toward what we might call "the inescapably real" in theory, more recently, under the spur of rapid global warming, the discourse of the Anthropocene has become the site upon which all of these elements, and these desires too, are assembled and reassembled, often in retooled attempts to be the latest version of what had been called, during the heyday of Object Oriented Ontology and Speculative Realism,

cary wolfe

WHAT "THE ANIMAL" CAN TEACH "THE ANTHROPOCENE"

"Flat Ontology." Of course, my version of posthumanism shares this desire to radically decenter the human in relation to the rest of the world, disallowing any prima facie ontological divide between "what calls *itself* man" (to borrow Jacques Derrida's judicious phrasing) (*The Animal* 30) and the rest of creation. In this context, what we might call the increasing "ecologization" of the "question of the animal" is a welcome development. Indeed, my particular posthumanist understanding of "the animal" has always been an "ecologized" one, with the fundamental evolutionary and developmental unit being, as Gregory Bateson put it long ago, not organism-as-printout of a genetic code, nor even organism-as-printout varied in its successive copies by random genetic mutations, but rather "flexible organism-in-its-environment" – all vs. the neo-Darwinian identification of the "unit of survival" as "the breeding individual or the family line" (451). But as I argued in *What is Posthumanism?*, when it comes to the decentering of the human, the issue isn't just *what* you're thinking, it's *how* you're thinking it. And here, one might draw a bright line between so-called Flat Ontologies and my insistence later in this essay on what one might call instead "jagged ontologies," ones that pay attention to differences and to how, as Bateson puts it, those differences *make* a difference: in this case, to formulating the discourse of Anthropocene (453).

In this context, toward the end of this essay I'll engage Bruno Latour's *Facing Gaia*, with its admirable desire to assert what he calls the "outlaw" character of Gaia as a stay against both holism and humanism and their understanding of Gaia as a kind of mythical superorganism. As we'll see, however, the discourse of Gaia and the Anthropocene, at least in Latour's influential rendition, has abandoned "the question of the animal" prematurely, because what the site of "the Animal" shows is that Flat Ontologies (and finally Latour's own Actor Network Theory) evacuate the radical discontinuity between qualitatively different orders of causation that obtain in living vs. physical systems – different orders that impact in fundamentally different ways the evolution of the biosphere, climate change, and, ultimately, the entire concept of Gaia. As we'll see later, with Latour's mobilization of Actor Network Theory in *Facing Gaia* as my example, what looks anti-reductionist often isn't anti-reductionist at all – and this is far from a "merely academic" matter.

Why is this important at this particular moment? While I can't make the argument within the confines of this essay, I'd suggest one answer: that we find ourselves at a crucial epistemic juncture – a shift away from forty years (or more, depending on how one wants to date it) of hegemony by the neo-Darwinian reductionist paradigm and its infatuation with the genome as "the book of life," a book that is itself idealized as essentially quantitative and mathematizable, which in turn lends itself readily to an engineering paradigm of the problem of "Life" and its manipulation. Thanks in no small part (and again, I can't make the argument here) to new developments in immunology, epigenetics, and the study of the biome (both micro- and macro-), we are on the cusp, I think, of a return to an anti-reductionist thinking of the question of "Life," which involves thinking the organism/environment relationship in all its (often paradoxical) dynamic complexity. This is to push back in a big way against the "central dogma" that has dominated the conversation about life in the biosphere for the last fifty years. That dogma, famously formalized by Francis Crick and institutionalized by molecular biology and popularized by figures such as Richard Dawkins, holds that in evolutionary heredity, inheritance that has evolutionary significance is limited to the "vertical" transmission of DNA sequences; that the only variations that are heritable in organisms take place in DNA sequences; and that variations in organisms do not occur as a result of somatic changes or environmental pressures, but only by means of random mutations in DNA sequences (Winslow 70). But as many thinkers inside and outside science have noted, well-known biological phenomena such as "horizontal inheritance," epigenetic inheritance, and niche construction make it clear that the understanding "in which identities are fundamentally tied to family lineages of vertical inheritance must be replaced by something far more ecological" (Winslow xiv). In the so-called "Baldwin effect" of niche construction, for example, an organism moving to a new niche "can change the course of evolution even with no mutations whatsoever," as biologist Denis Noble points out, resulting in "an evolution of the genome by combinatorial selection, not selection of new random mutations" (222). Indeed, as Richard Lewontin puts it in his typically no-nonsense way,

> the claim that the environment of an organism is causally independent of the organism, and that changes in the environment are autonomous and independent of changes in the species itself, is clearly wrong. It is bad

biology, and every ecologist and evolutionary biologist knows it is bad biology. (Qtd in Winslow 117)

With this larger context in mind, let me briefly address an equally large topic: the discourse of the Anthropocene. I have to admit, I'm a little tired of talking about it, not because it's not important, of course, but because I think we are clearly in a phase of diminishing returns with regard to the concept's periodizing vigor and analytical power, which has in turn generated a sort of backlash that is not far to seek in academic debates about the term and its usefulness – as in, for example, Bruce Clarke's observation that the Anthropocene is a slogan that "has been invented and presented to our attention for a cluster of reasons that are significantly other than scientific" (101). One of my main reservations about the Anthropocene is voiced by Latour himself in *Facing Gaia*, where he suggests that the problem with the concept is not so much that it constitutes "an immoderate extension of anthropo*centrism*," but rather its invocation of "the human as a unified agent," a "universal concept" (122). More seriously still, the Anthropocene concept threatens to authorize "a premature leap to a higher level *by confusing the figures of connection with those of totality*" (131), which leads in turn to what he calls a "deanimation" of the agents and actants (most of them non-human, of course) caught up in what William James once called the "pluriverse," where "we have to agree to remain open to the dizzying otherness of existents, the list of which is not closed, and to the multiple ways they have of existing and relating among themselves" (Latour 36).

Bruce Clarke gives an even more pointed critique of the "deanimation" and "totalization" noted by Latour. As he notes, what started out as a disciplinary designation in the discipline of geology gets amplified over time in ways that belie the Anthropocene concept's supposed posthumanism. As Clarke puts it, while "in a modest way 'the anthropocene' is certainly conceivable as a concept indicating a potential threshold for archaeological stratigraphy," in its actual deployment in the International Geosphere–Biosphere Programme (IGBP) – the globalized administrative body charged with coordinating academic and governmental activity related to the phenomenon named by the concept – what we get instead is "a hunk of traditional geology with an overlay of living beings but without closed systematicity" (102). Lurking in the background here, Clarke suggests, is the disciplinary squabble between Earth Science and Climate Science. The paradoxical (and autopoietic) fact that the earth is a "system with a panoply of feedbacks interconnecting biotic and abiotic systems into metabiotic ecosystems," in which the earth itself is "the system that arises as the sum effect of the operations of all those variegated subsystems" tends to be forgotten, so that what we are left with is, at one end, this thing called "The Planet," and at the other, this thing called "Life" that happens to live on it (102).

Meanwhile,

the full force and profound implications of a biosphere operationally integrated for over three billion years with its atmosphere, hydrosphere, and geosphere under the fall of solar energy – in relation to which the emergence of Homo sapiens is a rather minor detail – is allowed to dissipate, while human self-importance pushes its way back to the front of the line. (Clarke 102)

What we end up with, Clarke argues, is a detachment of geology from biology which is bad science, "except insofar as human beings are to stand for the whole of Biology" (103). But in fact – as James Lovelock and Lynn Margulis argue – "the biosphere is run by the microbes," and its evolution "has been driven hardest and longest by the ongoing evolution of bacteria" and their release of oxygen into the atmosphere (103). In this light, the concept of the Anthropocene is "a last-ditch firewall against the hard truth that humanity does not possess any 'controlling hand' over the Earth system" (103). And indeed, in Clarke's amped up reading (invested as he is in the concept of Gaia and the specific valence it is given by the work of Lynn Margulis), the Anthropocene is "the masculinist obverse of the Earth Mother," "a neo-patriarchal, equally inappropriate all-powerful geo-engineering father figure making Earth System science safe for (hu)man-centeredness" (104). So once again – to remember the point I emphasized earlier from *What is Posthumanism?* – the takeaway from Clarke's interrogation of the supposed posthumanism of the Anthropocene concept is this: the issue isn't just what you're thinking about, it's *how* you're thinking about it.

It may be, then, that the concept of the Anthropocene presents us, in Timothy Clark's words, with a new imperative to "think on a planetary scale" (21), but one has to ask, what would such a thing look like, exactly? After all – keeping in mind Bateson's reminder that "*the map is not the territory*" (449) – whenever we try to think the planetary, we are always thinking it in terms of *some* set of coordinates, *some* schema: in short, some map. But those maps have, of course, proliferated exponentially over time under the spur of modernization as a phenomenon of increasing complexity, functional differentiation (to Niklas Luhmann's term) and disciplinary specialization (Luhmann, *Social Systems* 190–91) – a far from trivial point if you're trying to be empirical and scientific about things. For these reasons, the object of investigation called "the Planet" has become more and more complex, and unavoidably so, over time. And what *that* means is that this proliferation of ever more differentiated disciplinary forms of knowledge, ever more differentiated and finely grained "maps," produces an object of knowledge called "the Planet" that is, in a very important sense, a *virtual* object. As Luhmann puts it in his analysis of "semantic over-burdening" in *Social Systems*,

> A system like science, one that observes other systems, analyses them functionally, uses an incongruent perspective in relation to them. It does not simply trace how these systems experience themselves and their environment. And it does not simply duplicate the view of the self it observes. Instead, the system is covered over with a procedure of reproducing and increasing its complexity that is impossible for it [...] [M]ore complexity becomes visible than is accessible to the observed system itself. As a technique of scientific observation and analysis, the functional method allows its object to appear more complex than it is for itself. In this sense it over-burdens its object's self-referential order. (*Social Systems* 56)

This virtualization, however, is not simply an epistemological matter. Indeed, as we know from the contemporary life sciences stretching back to the work of Jakob von Uexküll, ecological space is above all *virtual* space (Uexküll 52–54). Why? Because any such space is populated by a myriad of wildly heterogeneous life forms who create their worlds, their environments, through the embodied enaction, unfolding dynamically and in real time, of their own self-referential modes of knowing and being, their own autopoiesis (to use Maturana and Varela's term) (Maturana and Varela 43). Because of this multi-dimensionality and over-determination, however, "virtual" here doesn't mean "not real" or "less real," it means "*more real*." Indeed, biologist Humberto Maturana calls such a perspective "super-realist," in the sense of one "who believes in the existence of innumerable equally valid realities," which cannot, however, be called "relativist" because "asserting their relativity would entail the assumption of an absolute reality as the reference point against which their relativity would be measured" (Maturana and Poersken 34) – what Donna Haraway long ago called "the god-trick" that "fucks the world," often tacitly at work, as Latour has already noted, in the discourse of the Anthropocene (Haraway 189). Such an assertion would entail the all too familiar humanist desire to escape our own ecological embeddedness, our own finitude (to use Derrida's term) (Derrida, *The Beast* 99) – what Haraway, during that same period, characterizes as the "situatedness" of our knowledge and experience of the world (188).

Were one to couch the point in a more cultural studies fashion, one might say, then, that a fundamental problem of the discourse of the Anthropocene is what Stacy Alaimo has characterized as the "externalization" of "world" and "environment" in relation to the ongoing embodied enaction of living beings, which in turn "removes us from the scene and ignores the extent to which human agencies are entangled with those of nonhuman creatures" (144). As she argues, it's this removal and externalization that is, ironically enough, extended in the standard formulations of "sustainability" within the discourse of the Anthropocene, where *what* is sustained above all is "our" ability to remain insulated from, the better to manage and steer, this entanglement. My point here – as you will have already guessed by detecting the tones of Heidegger's "The Question Concerning Technology" and its discussion of *bestand* ("standing reserve") in the sentence you just read – is not just a pragmatic one. It's also the *philosophical* and *ethical* point made by Peter Sloterdijk in what can only be called a massive conjugation of the discourse of the Anthropocene with the problematic of biopolitics in his *Spheres* project (much admired by Latour, by the way): that the deeper problem in all this is the picture of "man" – as "rational animal," as Man the Manager – in relation to the question of Being and *Dasein* that we find underneath these canonical discourses of the Anthropocene. As Latour notes in his own way, Sloterdijk's *environmental* challenge to us is in his effort to think the questions of "world," "environment," "life," and so on in a rigorously posthumanist fashion (Latour 124).

So one way to frame the next section of this essay is to say that Derrida, Sloterdijk, and Latour all share the understanding – as Derrida puts it in the second set of seminars on *The Beast & the Sovereign* – that "there is no world" (Derrida, *The Beast* 9). And more importantly, they share the understanding that (counterintuitive as it may seem) this is, in fact, a radically ecological assertion. As Latour puts it in his own way in *Facing Gaia*, emphasizing the plurality of "world" underscored by Derrida,

> Ecology is clearly not the irruption of nature into the public space but *the end of "nature"* as a concept that would allow us to sum up our relations to the world and pacify them [...] The concept of nature now appears as

a truncated, simplified, exaggeratedly moralistic, excessively polemical, and prematurely political version of the otherness of the world to which we must open ourselves [...] [F]or Westerners and those who have imitated them, "nature" has made the *world* uninhabitable.

And this is why, he says, we need "to try to descend from 'nature' down toward the multiplicity of the world" (36). Or as Derrida voices it in *The Beast & the Sovereign II*, "there is no world, there are only islands" (9) – a more radical claim, it turns out, than Latour's, and for reasons that are crucial to avoiding the ontological flattening that we end up with in Latour's Actor Network Theory version of the claim, as we'll see in a moment.

What I want to show in the last section of this essay, however, is that the radically ecological character of the assertion "there is no world" is not dependent upon the *phenomenological* register of the term "world" that stretches from Kant, up through Uexküll, to Heidegger and then to Derrida. Indeed, we can redescribe the claim in robustly naturalistic and biological terms, as we are about to see. And in doing so, we can show that what the Anthropocene needs from "the Animal" is not just the ultraphilosophical assertion of the non-empirical character of "world" insisted on by Heidegger and respected by Derrida, but also, and more importantly for my purposes here, the non-reductive differentiation of *biological* from physical principles that are crucial to understanding the role of life in what Latour calls "the new climatic regime" of the Anthropocene. Here, I'm going to provide a much-shortened version of the material I cover in the third chapter of my recent book, *Ecological Poetics, or, Wallace Stevens's Birds*, focusing on the work of MacArthur fellow and Santa Fe Institute co-founder, Stuart Kauffman. Central to my argument is Kauffman's claim in his book *Humanity in a Creative Universe* from 2017 that there are no "entailing laws" that predetermine the evolution of the biosphere (hence the "creative universe" of the book's title).

In the section of Kauffman's book that I am most interested in, he assumes, almost exclusively, classical chemistry and physics, and "the point is not to show that Newton's laws do not often work (they do) [...] but to begin to demolish the hegemony of reductive materialism and its grip on our scientific minds" (40). The central thrust of this section of the book, which forces us to rethink not just the evolution of the biosphere but the entire concept of ecology, is that "at least part of why the universe has become complex is due to an easy-to-understand, but not well-recognized, 'antientropic' process that does not vitiate the second law [of thermodynamics]" (41). He continues,

> Briefly, as more complex things and linked processes are created, and can combine with one another in ever more new ways to make yet more complex amalgams of things and processes, the space of possible things and linked processes becomes vastly larger and the universe has not had time to make all the possibilities [...] There is an indefinitely expanding, ever more open space of possibilities ever more sparsely sampled, as the complexity of things and linked processes increases [...] [T]here is a deep sense in which the universe becomes complex in its exploration of these ever more sparsely sampled spaces of what is next possible because "*it can.*" (42)

One of the more compelling examples Kauffman gives of this principle obtains at the level of organic chemistry, before we even get to the domain of autopoietic organisms, or what he calls "Kantian wholes," where we would more likely expect to find such forms of complexity. In a key passage in the book, he writes, "Proteins are linear strings of amino acids bound together by peptide bonds. There are twenty types of amino acids in evolved biology. A typical protein is perhaps 300 amino acids long, and some are several thousand amino acids long." He continues,

> Now, how many possible proteins are there with 200 amino acids? Well, there are 20 choices for each of the 200 positions, so 20^{200} or 10^{260} possible proteins with the length of 200 amino acids. This is a tiny subset of the molecular species of CHNOPS [Carbon, Hydrogen, Nitrogen, Oxygen, Phosphorus, Sulfur] with 100,000 atoms per molecule. Now the universe is 13.7 billion years old and has about 10^{80} particles. The fastest time scale in the universe is the Planck time scale of 10^{-43} seconds. If the universe were doing nothing but using all 10^{80} particles in parallel to make proteins the length of 200 amino acids, each in a single Planck moment, it would take 10^{39} repetitions of the history of the universe to make all the possible proteins the length of 200 amino acids just *once*! [...] [A]s we consider proteins the length of 200 amino acids and all possible CHNOPS molecules with 100,000 atoms or less per molecule, it is obvious that the universe *will never make them all*. History enters when the space of what is possible is vastly larger than what can actually happen [...] A next point simple and clear: Consider all the CHNOPS molecules that can be made with 1, with 2, with 3, with 4, with n, with 100,000 atoms per molecule. Call the space of possible molecules with n atoms of CHNOPS the phase space for CHNOPS molecules of n atoms. That phase space increases enormously as n increases. Consequently, in the lifetime of the universe, as n increases, that phase space will be sampled ever more sparsely. (43)

As Kauffman shows, this "nonergodic" principle obtains even more radically and obviously at the level of the biosphere, in which

> its becoming cannot be prestated, is not "governed" by entailing laws, in which what becomes constitutes ever-new Actuals that are "enabling constraints" that do not cause, but enable, ever-new, typically prestatable, Adjacent Possible opportunities into which the evolving biosphere becomes. (64)

And when we reach the level of what he calls "Kantian wholes," or autopoietic organisms, this process is (not surprisingly) even more striking (67). If we think about the concept of biological function, for example, it is clear that while "in classical physics there are only 'happenings.' The ball rolls down the hill, bumps a rock, veers," and so on, in biology we have to distinguish function from mere physical happenings. "The function of the heart is to pump blood," Kauffman notes, but the heart "causally also makes heart sounds, jiggles water in the pericardial sac," and so on (65). Classical physics will not help us here, because "the *function* of the part is its causal consequences that help sustain the whole"; "function" is causal, in other words, but *causal in a qualitatively different way from classical physics* (66). As Kauffman notes, another nail in the coffin for the reductionist approach is the fact that "this capacity to define a function as a subset of causal consequences that can be improved in evolution further separates biology from physics, which cannot make the distinction among all causal consequences into a subset which are functions" (67).

Paying attention to these qualitatively different orders of causation in physical vs. biological systems is absolutely crucial to understanding what are sometimes called the "mereological" relations in living systems, where the relationship between the part and the whole is radically different from what we find in physical systems. We typically think of causation in the scientific domain as bottom-up (as we do in the "central dogma" of neo-Darwinism, where the lines of causality run from the gene to the physical characteristics, biomorphology, and so on, of the organism). But in the dynamic, self-organizing, autopoietic forms of life in the biosphere, we find a much more complex relationship between component (or element) and system, because causality often operates in a top-down and distributed fashion as well. As Alicia Juarrero notes, these "mereological" relationships have "bedeviled philosophers of science for centuries" (510), but what we can now see is that "the unpleasant whiff of paradox" that "remains in any mention of recursive causality" in living systems is unavoidable, and indeed a crucial part of explaining such systems (511). What we find in autopoietic biological systems, in fact, is what she calls a "decoupling in the locus of control: the components' behavior suddenly originate in and are under the control, regulation, and modulation of the emergent properties of the macro level, *as such*," which in turn "*loosens the one-to-one strict determinism from micro to macro level*" (519). In contrast to physical systems, even those that show emergent self-organization – dust devils, tornadoes, Bénard cells, and so on – where "external agents or circumstances are responsible for the conditions within which physical self-organization takes place," in autopoietic systems, those conditions and constraints are introduced and maintained *by the system itself*, resulting in a strong "downward causation" in which systemic closure becomes "a closure of constraint production, not just a closure of processes" (512–13).

This means (as Juarrero notes, quoting Kauffman) that "it is impossible to predict emergent properties even in principle because the 'categories necessary to frame them do not exist until after the fact'" (518). And of course, if everything we have said of biological organisms is also true of *us*, it is, in fact, *all the more the case* with us – and for the reasons Juarrero notes: the more complex the autopoietic life form, the more we find a "dynamic decoupling" of the causative relationships between the micro- and macro-levels. Or as she puts it:

> System and environment co-evolve over time in such a way that the identification between macro-property and specific configuration becomes irrelevant; as we go up the evolutionary ladder, the go of things issues more and more from higher and higher levels and according to criteria established at progressively emergent levels. Just as living things are autonomous and self-directed in a way that physical dissipative structures are not, sentient, conscious, and self-conscious being are even more autonomous and self-directed. (520)

But here, I think, we need a stringent dose of deconstruction: specifically, Derrida's critique of what he calls the "auto-" of autonomy, autoaffection, autobiography, and the like – in short, his critique of intentionality and of related concepts such as "agency" (*The Animal* 47, 56, 67). It's not that autonomy and self-directedness don't increase, as Juarrero suggests, with the increasing decoupling of micro- and macro-structures and the growing importance of downward causality. They do. It's just that the picture that intentionality and autonomy *gives to itself* (as Derrida characterizes it) of its situation is unavoidably partial, reductive, and blind to its full infrastructural conditions of possibility for emergence (or what we have already called its "ecological" embeddedness) (*The Animal* 12, 30).

When we move from the level of the organism to the biosphere, we find the same recursive logic at work on a different scale. Having established the importance of the concept of biological function, Kauffman hypothesizes that

> we cannot prestate the evolution of new functions in the biosphere, hence cannot prestate the ever-changing phase space of biological evolution which includes precisely the functions of organisms and their myriad parts and processes evolving in their worlds. But these ever-new functions, constitute the ever-changing *phase space* of biological evolution. (70)

And what this means (logically enough) is that "we can have *no entailing laws* at all for biological evolution" (70). Kauffman offers a nice, compact example of this process in his discussion of what are called Darwinian "pre-adaptations" or "exaptations" – the emergence of new, possibly useful, traits through random genetic mutation (staying with the discourse of the neo-Darwinian orthodoxy for the moment).

Kauffman's especially winning example of this process – where a side effect generated by random genetic mutation can become a functional asset for an organism under different environmental conditions, as Darwin himself surmised – is the emergence of the swim bladder in fish. The Darwinian exaptation whereby some early versions of fish had lungs, enabling them to bounce from puddle to puddle, led in time to the biological *function* of a ratio of air and water in fish who now live wholly in water, which allows, in turn, neutral buoyancy in the water column. Did this change the future evolution of the biosphere?, Kauffman asks. "Yes, and in two vastly different ways. First, new daughter species of fish with swim bladders and new proteins evolved." But second,

> once the swim bladder exists, it constitutes a new Actual condition in the evolving biosphere. The swim bladder now constitutes a new, empty but Adjacent Possible niche, or opportunity for evolution. For example, a species of worm or bacteria could evolve to live, say exclusively, in the swim bladder. The Adjacent-Possible opportunities for evolution, given the new swim bladder, do not include all possibilities. For example, a *T. Rex* or giraffe could not evolve to live in the swim bladder. (72)

One of the key theoretical points here arises when Kauffman asks, "do we think that selection, in any way at all, 'acted' to achieve the swim bladder as *constituting a new adjacent-possible empty niche* in which a worm or a bacterial species might evolve to live? No." Further, he adds,

> does the swim bladder, once it has come to exist, *cause* the worm or bacterial species to evolve to live in it? *No*. The swim bladder *enables, but does not cause, the bacterial or worm species to evolve to live in it*. Instead, quantum random mutations to the DNA of the bacterium or worm yield variations in screwdrivers that may be selected at the level of the whole organism by which the worm or bacterial species evolves to live in the swim bladder. (72)

More radically still, this means that "there is, therefore, no noncircular way to define the 'niche' of the organism separately from the organism. But that niche is the boundary condition on selection. The 'niche' is only revealed *after* the *fact*, by what succeeds in evolution" – hence the mystery of what Darwin called "the arrival of the fittest" (75).

It is hard to imagine a clearer articulation, in robust naturalistic, biological terms, of what Derrida calls "the becoming-space of time and the becoming-time of space" (Hägglund, *Radical Atheism* 2), the "will have been" of that which is "to come," unprestatable and unanticipatable, with Darwin's "pre-adaptations" being precisely the material substrate, the trace, on which retentions of the past and protentions of the future are inscribed. As Martin Hägglund explains:

> Given that every temporal moment ceases to be as soon as it comes to be, it must be inscribed in a trace in order to be at all. This is the *becoming-space of time*. The trace is necessarily spatial, since spatiality is characterized by the ability to remain in spite of temporal succession. The spatiality of the trace is thus a condition for the synthesis of time, since it enables the past to be retained for the future. The spatiality of the trace, however, is itself temporal. Without temporalization a trace could not remain across time and relate the past to the future [...] In order to remain – even for a moment – a trace cannot have any integrity as such but is already marked by its own becoming past and becoming related to the future. Accordingly, the persistence of the trace cannot be the persistence of something that is exempt from the negativity of time. Rather, the trace is always in relation to an unpredictable future that gives it both the chance to remain and to be effaced ("The Trace of Time" 39)

– exactly in the manner by which Kauffman describes the non-entailed evolutionary process of the biosphere.

Equally important (and I think this helps to underscore and indeed clarify an aspect of Kauffman's argument that is often only implicit) is what Hägglund calls the fundamental "negativity" of time,

> which undermines *both* the idea of a discrete moment *and* the idea of an absolute continuity. Only if something is *no longer* – that is, only if there is negativity – can there be a difference between before and after. This negativity must be at work in presence itself for there to be succession. If the moment is not negated in being succeeded by another moment, their relation is not one of temporal succession but of spatial coexistence. ("The Trace of Time" 43)

It is precisely the combination of this negativity of time with what Hägglund calls the "archemateriality" of the trace that makes Kauffman's non-entailed evolution of the biosphere thinkable. "Precisely because every temporal moment negates itself," Hägglund writes, "the duration of time can never be given in itself but depends on the material support of spatial inscription" in the form of the trace; "without the later inscription nothing could persist and there would be no movement or passage of time" ("The Trace of Time" 43).

Indeed, we find here the site of a *double* inscription, not just on the material substrate of the living being (as in the pre-adaptation of the swim bladder), but also in the dynamic contingency of the organism/environment relationship in which that ontogenetic inscription happens, which can make the "same" inscription function differently at different points in time. As Bateson points out in his discussion of "iconic genotypic signals," it is common to find what he calls "a secondary statistical iconicism" in the animal kingdom of the following type:

> *Labroides dimidiatus*, a small Indo-Pacific wrasse, which lives on the ectoparasites of other fishes, is strikingly colored and moves or "dances" in a way which is easily recognized. No doubt these characteristics attract other fish and are part of a signaling system which leads the other fish to permit the approaches of the cleaner. But there is a mimic of this species of *Labroides*, a sabertoothed blenny (*Aspirdontus taeniatus*), whose similar coloring and movement permit the mimic to approach – and bite off pieces of the fins of other fishes.
>
> Clearly the coloring and movements of the mimic are iconic and "represent" the cleaner. But what of the coloring and movements of the latter? All that is primarily required is that the cleaner be conspicuous and distinctive. It is not required that it represent something else. But when we consider the statistical aspects of the system, it becomes clear that if the blennies become too numerous, the distinctive features of the wrasses will become iconic warnings and their hosts will avoid them. (418–19)

If theoretical biology reminds us of this fact of double inscription, deconstruction reminds us that there is no evolution without the negativity of time and its inscription in the arche-materiality of the trace, figured on a larger biological canvas as the dynamic complexity of the organism/environment relationship. No negativity of time, no evolution; but also: no materiality of inscription in the trace, no evolution.

We're now in a better position to specify exactly what is wrong with Latour's Actor Network Theory ontology in *Facing Gaia* – and to specify, moreover, why those problems are tethered to an insufficient understanding of the difference between first-order and second-order systems theory and how those, in turn, bear upon our understanding of the "mereological" relations of organisms and the qualitatively different orders of causality that obtain in biological vs. physical systems. A crucial underlying problem, I think, is that Latour continues to understand the terms "system" and "autopoiesis" as if they were simply synonyms for homeostasis and command-and-control, and the fingerprints of this misunderstanding in *Facing Gaia* are all over his use of the term "cybernetics." When Latour writes that the figure of the *"loop"* is "the only way to draw a path between agents without resorting to the notions of part and a Whole that only the presence of an all-powerful Engineer – Providence, Evolution, or Thermostat – could have set up," he immediately cautions us to "not hurry to identify this movement [...] with feedback loops in the cybernetic sense: we would revert at once to the model with a rudder, a helmsman, and a world government" (137). What he doesn't understand here – and what he doesn't understand when he suggests that Gaia is "the outlaw, the anti-system" (87) – is a fundamental point I explore in great detail in *What is Posthumanism?*: that second-order systems theory (of the sort mobilized by Maturana and Varela, Juarrero, and Kauffman, among many others) is best understood, as Dirk Baecker puts it, "as an attempt to do away with any usual notion of system, the theory in a way being the deconstruction of its central term" (61).

Latour is right, of course, in his discussion of Lovelock, that "all the sciences, natural or social, are haunted by the spectre of the 'organism,'" but he is wrong when he says that that figure

> always becomes, more or less surreptitiously, a *"superorganism"* – that is, a dispatcher to whom the task – or rather the holy mystery – of successfully coordinating the various parts is attributed [...] As soon as you imagine parts that "fulfill a function" within a whole, you are inevitably bound to imagine, *also, an engineer* who proceeds to make them work together. (95)

But as we have already seen with Kauffman's discussion of the concept of biological *function* in the larger context of the evolution of the biosphere with *no entailing laws*, this is an unwarranted assimilation of the concept of the organismic closure in what Kauffman calls "Kantian wholes" to a *first*-order notion of holism and homeostasis. Sometimes, Latour associates this first-order notion of holism and homeostasis with "an encompassing, preordained system of retroaction" of the sort we find in appeals to the "equilibrium of nature" or the "wisdom of Gaia" invoked, for instance, by Deep Ecology during its heyday (142). And sometimes he associates it with the hackneyed and rudimentary tropes of the "Governor figure" and "technological metaphors like that of the thermostat" (98). This in turn authorizes for Latour an engineering, command-and-control understanding of causality in systems theory as "-centric," rather than decentered and "decoupled," as Juarrero notes, whereas the whole point of Kauffman's non-ergodic, unentailed evolution of the biosphere is that it makes such an engineering fantasy literally unthinkable. So it should come as no surprise that Latour cannot understand that, in second-order systems theory, the account of the relationship between the "part" and the "whole" – those "mereological" relationships that we saw Juarrero discussing a moment ago – is actually the *opposite* of the caricature he offers here. Indeed, as Yuk Hui has pointed out,

> in contrast to Lovelock's strong form of Gaia, consisting of a single organism, Margulis forced Lovelock to admit that Gaia [...] is

rather a symbiogenesis of a great variety of organisms, including plants, animals, fungi, protists, and bacteria. The concept of symbiogenesis in turn comes from Varela and Maturana's concept of autopoiesis,

and in fact, he suggests, "with the participation of Margulis, the Gaia theory moves from first-order cybernetics to second-order cybernetics" (83).

We find the same elisions in Latour's rendering of the "inside" and "outside" of the organism/environment relationship, where he simply collapses the "inside" of autopoietic distinction in second-order systems theory into what he calls the "selfish" position – and the economy of optimization in neo-Darwinian reductionism – associated with Richard Dawkins and his "selfish gene" theory (103). On the one hand, he seems to understand the second-order systems theory rendering of the organism/environment relationship when he writes that

> Properly speaking, for Lovelock and even more clearly for Lynn Margulis, there *is no longer any environment* to which one might adapt. Since all living agents follow their own intentions all along, modifying their neighbors as much as possible, there is no way to distinguish between an environment to which the organism is adapting and the point at which its own action begins. (100)

So far, so good. Latour seems to grasp here the fundamental point that, in second-order systems theory (as we find it in Maturana and Varela in biology or Luhmann in sociology), the environment is not antecedent or pre-given but is always understood as the environment *of* the system – a strict corollary, of course, of the fact of autopoietic self-reference (what Latour calls, in a remarkably imprecise locution, "intention" (100)).

But the theoretical coherence of Latour's discussion goes completely off the rails when he glosses the following passage by one of Lovelock's collaborators, Timothy Lenton, who writes that, in Gaia, "the evolution of organisms and their material environment" are "so closely *coupled* that they form a *single, indivisible process*. Organisms possess environment-altering traits because the benefit that these traits confer (to the fitness of the organisms) outweighs the cost in energy to the individual" (qtd in Latour 100–01). Latour gleefully reads this passage as saying that

> The inside and outside of all borders are subverted. Not because everything is connected in a "great chain of being"; not because there is some global plan that orders the concatenation of agents; but because the interaction between a neighbor who is actively manipulating his neighbors and all the others who are manipulating the first one defines what could be called *waves of action*, which respect no borders and, even more importantly, never respect any fixed scale. (101)

But the obvious and question-begging problem here, of course, is how one can speak of "neighbors" and their "intentions" (so important to the premium that Latour places on the disruptive and unpredictable play of "agents," after all) when "the inside and outside of all borders are subverted."

What Latour is unable to theorize here is the relationship – indeed what one could call the *deconstructive* relationship – between "inside" and "outside," "neighbor" and "environment," because he doesn't grasp the key insight of second-order systems theory and the theory of autopoiesis: that the *contingency* of the self-reference of autopoietic organisms *is* the "wild card," the "outlaw," at the core of everything Latour wants from the unpredictable "agency" and "intentions" that push back against reductive totalization and the engineering fantasies of "life" and "nature" that emerge from it. To be even more specific about this: the "outlaw" character of the biosphere (and therefore its impact on the larger earth system of Gaia) is to be located not *just* in the contingency of the organism's self-reference and how it selectively determines its environment, its "world," but also in the fact that that self-reference provides the conditions of possibility for the *recursive* operations of biological organisms in real time, and how that recursivity can make environmental differences *make* a difference (to paraphrase Bateson), establishing the "decoupling in the locus of control" and the "downward causality" that we saw Juarrero explaining earlier. What does this do? It enables – and this is my third point – what I call the second-order turn of "openness from closure" that I explore in some detail in *What is Posthumanism?* Closure and the recursive selectivity that goes with it – a selectively forced upon organisms by the fact that any environment is always already exponentially more complex than any individual system – increase the differences that can *make* a difference in the organism's environment. Or as Luhmann succinctly puts it, self-referential closure

> does not contradict the system's *openness to the environment*. Instead, in the self-referential mode of operation, closure is a form of broadening possible environmental contacts; closure increases, by constituting elements more capable of being determined, the complexity of the environment that is possible for the system. (*Social Systems* 37)

What separates us from the world is precisely what connects us to the world.

So – to slice this a little more finely – there are actually *three* "wild cards" in the deck here. There's the contingency of self-reference that we find in "Kantian wholes" or autopoietic organisms, in which the meaning of an element is conferred by its functional role in the whole organism, as we find in the distinction between what Maturana and Varela call "structure" and "organization": "Autopoietic unities," they write,

> specify biological phenomenology as [...] distinct from physical phenomenology [...] not because autopoietic unities go against any aspect of physical phenomenology – since their molecular components must fulfill all physical laws – but because the phenomena they generate in functioning as autopoietic unities depend on their organization and the way this organization comes about, and not on the physical nature of their components (which only determines their space of existence). (51)

Second, there's *recursivity*: the circular process by which that self-reference operates dynamically in real time in the production of what Juarrero calls "constraint closure" as not merely mechanical but processive, which enables differences (in the environment) to make a difference (in the organism) in the services of adaptation to a changing environment. And third, there's how that recursivity structures the organism/environment relationship in an ongoing way, not only on the side of the organism, but also on the side of the environment, as we see dramatically illustrated in the phenomena of niche construction, the so-called "Baldwin effect," and so on.

As Alexander Wilson notes, in the kinds of "evolutionary arms races" dramatized in niche construction, we find highly selective feedback loops that recursively compound themselves – and change the biosphere for doing so. For example,

> a bat evolves echolocation, which allows it to locate moths, in turn provoking the moths to evolve a capacity to hear the bats and maneuver evasively, which in turn presses the bats to evolve better maneuverability, and so on [...]
>
> These "runaway" effects occur everywhere in nature [...] Arms races and niches necessarily *close themselves off* from the overarching environmental influences and take off, playing their own private games, and therefore drift along unpredictably. This leads to the proliferation of complexity and nonlinear relations between species and their environments [...] The niche reinforces the *specialness* of its particular character [...] They are local *top-down* selectors, where the competition between individuals drives a progressively intensifying race to grow longer plumage or devise more complex songs and dances. (91–92)

In other words, when it comes to the biosphere and its role in the larger system of Gaia, second-order closure and the recursivity it enables between organism and environment *is* the joker in the deck, both ontogenetically and phylogenetically, the most unpredictable source of the "outlaw" characteristics of alterity and contingency that Latour wants from Gaia to mobilize against "nature."

Now, one might ask why that alterity can't simply be located at the level of what Latour calls "connections" and "waves of action." Well, it *is* located there, of course, but the important point is that the *kinds* of connections that an entity is *capable* of having are heavily constrained – *enabled* but not *determined*, as Kauffman puts it – by the closure and self-reference of the entity in question, and how that effects the causative relations between the elements in the system, the locus of control, and the environment. Here, it is important to simply note something that is ignored and even occluded in Latour's theory: that most of these entities are in fact overwhelmingly *not* connected to anything else in the universe – not because they are solipsistic or "autonomous," or "selfish," but simply as a matter of their survival in an environment exponentially more complex than they are. And if we don't pay attention to these underlying conditions of possibility for "connections," these constraints – a need that really gets ratcheted up, as Juarrero and Kauffman note, when we come to the level of multi-cellular organism and Kantian wholes – then we threaten to fall back into the flattening of living vs. physical systems, and their radically different modes of causality and organization, that occludes their specific roles in the larger dynamic of climate change.

One of the things "the Anthropocene" can learn from "the Animal," then, is that the alterity, "creativity," and "outlaw" relations that obtain among what Latour calls "actants" are, for the reasons we have been outlining, much more unruly and unpredictable among biological life forms and their environmental relations than between, say, stones or vacuum cleaners. And here, of course, we can add yet another layer of recursivity that gets flattened in Actor Network Theory – the "not" and the "no," the domain of the negative, introduced by the goal-directed behavior of Kantian wholes. Again, Juarrero: "Just as living things are autonomous and self-directed in a way that physical dissipative structures are not, sentient, conscious, and self-conscious being are even more autonomous and self-directed" (520). Here, as Hui suggests, "teleonomy," not "teleology," is the term we want (142); goal-directed and purposive doesn't mean linear and pre-programmed, but quite the contrary, because "recursivity is not only a mechanism that can effectively 'domesticate' contingency [...] it is also a mechanism that allows novelty to occur, not simply as something coming from outside, but also as an internal transformation" (139). And this, of course, can and does feed back into the environment, as Wilson has already noted. As theoretical biologist Denis Noble observes of the "Baldwin effect" and so-called "adaptability drivers" in niche construction, when organisms choose new niches in which to flourish, "the process is an active choice of organisms, including learnt behavior. The causality involved here is very far from random" (223) – that is, it is not a statistical feature of "genetic drift," as neo-Darwinians like to argue – even though it is a product of the complex, ongoing, dynamic relationship of contingency and recursivity in living organisms and how they change the environment that changes them.

So, let me conclude by summing up some salient points. First, physics is not biology. Qualitatively different orders of causation and complexity, in which the "negativity" of temporality plays a crucially irreducible role, are involved. It's not that biology can flout the so-called laws of physics; rather, it's a simple "necessary" vs. "sufficient" distinction. The particular modes of organization and causality that obtain in the biosphere cannot in any way be assimilated, as an "equal partner," to a more general Actor Network Theory, much less to any kind of flat ontology. Could we come up with an algorithm for the difference between these unequal partners? I believe – and I believe Latour believes – that the answer is "No." Second, what Latour means by "outlaw" is really, as far as I can tell, just contingency, but as we have seen, this needs to be parsed in a much, much finer way. There's the kind of contingency that we find in Kauffman's CHNOPS proteins example, which is essentially mathematical and combinatory (though already, he argues, non-ergodic, so even here, "history enters"); then there's the *recursivity* that we find in Kantian wholes, in which the functional uptake of those combinatory possibilities by biological entities takes a second-order turn, dynamically and in real time, both ontogenetically and phylogenetically, so that selection and closure become the drivers of complexity and creativity, as we saw with niche construction; then there's the recursivity of the domain of the "not" and the negative in biological organisms that we see in the "Baldwin effect" and in what we call proportionate learning and creative teleonomy among a wide range of organisms.

In a metatheoretical context, it is important, I think, to insist on these distinctions, for the reasons I noted at the outset: the importance, at this precise moment, of developing a robust, interdisciplinary anti-reductionism, a side project of which (but a central strategic goal of which) involves doing our part to bring an end to the hegemony of the neo-Darwinian paradigm. On this terrain, Latour and I are, of course, on the same team. Here, however – to reach back to my opening comments from *What is Posthumanism?* about the importance of not just *what* you're doing but *how* you're doing it – I would insist on the importance of working hard to theorize an *anti-reductionist* anti-reductionism. And here, I think, Latour and I are *not* on the same team, at least not on the terrain explored in this essay, even though we share the same theoretical and existential desire to push back against reductionism in all its forms. In that context, I would insist that the discourse and problematic of "the animal" is not done just yet – far from it – even though the current fashion is to see it as perhaps an early and already obsolesced mode of posthumanist intervention. Paying serious attention to "the question of the animal" can force the discourse of the Anthropocene to pay attention to something that reaches far beyond the question of climate change and should shape the current theoretical horizon: that what's needed here is not flat but ever more jagged ontologies.

disclosure statement

No potential conflict of interest was reported by the author.

bibliography

Alaimo, Stacy. *Exposed: Environmental Politics and Pleasures in Posthuman Times*. Minneapolis: U of Minnesota P, 2016. Print.

Baecker, Dirk. "Why Systems?" *Theory, Culture, Society* 18.1 (2001): 59–74. Print.

Bateson, Gregory. *Steps to an Ecology of Mind*. New York: Ballantine, 1972. Print.

Clark, Timothy. *Ecocriticism on the Edge: The Anthropocene as a Threshold Concept*. London: Bloomsbury Academic, 2015. Print.

Clarke, Bruce. "'The Anthropocene,' or, Gaia Shrugs." *Journal of Contemporary Archaeology* 1.1 (2014): 101–04. Print.

Derrida, Jacques. *The Animal that Therefore I Am*. Trans. David Wills. New York: Fordham UP, 2008. Print.

Derrida, Jacques. *The Beast & the Sovereign*. Trans. Geoffrey Bennington. Vol. 2. Chicago: U of Chicago P, 2011. Print.

Hägglund, Martin. *Radical Atheism: Derrida and the Time of Life*. New York: Fordham UP, 2008. Print.

Hägglund, Martin. "The Trace of Time: A Critique of Vitalism." *Derrida Today* 9.1 (2016): 36–46. Print.

Haraway, Donna J. *Simians, Cyborgs, and Women: The Reinvention of Nature*. New York: Routledge, 1991. Print.

Hui, Yuk. *Recursivity and Contingency*. Lanham: Rowman, 2019. Print.

Juarrero, Alicia. "What does the Closure of Context-Sensitive Constraints Mean for Determinism, Autonomy, Self-Determination, and Agency?" *Progress in Biophysics and Molecular Biology* 119 (2015): 510–21. Print.

Kauffman, Stuart A. *Humanity in a Creative Universe*. Oxford: Oxford UP, 2017. Print.

Latour, Bruno. *Facing Gaia: Eight Lectures on the New Climatic Regime*. Trans. Catherine Porter. Cambridge: Polity, 2017. Print.

Luhmann, Niklas. *The Reality of the Mass Media*. Trans. Kathleen Cross. Stanford: Stanford UP, 2000. Print.

Luhmann, Niklas. *Social Systems*. Trans. John Bednarz, Jr. with Dirk Baecker. Stanford: Stanford UP, 1995. Print.

Maturana, Humberto R., and Bernhard Poersken. *From Being to Doing: The Origins of the Biology of Cognition.* Trans. Wolfram Karl Koeck and Alison Rosemary Koeck. Heidelberg: Carl-Auer, 2004. Print.

Maturana, Humberto R., and Francisco J. Varela. *The Tree of Knowledge: The Biological Roots of Human Understanding.* Rev. ed. Trans. Robert Paolucci. Boston: Shambhala, 1992. Print.

Noble, Denis. *Dance to the Tune of Life: Biological Relativity.* Cambridge: Cambridge UP, 2017. Print.

Uexküll, Jakob von. *A Foray into the Worlds of Animals and Humans with A Theory of Meaning.* Trans. Joseph D. O'Neil. Minneapolis: U of Minnesota P, 2010. Print.

Wilson, Alexander. *Aesthesis and Perceptronium: On the Entanglement of Sensation, Cognition, and Matter.* Minneapolis: U of Minnesota P, 2019. Print.

Winslow, Russell. *Organism and Environment: Inheritance and Subjectivity in the Life Sciences.* Lanham: Lexington, 2017. Print.

Cary Wolfe

Editors' Note: The following is culled from many hours of taped conversations among members of the Ontogenetics Process Group that took place in separate meetings over a roughly two-year span in Santa Fe, New Mexico and Scottsdale, Arizona, from April 2017 to February 2018. The material is presented in chronological order, and has been only lightly edited locally. It has been edited globally for continuity and to indicate the range of interests of the Group for current and future research. Extended ellipses indicate where sections of the original recordings have been omitted.[1]

ONTOGENESIS BEYOND COMPLEXITY
conversations

scottsdale, i: ontogenesis, biogenesis, genetics, and "life" ...

Stuart Kauffman (hereafter, Stu): I think there's a deep parallel between atomism in chemistry and the foundations of genetics. There's a guy named Eors Szathmary whose name you all should know. Eors is an old friend. Eors wrote a major book with John Maynard Smith called *The Major Transitions in Biology*. He and I hung out for a week a year and a half ago in Budapest, and we shared this [...] We have exactly the same hypothesis about what was going on in Mendel's mind. It's a hypothesis, okay? But since Eors and I have the same one, and he's a really good evolutionary biologist, I give it some credence.

Stu: So, here's Mendel. Mendel dabbles around. Atomism is ripe in the day, right? Notice that a lot of chemists were not convinced that atoms were real things. Right? It's Einstein who convinces physicists that atoms are real things in 1905. So, Eors and I both think the following: here's Mendel. He's thinking about heredity. Kids look like mom and they look like dad, there must be some basis to heredity. Atomism [...] So, here Eors and I converge on the same thing: the atom is ripe, it's in the air. What if he thinks the following? I wonder if there are atoms of heredity? Then he thinks through the consequences. Well, mom and dad have different traits and the offspring have some traits of mom and some traits of dad, roughly speaking. There must be atoms of heredity that code for the different traits — somehow make the different traits, not code for it. But I look like mom, I look like dad.

Therefore, I must have atoms from mom and I must have atoms from dad.

Stu: But mom and dad have parents, so they must have atoms of heredity from their parents, and that goes back indefinitely many generations. I must be absolutely full of atoms of heredity from my great great great great great great great great grandparents all the way back in this exponential tree, right? Well, that's no good. I mean, as time goes on, I'd have infinitely many atoms of heredity. I must have some way of getting rid of half of the atoms of heredity because I get some from mom and some from dad. I better get rid of half of the atoms of heredity at every generation.

Stu: Well, the easiest thought then is that I have one atom from mom and one atom from dad, and at meiosis, at making the egg, somehow or another, half of them are lost. Once you say that, and do Mendel's experiments, okay [...] You go and say, "Well, can I see these atoms passing into progeny?" Well, dominance and recessive is not obvious from that line of thought. Then he discovered dominance and recessive, and he goes through Mendelian ratios: red eyed is wild type and white eyed is homozygous recessive, therefore if you take red-eyed homozygous mom and a white-eyed homozygous dad, and you mate them, you'll get [...] The F1 is genetically red and white, but phenotypically it will be all red eyed. But if you mate them, one quarter of the offspring will be white eyed, okay? And that's what they find in sweet peas. Except that his statistics are too clean. Do you know this?

Stu: It's been concluded that he cheated. His data is too close to a three-quarters and one-quarter. He certainly couldn't have gotten that by chance, goes the argument. Therefore, either he or one of his technicians [...]

Stu: And that may be right. Anyway, what I like about this is that Eors and I woke up to the same idea: how the whole thing got started then becomes the functional idea of the gene as atoms as factors of heredity that behave discreetly and autonomously. I think there's a reasonable chance that Eors and I are right. Obviously, I don't know that.

Phillip Thurtle (hereafter, Phil): And it's also really fascinating too. So, there's a couple counterpoints to this I think that really solidify your argument too. First of all, William Bateson and why the chromosomal theory people hated Bateson, Gregory Bateson's father, William Bateson, is because he was trying to come up with a wave theory of heredity and development. But then, the other thing that's really cool is that once scientists reduced genetic placement down to the one-dimensional space of genes as beads along a string, they came up with a lot of really interesting anomalies, mutations, and they map these through linkage analysis [...] But according to Mendel, this shouldn't work, because one of Mendel's laws is independent assortment, and you can't have totally independent assortment on a chromosome, otherwise you wouldn't have linkage groups. But then they find that genes that are right next to each other on the chromosome, might be able to help each other. These are the experiments that lead to thinking about genetic expression through Ed Lewis's work.

Adam Nocek (hereafter, Adam): Yeah, gene regulatory networks [...]

Stu: Very good history. Thank you.

Gaymon Bennett (hereafter, Gaymon): It opens up a lot in contemporary work. So I work with these guys who make stuff. Make stuff with biology – synthetic biology [...] Seems to me a couple of things that are quite powerful about what you're suggesting here and the way in which you're systematically spelling it out. First is, I don't think that's changed; there is a persistent unresolved tension between an imagined atomization and interplay. I think that, in fact, the gene is still a kind of conceptual multiplicity that doesn't need to have a kind of settled material basis. But, I think there's a twist on it, which is that, since the genome projects, the genome sequencing projects, there has been the working assumption that the question "What is a gene in its physiochemical dimensions?" has been answered. But, in fact, the question just got operationally skipped over in favor of a kind of pragmatic assumption: "we must know what a gene is; we can build machines that map them."

Gaymon: Today we're living in something like the afterlife – a conceptual *Nachleben* as Aby Warbug put it – of the belief that the question of the gene has been settled physiologically. That afterlife has allowed bioengineers to now do these deep ontologies of the gene, and they use the deep ontologies of the gene and the functional characterization of those deep ontologies to build tools that they think will allow them to manipulate living systems at a genetic level, and even design them, in such a way that the informational future of the organism is more or less open. And the cultural memory that "we know what a gene is," even though we don't actually know what a gene is in terms of its physiochemistry [...] Labs, of course, have in-practice approximations of all of this. I mean, it's not handwaving or something, it activates a whole range of interventions. But nothing really hangs on it conceptually. Like you don't need the gene, you just need to refer to it when you're in the middle of building a genetic construct or something. Yet the catch is, with these guys doing design work, who propose designs for, say, novel gene functions, they actually need the ontology to sit still. They need to know where, say, that ribosome binding site is, where the gene ends, physically, and they need to know that you can name physical and functional bits, measure them, and stick that information in a relational database.

Adam: It's the only way you can have bioengineering.

Gaymon: Yeah, and these other conversations we've had, quite powerful conversations around the tendency to treat living things as algorithmic things [...] To treat them as prestatable, is bound up in the ability to read a gene as a set of specified interactive components that make up the gene that can be rendered physiologically discreet, and therefore abstracted and managed within a database. But then the database itself, of course, is regulated by the logical parameters of relational databases and the needs of the computer, and that's a much longer conversation. Then the idea that you can build a whole set of machineries that can operate on those data and ontologies and do the design work in a mediated fashion, or at least help you bootstrap the design work [...] all indexes back in a certain kind of way to the belief that, out of the genome project, you have genes.

Sha Xin Wei (hereafter, Xin Wei): But let me just ask you, then, what's happening in synthetic biology as a big deal, biomimicry and biodesign are a big deal here at ASU [Arizona State University], right? What do you see happening? Because you see, these ontologies *don't* sit still, so these products get released into the wild. They go wild, with unintended consequences; and we need to have much bigger stabilizing institutions, like what the Federal Reserve does with the money supply, right? So, what do you see happening now at the institutional level? There must be [...] Is it like new kinds of lawsuits, class-action lawsuits, you know what I mean? Regulatory agencies that don't exist or should exist? We don't see any new institutions arising with this [...]

Gaymon: There are very few new institutions arising with this space that are, we could say, ontologically updated. The old institutions believe, again operationally, that they can simply be adjusted to fit the new ontologies needed for design and engineering. So, for example, I can still do intellectual property in biology within the existing systems of intellectual property law [...] I mean, if there was a place in which the gene concept got reified, it was in intellectual property. You have to have a gene to own the value that comes from engineering it.

Xin Wei: See, this is where the lawsuit stories intersect with that story. It's pretty powerful.

Gaymon: And it's really powerful when you consider that once you start getting big dumps of money into biotech, even in these sort of invisible ways where, you know, in the early 1990s, big pharma looks to the biologist to help them do the chemistry of drug discovery better. Pharma gets early on, or thinks it gets, that bioengineers offer a way to be more efficient in all this. They only are going to invest in molecular biology if they think that they can get more out than they put in [...] If they can really lock down intellectual property, we might say ontologically, and the intellectual property isn't just about patenting processes or tools. It's about objects.

Xin Wei: To make property out of things that are not really amenable to becoming property, or shouldn't be. Like, intellectual property, for me, for twenty years, has been an oxymoron. Gaymon, you're pointing very concretely to how some of that's working in the bioengineering domain. We're petrifying certain entities [...]

Adam: Well, it's a really interesting way to start thinking about information capital, or in any case, what is required in order for something, like the gene, to become informationalized. What you're suggesting is that we have to make this abstract thing called a gene, molecular, and ultimately, capable of being broken up into discrete bits. We have to make the gene discreet, we have to make it ready or amenable to capture [...]

Gaymon: One of the ways in which you can make it discreet if you're a synthetic biologist is keeping it as a reference point in the background that only gets gestured to. It gets gestured to both as the warrant for the way in which you're promising to generate physiological reifications of parts of the gene [...] There's that. And there's also the political economy reference, which is, you know, we want to make sure we can do an entire database of all the possible ribosomal binding sites for this construct. But we don't know whether or not we have freedom of operation because somebody might have a patent on the gene.

Phil: The other thing that Gaymon said that I think is really important: so, it's not just about stability in space and time, it's also about the operational nature of the gene through the coding problem. It's the fact that this is a specific code that then you can treat in a certain way. That's the assumption. But that wasn't the assumption of the early experimentalists and, matter of fact, the early stuff by the theoretical coding people [...] was a failure. It was biochemists working pragmatically who solved it, Marshall Nirenberg and Johann Matthaei, and even the well-referenced article of Jacob and Monod, ideas for those experiments came out of a really phenomenologically centered bacteriologist, Arthur Pardee, who was interested in feedback groups in bacterial enzymology, right [...]

Gaymon: [...] right, because they shifted from metaphors of code to metaphors of regulatory networks.

Phil: Yep, yep. So that ends up working between the material and the operational and ends up giving a huge [...]

Gaymon: And a return to the language of code during the genome projects is actually a different reference to code than what you or I would argue.

Stu: And it's also, mind you – I think I'm still sort of a relevant biologist – there's been a catastrophic mistake. Not gene-coding. The DNA code is the DNA code. The notion that the organism, the egg, or the genome, contains a code for the adult, a master code like a computer program, is just wrong. That's not what's happening at all, and it's misled us for fifty years. Brian Goodwin first said this in maybe 1982.

Gaymon: And this is just something – just look at the material ramifications of this. Once you start treating it as a program then the bioengineering department at Stanford starts looking more and more like a computer science department. It's filled with people who now say they do RNA engineering. "Why do you do RNA engineering?" "Because I don't work on circuits, I work on software."

Gaymon: And, you know, it's clever and it's communicable, but it also sets into motion a whole set of regimes that govern how you do work, who you train, who you attract into the field [...]

Stu: What do you mean "I don't work on circuits, I work on software"?

Gaymon: Yeah, that you can think of the machinery of the cell, the encoded machinery of the cell as like the binary code that needs a program in order to do something.

Stu: As a computer programmer.

Gaymon: As a computer programmer.

Stu: And circuits would be what?

Gaymon: Basically, the DNA. It's hand-waving, but it's basically, "We don't engineer the DNA, we engineer the RNA."

Stu: Oh okay, I see.

Adam: It's so funny the way in which synthetic biology has just reified all of this crap. I mean, the early days of biotechnology were far more experimental and interesting than what you're talking about [...]

Gaymon: Yeah, I mean, on one level, this is my shtick lately in terms of – and I don't want to shift this to my research – but just to say that I think it's less that synthetic biology is an actual driver of all this stuff – there's lots of other experimental work going on – and more that synthetic biology has provided the systematic articulation of a whole set of tacit imaginaries that started circulating in the early 2000s.

Adam: Yeah yeah [...]

Phil: This might be the operational point, for me [...] Because these types of histories tend to be very deterministic. Like CODE COMES IN and it displaces biochemical ways of thinking, right? When it's really there's a whole set of issues out there that both informatics and biochemists are working on, and they're reaching towards how to build things back up again. So, I think that's a historiographical issue as well.

Gaymon: There's this – I mean, to use insider jargon – there's a way in which the synthetic biology people – as just one of the cast of the characters in the biotech mix, and of course there's dozens and dozens – they're like operating in a high-tech imaginary, in Charles Taylor's sense of all those unthought presumptions that allow us to build worlds together and inhabit them. And what the synthetic biologist does is he brings that imaginary to articulation for a certain biotechnical program, but the reason it's super successful is because it allows the synthetic biologist to become "a man of his time," a man in a world of high tech. That is to say, it's culturally coherent to the other people who also want to do this stuff. And so the reification of a kind of code – it's not just code language, but the reification of a whole set of dispositions and practices around the making of digital technology as adequate to the making of biotechnologies.

Stu: So, can I bitch for a moment? If you ask these guys, "What's a cell type?" They have no answer whatsoever. Jacob and Monod did. Jacob and Monod said a cell type is a stable pattern of gene expression. These guys don't think that.

Gaymon: No, they don't.

Stu: They don't think about it at all. They have no idea, and it pisses me off [...]

Gaymon: Yeah, but part of it is their inheritance of the huge data dump of genomics, which was underwritten by the idea that at some fundamental level, all living processes are informational processes, and all informational processes are digital processes, and all digital processes can be captured in digital ontologies. And so, as it goes, what makes one particular cell type significant to the engineering of some construct ultimately will be shown to be non-fundamental. That is to say, that the motifs that they're operating with at the level of, say, ribosome binding sites, will allow you to create a "basis set" of informational motifs at the level of DNA, RNA, and protein that will allow you to be agnostic about which form of life, which cell type, we're working with – that *all* of life will be able to be reduced to informational motifs, which can be mixed and matched.

* * *

scottsdale, ii: technology, modeling, and contingency in social forms

Stu: So I'm going to tell you guys about some work that's been underway for about ten years, two years, two months and three days.

Stu: If you think about the diversity of the global economy [...] goods and services fifty thousand years ago [...] perhaps there was a thousand, ten thousand goods and services. There's a billion goods and services today in New York City alone. Ask the economists why and they really don't have an answer. I will try to broach an answer.

Stu: The fundamental idea is that a good or a service [...] a new good or service creates a niche or an opportunity for still further goods and services to come into existence. And the same is true for laws. Laws create the conditions for new legal opinions which wind up becoming new laws, which wind up creating new legal opinions which wind up creating new laws. So I'm going to give a model that I think is too simple but it's kind of [...] it might be better than I think it is. But before we do just think of the following history.

Stu: In 1933, or whenever it was, Turing invented the Turing Machine. It *enabled* but did not *cause* von Neumann to invent the mainframe computer. Right? Then that was part of the coming into existence of the first computer, the ENIAC during the war then – ENIAC then von Neumann. So von Neumann, by inventing the mainframe computer, did not *cause* but *enabled* IBM to start making mainframe computers. Which then got sold. Well, getting sold created a market for computers, right? I remember it, when I was using computers for the first time, in '65, with IBM computers and Dell [...] DEC, DEC or Dell computers [...]

Michael Epperson (hereafter, Mike): DEC.

Stu: DEC. DEC computers. The invention of the chip and the wide market created by IBM made it possible – did not *cause* but made it possible – to invent the personal computer, whose invention created a niche. It created a niche, it did not cause it. It created a niche for word processing and Microsoft came along, right?

Stu: Microsoft and word processing meant that we had files on our computers which afforded an opportunity to share files, and so we invented the modem. But the sharing of files did not cause, but it invited – it created a niche for – the invention of the World Wide Web. And the World Wide Web created the capacity to sell on the Web. It didn't *cause* it, it created the capacity to sell on the Web. And eBay and Amazon came along, right? eBay and Amazon came along and we were all on the Web, that put a lot of content on the Web, and that enabled Google to come along, right? See how goods and services create niches for the next new goods and services that come along?

Stu: The economists don't know this. I certainly promise you there are some areas that they don't know. And one of the reasons they don't know it is the unprestatable uses of screwdrivers – because of this unprestatability, they can't make a mathematical model of the specific things that will happen. I've been thinking about that for years and last summer, in desperation, I wrote an equation which I'm going to tell you what it says and pass it around, if you can read my writing [...]

Gaymon: So just thinking of an example as you were talking. I was thinking about in the last two decades the way in which the behemoth technology corporations in the Bay Area have vacillated between a shift towards a kind of conservative relationship to innovation. The iPhone: Apple wants to produce things like the iPhone but once they produce the iPhone, they don't want other people to innovate because now they want to act like, you know, like the clothing company GAP used to, where they produce a new line of products every six months or whatever and so you throw away all your old clothes and you buy a bunch of new clothes. They don't want any substantial shifts [...]

Stu: [...] so they want [...]

Gaymon: And yet, then companies like Google realize that they see the life cycle of their own wealth generation and they realize that they've got to start inventing a lot of other things to produce the equivalent of a smart phone X days down the road if they want to continue their growth trajectory. And so you get these binds within the niches themselves.

Stu: Can I come back to you with something we've talked about before. Sometime ago [...] you know I've had this idea of the adjacent possible, we've all talked about it. And I've got this idea of sub-critical and super-critical growth. Super-critical growth is usually just exploding, and so the question is, "Is there anything that gates our entry into the adjacent possible?" "Why don't we go faster and faster and faster and faster and faster to the adjacent possible?" And economically one answer is, if the rate of entry into the adjacent possible is so fast that the life cycle, the lifetime of the new good or service, is too short to make a living on it,

then we slow down. And that's what you just talked about.

Gaymon: Yeah. You need a certain durability to the niche in order for it to produce diversity and ramify out.

Stu: So you're saying what's happening is that it's spreading wider. So I've got you, do I have you right? I can't innovate my own main product faster because I need seven years to get my investment back on it, or one year, or whatever. Therefore, I'll invent something else over on the side [...]

Gaymon: That's right. I'll invent a quasi-monopoly with regard to [...]

Stu: [...] oh, that's neat [...]

Gaymon: So it'd be interesting to plot whether or not these changes in, essentially cultural practice around innovation, are significant enough to change the rates of probabilities. That was just one example and I don't want to talk very much about it. It would be interesting to [...]

Stu: [...] but can I just absorb it. So what you just said is – I think – that I can't innovate on my mainline fast enough because there's a lifetime for my product that must be running for me to make a profit on it. But I still want to innovate like mad to expand the market, therefore I better innovate on the side somewhere. And I wonder how you want to put that into an update on this model.

Cary Wolfe (hereafter, Cary): Can I ask a question here? Kind of a second-order question: to what extent does the financialization of real goods and services make a difference? So I'm thinking about, ok [...] I'm innovating something and the issue is not is the thing going to work or not. The issue is can I make money on the financialization of the risk?

Stu: What do you mean by financialization of the risk?

Cary: Turning it into an investment vehicle so it becomes purely abstract and it's not [...] I know it's going to fail, but I'm still going to make money on it.

Gaymon: So I'm going to make a ton of money off people buying iPhones but I'm also going to make a shit load more off the growth in the stock prices [...]

Cary: Exactly. I mean, the '08 bubble is Exhibit A [...]

Adam: [...] and also you get people making money on failure [...]

Cary: [...] you financialize mortgages that you *know* are going to fail. So innovation becomes something different under financialization.

Adam: What you're asking though is about historical specificity. The rates can change [...]

Gaymon: [...] or does it? I mean how [...] maybe you see some regularities [...]

Adam: [...] that would be very interesting [...]

Mike: Can I just say, because it connects to all of this and we've had this discussion about graph theory before. I don't think it's adequate to do what you want to do for this reason: it's not compatible with how we defined the global earlier in our conversation. Failed products, or the locally unrealized *potentia* of these failed products, aren't representable globally in the graph theoretic model. You don't have any feedback mechanism with acyclic directed graphs. It's definitely relevant in the type of dynamic you're talking about.

Stu: You can have a graph that has cycles in it.

Mike: Yes, but that's not what you were originally describing with the directed acyclic graphs. And even with cyclic graphs you can't model novel potential relations and their potential overlaps the way you'd need to. When you talk about the innovations involved in going from the invention of the solid state, of the ENIAC and MULTIVAC to UNIVAC to word processing, etc., you defined that in a nice clean directed acyclic graph theoretic way. But I think the reality of that evolution was a little different. There were a lot of technologies that were developed, intermediate technologies that were discarded as irrelevant, yet nevertheless introduced novel local *potentia* that influenced the global state history.

Mike: In that sense, almost everything we know about modern computing and the internet doesn't really come directly from that computing lineage that you define – ENIAC to UNIVAC to PCs. You could make the argument that the modern PC actually descends more directly from the photocopier. Because all the innovations that drive modern computing came from PARC, from Xerox – their Palo Alto research group. They didn't initially know what they were going to build with PARC. Xerox just said "Hey we have all this money from our photocopying empire, we don't even know if these technologies are going to be viable, we just want to put you guys in a room and see if you come up with something. We have no idea what that might be [...]"

Mike: One of those technologies was the laser printer, which Xerox, ironically, said, "Fuck it, we don't want it. It's going to compete with our photocopiers and lose us money." Ethernet and TCP IP were developed there, the current internet transfer protocol was developed at PARC to network computers. The language that makes the modern internet possible was developed there at PARC. The graphical user interface [...] all thanks to the Xerox photocopier money.

Mike: All those things that are integral to modern IT today derive from innovations that came from PARC. And all of that lineage of actualized *potentia* and enabling constraints involves feedback, all these crazy feedback loops – relations of unrealized *potentia*. So my feeling is if we're going to use the definition of global that we were talking about earlier, combined with your idea, what you'd need instead of an acyclic directed graph, or even cyclic graphs, which don't capture global state change as relations among novel local *potentia* […] I think you'd need something that captures these weird relational overlaps of novel local potential states to represent the global state that you're talking about. I think you'd need something like category theory to represent that.

Xin Wei: No, you wouldn't necessarily use category theory, not for this. But there are other things you might want to use before that point […]

Mike: Category theory plus topology, then. Sheaf theory, to follow these potential relations topologically. Now that's not the only way, of course. I'm thinking of it in terms of physics, which is my reference point. The way that we would define a global state that involves these kinds of overlapping local contexts would be something like sheaf theory because there's a structure-preserving mechanism that's emergent, because the global state's constantly changing. You need a way of going back and showing how an irrelevant product way back in the lineage all of a sudden becomes rehabilitated as relevant because of some new potential. In other words, the *potentia* don't go away, the *potentia* remain embedded structurally in the global state history.

Stu: I think that can be shown – and I heard what you said and I think you're right. You all know about Schumpeterian gales of creative destruction? So, Brian Arthur taught me years ago: the automobile comes in and it kills the horse as a mode of transport. With the horse goes the buggy, the buggy whip, the saddle, the pony express. A whole lot of things die out of the economy and with the car you get an oil industry, gas industry, paved roads, traffic lights, traffic courts, fast food restaurant, hotels, and so on. So that's a Schumpeterian gale of creative destruction. But it killed the horse, that's not in this model. That's what I wrote Roger about; I said "There's no death in the model" he said "yeah, but for a start don't worry about it."

Xin Wei: Can I just? […] There are some questions. For example, I think this is fantastic but we don't have time to talk about it all today at the level that it deserves. But just let me make a few bookmarks and come back to it another day. One of the serious issues is what constitutes an innovation. Another is what constitutes a product. So, for example, a lot of these effects that you're pointing to, yes they're one passing effect, but another effect would be iTunes, and then another side effect of that side effect would be the possibility for musical ensembles to try to make a practice […] make a living playing concerts again. Not through selling LPs and CDs – they don't exist anymore – but because of the rise in attention, larger fields of attention paid to these small ensembles. So can't you go out there and say "We're going to do a concert and have people come to that concert," see what I'm saying?

Xin Wei: And these side effects are entirely on different levels in ontology, which are not addressed by the single curve. Now: yes, there's innovation, but it's in whole different parts of the ontology. Second point is, David Graeber wrote a very nice article, "Of Flying Cars and the Declining Rate of Profit," in *The Baffler* in 2012, that said something like why don't we have flying machines and teleportation devices? I forget what the long version was, but what happened to innovation?

Gaymon: Right, right […]

Cary: […] yeah, where's my flying car?!

Xin Wei: And Mackenzie Wark, two days ago said there *is* no innovation in Silicon Valley. And being part of that, I know what he said is the case. There is no innovation. Basically, what happens is after a while, maybe when Anatol Holt was working when he was a first programmer for the UNIVAC (the first general purpose electronic digital computer design commercial computer) in Philadelphia in 1958, there was innovation there but by the time it got to Silicon Valley there was less and less and less innovation. So, in fact, it's the *repackaging* of products, which can happen.

Xin Wei: So the financialization question is very important, because you can make money even in the absence of innovation [...]

Xin Wei: Now China – for example the medium question comes up. Actually, if you think, you look at say literary practices in China after say the "Wusi" May Fourth movement in the early twentieth century, there's a tremendous amount of innovation in China but it happened to be in the literary as well as political domains. In the popular fiction domain, not in technology. So the question is "By what measure are we talking about measuring innovation?"

Xin Wei: Another point is that the exponentiality of the curve is nothing remarkable, because as soon as we have a $dp/dt = \lambda p$ we get exponentiality. Yes, I think as a proof or a theory, this is true. But it's true of all sorts of phenomena. Including biology with diversity.

Xin Wei: Another point: you know, we have this theory of Punctuated Equilibrium. We can have local exponentiality, still punctuated, you know this very well. So it functions so that the global diversity does not increase monotonically with history – it doesn't have to increase monotonically. You can have *local* increase without monotonic increase over all time. Of course. So the theory is true and also not true, or can be true and not true, it can be true on some schedule of time and not others.

Xin Wei: Another point: Saari has established some very interesting theorems about the Mathematical Complexity of Simple Economics (1991) [...] So in addition to products, we have to think about the *value* of products, because if you think about, this is a kind of observational theory that we would, if we are scientific, we would also be interested in, how do you say, a "how does it work?" kind of theory. Which gets us to proper nouns, a game with proper nouns. So read it this way: what are the actors, what are the agents and also what are the aspirations and desires and what are the forces at work that make these things change? So that's [...] there's a *huge* amount of physics involved. Even if we stay within economics, there's this notion of value and price. So, going back to Sraffa's famous theory of price – or going more forward to ten fifteen years ago, to the famous work by Soares, whose theorem said that "Any economy with at least three products and three consumers, it's prices will go generically to infinity," or minus infinity.

Xin Wei: This is a fundamental theorem. So it'd be interesting to have, in addition to this, on top of it, a theory of price that tells us a little bit about what drives things. This is a forward reference to Nicholas Damiris who is actually here in town, and I actually talked to Nicholas at dinner last night about this thing so he can actually probably speak more to it than I can. But put in price as a way to mark desire, then we're in deep waters. Deep waters.

Phil: So, in the intellectual history of political economy, the problem is that this particular point has been overshadowed by attention to Marx, but what you're suggesting is, what I've been hearing suggested here is, that this is much better explained by Thorsten Veblen.

Gaymon: Yeah, Veblen's all over this [...]

Phil: Yeah, he's *so* all over this because he's got an immanence theory of price, in *The Theory of the Leisure Class*. So when things become expensive precisely because high social class people start to use them [...] but things don't die in the same way, they become transformed into different functions. All of a sudden, horses are no longer used to plow fields they're used for equestrian dressage [...]

Cary: Right, right [...]

Phil: [...] and then he talked about the change in the business enterprise with the theory of the business enterprise and the move from industrialization to the notion of speculation in business [...]

Phil: So I think he could be a really key historical figure for this [...]

Gaymon: And I think Veblen's intellectual style injects a really nice sort of bootstrapping rhythm between, if you will, theories and models, and historiography and some sort of quasi-ethnography in which [...] like, his theory of Trained Incapacity. What happens to people when they begin to work in different sorts of workspaces? They learn not to be able to do other certain kinds of things.

Gaymon: And that all begins, with him, with this very close, fine-grained study of what happens to workers having their bodies and skills formed in certain kinds of factories, and then he bootstraps that to a theory. And it seems to me that this, you know, I don't know enough about how the math works in order to know what's left out of a certain kind of equation [...]

Gaymon: I mean, I hear what Michael's saying, and it totally makes intuitive sense. But there is a certain sense in which it seems that if models can be indicators, if we think there's something about these realities we're interested in that are non-prestatable [...]

Gaymon: That are characterized by the dynamics implied by the inductive global, that systems are autopoietic in some sorts of ways that are connected to these other two variables. Those sorts of things [...]

Gaymon: [...] one of the things that's powerful about a model is that it just suggests some places where you might pay attention.

Mike: Yeah.

Gaymon: And the question would be whether or not this gives you enough to see [...]

Stu: If I – sort of in defense of this, the group is working on this. There's only three of us or four [...]

Mike: We call it our Silly Model [...]

Stu: But maybe it's not so silly [...]

Stu: See, here's where [...] do you know competitive general equilibrium?

Gaymon: Hm hm.

Stu: Well, it's a fundamental theory, with Arrow and his group, published in '54 or something like that [...]

Stu: [...] and the problem they're trying to solve is the following: given supply and demand – I can say this in just a couple minutes – but the main thing is, you've got a prestated set of goods and services. So you have to have a prestated set of goods and services. And the question is, is there a vector of prices such that, given consumers and their vector of demands, is there a vector of prices such that markets clear?

Stu: The notion of equilibrium in economics, that markets clear. That's the equilibrium notion, supply and demand balance.

Stu: The problem's the following: you've got, you change the price of bread and you change the demand for bread. But what if you put butter on your bread and you change the supply of butter? What happens to the demand for bread? So once you've got more than one good, it's no longer so trivial, so there's a couple of things [...]

Stu: So Arrow and Debru proved a theorem in '55 showing that a rather general condition is met.

Stu: So yeah, in this model – which I can explain to you guys if you want – under very general conditions of competitive equilibrium, all markets clear, and basically, you've got agents and they've got probability distributions over what's going to happen in the future, which are the separate utility functions, and you've got a prestated set of goods and services, and then the economy unfolds in some stochastic way, and contracts come due or not, depending on what happens, and everything works out. It's a gorgeous theorem, the Fixed Point Theorem.

Stu: But it can't talk about new goods and services.

Mike: Yeah [...]

Cary: Right, right.

Stu: And it certainly can't talk about the fact that the new goods and services aren't prestatable. And that's why the economists don't talk about it because they want to write down equations.

Stu: [...] and what's funny about this little equation is that you can't state what the goods and services are, but you can state how many of them you've got.

Stu: Well that's actually something you could maybe study.

Cary: Well, I was going to just follow up Xin Wei's set of observations, but also yours, Gaymon. Going back to this thing about models vs. theories. I mean, one way to think about this is to step back and say, okay, a *huge* ideological and political problem that we live with right now is the confusion of the relationship between growth and innovation. That's a huge fucking problem [...]

Mike: Sure, yeah.

Cary: And so this can be an invitation to step back and say, hang on a second, let's think about the difference [...]

Mike: Yeah [...]

Cary: [...] *especially* under financialized late capitalism.

Cary: The difference between actual "innovation" and economic "growth," quote unquote.

Stu: Yeah, you could work on the growth with the same set of goods and services. You know [...]

Cary: Yeah. And this goes back to Xin Wei's point about Mackenzie Wark's talk about innovation.

Mike: You know, one thing, I just want to chime in before we leave, this is all very cool to me. I've often wondered why it is that some of the most ground-breaking innovations that produce the most exciting new *potentia*, that were *not* prestatable – at least in tech let's just say – because you asked earlier, why does it all come from Silicon Valley? [...]

Mike: [...] it didn't really come from Silicon Valley. It came from Norristown, Pennsylvania. It was MOS Technology, this tiny little company that made a really cheap micro-processor. The 6502, which competed with Intel's 8088. The idea behind that was "Hey, we make this thing cheap, everyone's going to be able to have a personal computer at home." And there was not one compelling financial model. All the big companies were pitched this, they all said no. They said, "Nah, there's no market. People wouldn't know what to do with a computer. No one's going to care."

Mike: So by some weird confluence of business currents, this really cool guy who wanted to design a cheap-ass processor, for no particular application, got together with this Polish immigrant who founded Commodore – which built typewriters and calculators – who just wanted to make money on some new product – somehow got *him* to say yes, when all the big companies said no. That produced the 6502, which then led to Apple and Atari and all the cheap PCs built around it.

Mike: And there's no compelling economic reason behind it. There was no market for it, which is why all the big companies passed on it. Nobody knew what to do with these home computers. And it was these crazy guys who had no business model, they didn't even know what the hell they were doing other than, hey, we *can* do this, let's do it. And then all of a sudden, all of these new possibilities exploded. And PARC of course is a similar example. It's so crazy.

Gaymon: That's right, because there really are these, there really is a multiplicity of genealogies that get reconfigured and attached to certain kinds of gravitational centers that allow for these [...] this scale of growth.

Mike: Yeah, and I remember as a kid. The Commodore 64 was my first computer. Amazing.

Gaymon: Programming the color screen change!

Mike: Yes! It would come with [...]

Gaymon: [...] Whoa, I just got a lime green! [...]

Mike: [...] Yeah, and it came with a manual that would teach you how to program. It was a big thick manual. And no one knew what the fuck to do with this thing, yet everyone wanted one. Everyone had to have one of these things.

Mike: And we would just, it was this amazing thing, even though it didn't have a specific purpose. It was pure unprestatable potentiality. It was a tangible example of that. It's like, I have this thing where I don't even know what the hell I can do with it. But that is enough to make me beg my mom to spend 300 bucks to buy this thing.

Mike: And when else do you ever see that? It's so rare [...]

Gaymon: [...] again this is the unprestatable. In the 1960s you have people like Doug Englebart and others, in Stanford, who are sort of a micro version of the office park, or the research parks, in which, like, okay the DoD is going to throw some money at these really smart people to like, work on their pet projects and kind of hover at the edge to see whether or not a missile technology is going to happen [...]

Mike: Yeah, yeah (laughing) [...]

Gaymon: [...] and meanwhile, they're all like super in love with Vannevar Bush – like "whoa, that'd be awesome!" – and then they're going to Esalen and dropping acid, or whatever, and being told: you know, if you achieve total control of your own psyche, you will discover that your psyche is coextensive with all psychic energy. And that the control of your own capacities is simultaneously a linkage to the cosmic self.

Gaymon: And they're like "whoa, shit dude, that's Vannevar Bush. We can program that shit!"

Xin Wei: It's Sargent Pepper's too!

Gaymon: Yeah! Okay, it's true, there are also technologies around and they were super smart and there's mathematics and there's money sloshing around and there's, you know [...] So it's not *just* the counterculture. But there's this way in which like there's these weird convergences that allow for the possibility of something.

Mike: The biggest fans of the PC in the Bay Area were *hippies*.

Mike: They even tried to develop their own computer company. I forget what it was called, but it was this idea of the hippie computer company. And, that's amazing to me. We don't have that any more. I mean, now all we have are these idiots building apps to do stuff that nobody needs [...]

Gaymon: [...] and save Oracle [...] (laughing)

Mike: [...] *and* save the world [...] (laughing)

Mike: It's like everyone's restricted their ideas of what's possible to what's actual *now* in the technology. And that's why we're stalling.

Gaymon: I *do* think that this inflated self-love of Silicon Valley, which keeps it blind to things – like, maybe we're not really innovating – is the same culture that's providing the energy to transform biotechnology in the image of high tech. It's self-congratulations and wealth in the high-tech industry that is the driver that makes this structure [...]

Stu: Question to you, I'm still a biologist, so, for example, I started in medicine and then in developmental biology. So, does anything that is going on in this biotech, synthetic biology area that you're talking about, have anything whatsoever to do with, for example, how a zygote develops into a human adult? Does it have anything to do with the origin of life? Does it have anything to do with what life is?

Gaymon: Yeah, no.

Stu: It's just doing things [...] My sense is in listening to you and looking at it distantly, is it doing what is technologically possible, certainly with synthetic biology. I remember when the first genetic circuits were engineered. I mean, the little oscillator that whoever it is made, the three genes that repress one another oscillate, it's called the oscillator or something like that [...]

Gaymon: [...] yeah, what's his name, at Caltech [...]

Stu: [...] yeah, I can't remember. Anyway, so it seems like, isn't an awful lot of this just doing what's technologically possible? It has no fundamental bearing on biology as a science?

Gaymon: I think the only bearing it has on biology as a science, is it's restricting the space within which biologists talk about and justify their work such that they need funding.

Phil: I think it's also changed such fundamental things like what it becomes to "know" in biology [...]

Cary: [...] and that's *huge* [...]

Phil: [...] because what it becomes to "know" is "we have to build it to know it."

Gaymon: And you know in 2000, there was something quite elegant about this. This was a push-back from blue-collar biology. The techs on the bench were like, "fuck you with all of your theories, I can *build* DNA. And you can't. I'm really good at building DNA."

Gaymon: And so, there's this blue-collar attitude that says, like, and then they pick up on this, precisely on this attitude, "you don't understand it until you build it." Or, you know, the one quote that I used to love from a synthetic biologist Drew Endy was, "I don't care how living things work. I want to know how living things can be *made* to work."

Xin Wei: Exactly.

Mike: And that's iterative. That's not about understanding. That's what *he* would say.

Xin Wei: That's it. That really describes the whole situation [...]

Gaymon: But to come back to the basic sciences, why I left the synthetic biologists, one reason I left the synthetic biologists in the Bay Area and went to the basic sciences at Fred Hutch in Seattle – I had the opportunity and you don't say no to that kind of opportunity – but also just because I was quite interested in the fact that this is this enclave of people like Roger Brent who are deeply ascetic about what it means to be a basic biologist. I mean, Roger's like, "no, I want to know the *truth*."

Mike: And, I'm quite interested in how the forms of living for somebody like Roger are being *changed* by the pressure of these other institutions.

Cary: Yeah.

Adam: How does he get along with Church and those guys?

Gaymon: Oh, he can't stand them.

Adam: I didn't think so.

Gaymon: Yeah, he can't stand them.

* * *

santa fe, i: can we find laws for the evolution of social forms?

Stu: There's no law that entails the becoming of the biosphere or the economy or law. But you need a historical account that's situated in the moment and the actualities of what's come to be and there's no view from the outside. Okay, all that stuff that we were saying before. Law is order, order is law. Like Newton and Einstein and quantum mechanics. And then we can begin to ask what other kinds of law are there, or are there other kinds of laws, or finding law like properties beyond the beauty of Newton, who gives us the three laws of motions and the determinism of the billiard ball on the table, and he tells us how to reason. Give me the initial conditions of the boundary conditions and here's the laws of motion of the system and given all of those things, one can deduce the future behavior of the system in the deterministic world. That's what Newton taught us how to deal with, with the differential calculus.

Stu: He taught us how to think. But it doesn't work in the becoming of a legal system. Why not? Okay. What other kinds of laws are there? Well, you can have stochastic differential equations which give up determinism, right? Because they say whatever happens is drawn out of some distribution at random. You could look for statistical laws, so for example could we have a theory of the rate of diversification of niches in legal systems? Or in economics – the global economy – or the biosphere? So we actually have a theory of the *statistics* of it, but we give up trying to predict in detail what it becomes? That'd be cool. And that's not impossible.

Cary: Yeah, but I don't think so with the law; I don't think it would really tell you where the action is in the law. I mean, it wouldn't […]

Stu: Which law are you referring to Cary? Legal law?

Cary: Yeah, I'm talking about the kind of niche formation that we were discussing earlier […]

Stu: Yeah, absolutely.

Stu: You could have a statistical theory that says, "here's how the niches beget niches," but it would not tell you the internal details of laws and precedents and […]

Cary: Yeah, and we haven't even talked about jurisprudence, which is a whole other thing, right? So yeah, I kind of come back to Mike's point, it's like, "well, ok, why would you want that?"

Mike: Yeah.

Cary: What would that do for you?

Stu: Want what?

Cary: What you're describing: a statisticalization of the rates of internal differentiation of niches within the law.

Stu: Well it's kind of a cool law. That's nice, but it doesn't tell you what's going to happen in *this* legal system, *this* circumstance, when Monsanto comes along with lobbyists, okay, and fucks us.

Cary: No.

Gaymon: Let me take a shot at […]

Stu: Can I say one more thing?

Gaymon: Yeah.

Stu: What you just said, Cary, is exactly the two cultures issue, because we want a nuanced discussion of how come Monsanto did what it did, in that detailed circumstance, right? That's a historical becoming that requires something that is the two cultures. It requires, let me just sort of say it, a historical account that's nuanced and understands the social context and all that kind of stuff. You won't get that out of a law, no.

Cary: No.

Stu: Fine, that's the union of the two cultures: we could have a law that's the statistics of the becoming of new niches, but not the specific way in which the niches become.

Cary: Well, I think what you could say, and in fact, a guy who wrote a book about Niklas Luhmann, this philosopher Hans-Georg Moeller did say this, you know, the theory of social complexity we're talking about is actually meta-biological, precisely on the model that you use to describe the evolution of the biosphere. I would say that helps you understand how the law actually works, and how specialization within the law actually works in ways that heavily constrain, especially legal decisions that might seem counterintuitive or just even stupid, but that happen all the time, and they happen because people who are experts within these areas know how to use those constraints to move the law to a certain kind of judgment. Now, at that point it seems to me you've got [...] it's like understanding the evolution of the law meta-biologically along the lines that you described with Darwinian "exaptations" or pre-adaptations and so on, which makes a whole lot of sense. But I don't see how trying to statisticalize that would get you any further purchase on saying, well let's try to figure out how this shit really works.

Mike: Yeah, all of it hangs, I think, Stu, on the difference between laws explicative and laws just merely descriptive, because do you think Newton's laws, as intended by him, were intended to be explicative or just descriptive?

Stu: I think it was explicative.

Mike: I think it was just descriptive, because when he was asked "well, where does gravity come from?," his answer is, "I have no fucking idea. My job is not to explain gravity."

Stu: Oh, you're right.

Mike: My job is to describe how it works.

Stu: Yes, you're right.

Mike: The kind of way you're talking about a law – to use the way that you're describing it – seems explicative to me, and I don't think there is such a thing as a fundamentally explicative set of scientific theories or laws that can be derived from description alone. It seems to me that the laws of science and theories of science are intended to describe the natural world in a way where one can reliably measure the success of the description. But how do you elevate that to a fundamentally explicative mode – i.e., one with no presupposed first principles or boundary conditions? I don't think it can be done scientifically. You can say, I have a *speculation* about how this description could rise to the level of explanation, and then it would turn into this thing [...]

Cary: Well no, and you can describe – and Luhmann's theory of modernity as functional differentiation, which increases specialization in social systems, basically says this – you can say "hey, I think I can give you the reason why we see increasing complexity, increasing specialization, increasing differentiation, within all the social systems, including the law, including the economy, including education and so on. Yeah, I think I can give you a really plausible explanation of why that's the drift of things, and it has to do with systems simply doing what they do to try to deal with an increasingly complex environment in which they find themselves," and there are historical reasons for that that he talks about, and so on. At that point, it's like well, really all you need is to say, "there is a systematic nature to how this thing unfolds that is constrained" – I mean, this comes back to your stuff, Stu – "it's constrained, but not entailing." Right? And that's where the action is, it seems to me, politically, ethically, in terms of how shit actually happens.

Gaymon: You know, with Luhmann, there's the expectation of a principle of regularity in which there are things in the world called social systems and they're comparable and you can see patterns at a kind of meta-level, and I think the conversations around what aspects of reality are non-prestatable and which ones aren't, what is the degree to which this is the case, even challenges that idea that these are comparable things called systems and they could obey certain kinds of principles [...]

Cary: Yeah, I think that's right, and I think what's useful about it, because where you really end up, what you end up focusing on, is "okay, what are the modes of structural coupling that are possible between the economic system and the legal system, or the economic system and the political system, *and not others*." So it's these articulation points, and you don't end up back in this kind of either/or-ist sort of explanation. You're having to pay attention to the details of structural coupling. So, with the law, and the relationship between law and the economy, it's like on the one hand, you can say "yeah, I think we all know that the more money you have, the more access you have to the legal system vis-à-vis access to legal expertise. I think we know that. But we also know that all the money in the world is not going to guarantee a particular judgment in a particular case." Right? So, *that's* where the complexity is.

Gaymon: And the constraint.

Cary: And the constraint.

Gaymon: And this is part of my nervousness around Luhmann is he thinks it's all complexity, but in fact there are patterns of constraint and consolidation and [...]

Cary: [...] oh, yeah, yeah. And his theory of the political system is all over this, because his theory of the political system is actually that what we call "the political" is hyper-distributed. There are bureaucrats, non-elected officials, elected officials, lobbyists, etc., so it's a super distributed [...] how the political system actually works is a super distributed asynchronous kind of network of relationships, you know?

Stu: Can I say something for the recording?

Cary: Yeah.

Stu: It's what I was babbling about before, and it ties in with what you were saying about Luhmann. What the legal system does, what the biosphere does, what the economy does, is that there's [...] whatever the current state of the system is [...] *that* creates what can arise next, which I call the adjacent possible. Then I use the phrase that – I like my phrase – we're *sucked* into the very adjacent possible that we, ourselves, create. Then that happens.

Cary: What's doing the sucking?

Stu: It's to our advantage to go into it to make money. For example, there's an economic opportunity. Our behavior creating the economic system created a new economic opportunity, and somebody goes and makes a living in that new economic opportunity – that's being sucked into it. It's not a force, I'm just using the phrase "sucked into it."

Cary: So, the "sucking" in the biosphere would be what, adaptive advantage?

Stu: It's adaptive advantage, yeah, I can become a new kind of snail, okay.

Cary: In the law, what would be doing the sucking?

Gaymon: The play of power and opportunity.

Stu: Yeah, whoever goes and tries the case and argues before [...]

Cary: It'd have to be a form of self-interest not reducible to economic self-interest, for the law [...]

Gaymon: Maybe not even self-interest. We can actually look at cases and figure things out.

Stu: I said "sucked" just to shock us [...]

Cary: [...] yeah yeah. I like "being sucked in" [...]

Gaymon: It has a kind of lure in that if a possibility space opens that implies other kinds of closures, and so there is a driving toward [...]

Stu: Right, and then the system goes into that, but that in turn creates a new adjacent possible, into which this becomes. And so, one of the things that I've thought about for a long time is, "is the adjacent possible growing or not?," meaning it's exactly the issue about the growing diversity of the law.

Cary: Well, I can answer that.

Stu: I think the answer's yes.

Cary: It *has* to be yes.

Stu: Yes, I think that in general the answer is yes. There's a deeper issue [...]

Gaymon: Although within niches, the answer is no.

Cary: Within niches, the answer is no. That's right.

Gaymon: So like, the things we've talked about before, the hyper-algorithmization of everyday life is a force that's constraining us [...]

Cary: Look at species loss, it's a perfect example.

Stu: So there's another issue, there's a big issue, "why did the universe get complex?," and this is just a crude intuition that I'm struggling with,

but it may be right. So: the universe has gotten really complex. Here's what the physicists say. They say, "isn't it neat that the universe is accelerating during its expansion?" That means that the maximum entropy of the universe is rising faster than the actual entropy of the universe. Therefore, there's free energy available to do work, and there always will be because of accelerating expansion. Okay, so hold that. Then they say "look, the constants of nature are finely tuned, so you get a complex universe." And they say, "isn't that cool?" That's what they contribute to the question of why the universe is complex, which you guys know, those are necessary conditions, they're not sufficient conditions. There's no argument that gives *sufficient* conditions for why the universe gets complex. Now, what we're talking about is why the legal system gets complex, why the economy gets complex. It's because they flow into an adjacent possible that they themselves create, right?

Stu: So let me give you guys an argument. Mike, I don't know if you've heard this babble of mine. You know what proteins are, they're sequences of amino acids. A typical protein in you has 300 amino acids, so now consider a protein with 200 amino acids. There's twenty kinds of amino acids. How many proteins are there made? 200. Well, 20 times 20, 200 times. That's 20 to the 200th, which is 10 to the 260th, right? Now let's ask if this means something. Could the universe have created all possible proteins, length 200 in the lifetime of the universe? No! Quick calculation.

Cary: As you said in the book, even if it's doing nothing but doing that on the Planck scale –

Stu: [...] right, couldn't do it [...]

Cary: [...] couldn't happen anyway, right. Not even close.

Stu: Yes. Can I just say it for these guys? So the Planck timescale is 10 to the −43rd seconds. There's 10 to the 80th particles. If they were doing nothing internal but making proteins length 200 on the Planck timescale and the universe is 10 to the 17th seconds old, it would take the age of the universe raised to 10 to the 39th power to make all proteins once, just once. Just once. This means something physical. Then I'm going to get to an intuition that I think is huge, but I don't know if it's right. It means that the universe is non-repeating, it's non-ergodic above the level of atoms. Okay, so history enters when the space of possibilities is vastly larger than what can happen. All the history we're talking about has to do with the universe being complex and non-ergodic, okay?

Cary: This is the core of the book [*Humanity in a Creative Universe*], as far as I'm concerned.

Stu: Yeah, part of it. So Cary, what I'm struggling with is the following: is there an anti-entropic process? You all know what the second law of thermodynamics is. Is there an anti-entropic process going on in the universe in which there's an infinite "space," "space" with scare quotes, upwards in complexity? The universe will never make all complex things, never. It won't make all possible organisms, it won't make all possible bladders, it won't make all possible rivers, it won't make all possible pebbles, it won't make all possible skyscrapers. It won't make all possible houses. Does this mean something physical, that there's a blossoming upward that's been going on in the biosphere since life started, and it's gone kaboom!, and it's created the biosphere, which has created an economy, which has created legal systems, which are all somehow released and becoming in this bubbling complexity, and I've got this intuition – it's too strong to say "intuition" – I've got this wondering, is there something vast going on that's right in front of us, and we can't say – yet? The universe becomes complex because it *can*, because there's infinite synch upward or indefinite synch upward in complexity, and the word "can" means it's not deterministic.

Cary: Right, and I would just add – the kind of Luhmannian piggyback on this would be – that that fact poses challenges for any autopoietic system that wants to continue to reproduce itself in a situation of increasing complexity. And how do systems deal with that? They deal with it through selectivity. And what does selectivity do? It increases the internal complexity of the systems that are trying to reduce environmental complexity. What does that do? It feeds back greater complexity into the aggregate environment.

Stu: Could we be saying the same thing?

Cary: So in terms of what the motor is, the motor is simply that systems, by doing what they do to try to get along in a situation increasing complexity, actually – in trying to *reduce* complexity – *increase* environmental complexity, and so you have the paradigmatic situation of increasing hypercomplexity. It's not for any *reason* in that sense, it's just that this is what any autopoietic system has to do to make its way in a world of increasing complexity.

Stu: That's great, Cary – that's great [...]

Cary: And you see this in the law, of course [...]

Stu: But you also see it in the biosphere.

Cary: Yeah, yeah, yeah.

Stu: Maybe you're putting your finger on it, or you and Luhmann are putting your fingers on it. If we buy that the autopoietic system, okay, creates its more complex world, into which it becomes and creates yet more complexity, okay, via the things that we were just saying before, right, look: then maybe we can get to this for the whole biosphere. Maybe we need autopoietic systems [...]

Stu: Maybe we need autopoietic systems. Which is fine for the biosphere. I mean organisms are autopoietic systems and corporations are autopoietic systems, right?

Gaymon: And legal niches are autopoietic systems [...]

Cary: Luhmann has a really Zen-like saying, he loves these little weird Zen-like formulations. He says somewhere, "only complexity can reduce complexity." And what he means by that is that systems that build up their own internal differentiation, or their own internal complexity – which is to say their own selectivity – have more ways of responding adaptively to environmental change than ones that only have an on/off switch, right? So the reason that you can respond to your environment and environmental complexity in myriad more ways than an amoeba can swimming up a sugar gradient is for that very reason.

Cary: And there's no *reason* for this except trying to continue your autopoiesis in this situation of increasing complexity [...]

Stu: Cary, that's [...] this is tying into [...] So I just finished my last book.

Stu: I'm sorry Mike if you've heard it. So the title of this book that's almost in press with Oxford is *A World Beyond Physics: On the Origin of the Evolution of Life*. One hundred pages. Of course, you can't do justice to the topic in 100 pages. So here's what it does. The first two thirds of the book is how to get to protocells from nothing. And the fundamental issue is how to make an autopoietic system. I used the idea of autocatalytic sets and an idea called constraint closure due to some guys in France – it's just astonishing – and some other things.

Cary: This is where you talk about the lipid bubbles.

Gaymon: The first time we met here in Santa Fe you walked us through this pretty carefully.

Stu: Did I? I really don't remember. It's just because I'm 78. There's a joke about it that I'll tell you guys.

Gaymon: Somehow you remember the jokes.

Stu: Everything but the punchline. The second part of the story is [...] Maybe I did tell you guys this. Once you've got protocells, the way they evolve can't be said – it's unprestatability. But they can *build* themselves. This is the constraint closure.

Cary: Exactly.

Stu: Did I tell you guys this idea? Of constraint closure?

Gaymon: Yeah. But walk through it again [...]

Stu: Okay I will in a second. I'll give you constraint closure and I'll do the two guys in France, Maël Montévil and Matteo Mossio. It's a system that builds its own boundary conditions. Boundary conditions are constraints on the release of energy that does work. You need constraints on the release of energy to get work. But you have to do work to get the constraints on the release of energy. Which is a notion that I came up with around twenty years ago, and these guys built on it to say you get a closure where you have a system that takes a set of non-equilibrium processes – like, say, three non-equilibrium processes – and each does work because there is a constraint on that non-equilibrium process so that it does work. So, there's three constraints and they're linked such that the system builds the very same constraints. That's constraint closure. It gives you something that's exactly what we want physically, but maybe not legally. It gives you a system that can build itself physically. Cells *build* themselves, they *construct* themselves. These two guys have come up with a fundamental notion that I think that is absolutely brilliant.

Stu: Now put it into a protocell, and the protocell *builds* itself. But it co-creates worlds with other protocells that differentiate. They do exactly the niche construction we discussed, so they create an ecosystem that goes and creates an adjacent possible into which they are sucked, and that's now the evolution of the biosphere.

Stu: It's a physical becoming upward into the indefinite complexity upward in the universe.

And it's physically becoming. And now we've got redwood trees. It's just astonishing we've got redwood trees. And if there are [...] there's now estimated to be 10 to the 22nd stars. Maybe 20 times 10 to the 22nd stars. And it's estimated that 10 percent to half of them have planets. What if on one thousandth of those there's biospheres? This becoming is happening all over the universe and it's *physical*. It's not just ideas. We're physical things, ok? We obviously are. So is the redwood tree. A redwood tree starts as a seed and constructs itself into a tree. Isn't that astonishing? It *builds* itself and builds a biosphere of trees that make room and niches for other trees and for rabbits. And they all become upward, in this indefinite complexity, higher, that I wonder if it's an anti-entropic process.

Stu: So that's what the book's about. Cary, it ties into exactly what you're saying Luhmann is saying. Let's try to define what we mean by an autopoietic legal system. Somehow a corporation is [...] Let's try to define what we mean by an autopoietic legal system that can then become [...] It conserves itself. IBM conserves itself and propagates IBM. Right? So if we can make the translation that's exactly what Luhmann says – that it's autopoietic, or I use the term autocatalytic – to make it into legal terms, then we've taken the ideas that we can drive all the way upward into legal systems, corporations, and other legal and social entities that create themselves, sustain themselves, and co-create a world in which they can become. So, Cargill does what it does. Well of course it does [...]

Cary: [...] right, but that [...]

Stu: [...] we're almost to a framework [...]

Cary: That's right. And that's the key. The big shift in Luhmann's thinking is when he actually takes the term autopoiesis from Maturana and says, "well, if you read the definition of an autopoietic system in Maturana, I don't see any reason why it doesn't apply to thinking about how social systems operate." And that's the big shift in his work. The key thing I would emphasize in what you're saying, Stu, is this: it's not for any *reason* [...]

Stu: Correct [...]

Cary: [...] and this is the difference between second-order systems theory of the sort that Luhmann's doing and the kind of stuff that you get in Bateson, for example – or one half of Bateson I would say. The key is that none of this is happening because all the things in the universe that are doing this want to be part of some large totality that's ever increasing and creative. It happens because of closure and selectivity. Constraint boundaries.

Stu: What do you mean right here?

Cary: The driver of this increasing complexity is not because all the entities who are involved in this are striving to be more complex or striving to be part of this larger totality. They are trying to reduce an increasingly complex environment, which they do through closure and selectivity. So, the second-order turn that people have trouble wrapping their head around is actually this openness from closure. Right? This closure that actually creates openness and creates complexity simply by systems doing what they do, what they *have to* do if they want to continue their autopoiesis.

Cary: And so, just to come back to my earlier point – going back to constraint boundaries that you were talking about earlier – it's through closure that systems are able to build up their own internal filters, you might say, their own internal selectivity, in relation to an environment in which they can't afford to have everything in the environment *count* in terms of whether they can continue their autopoiesis or not. They have to limit that shit, and they do it through their own internal filtering system, their own internal closure, their own internal –

Gaymon: And their own work on the environment.

Cary: And their own work on the environment. So, it's not like, "oh, I want to go be more complex." That's not what's going on. And that's why the process is blind and yet eventuates [...]

Stu: So this is my "getting sucked into" [...]

Cary: [...] Yeah. This is the sucking mechanism. You know, sucking or pushing, however you want to [...] I like sucking actually better. That's the second-order turn, it's to say "look, it's actually *through* closure that increasing openness to the environment is created." Go back to a bonobo vs. an amoeba. The bonobo has a zillion other ways to react to changes in its environment and deal with it adaptively than an amoeba has. Why? Because through selectivity it's built up its own internal complexity in relation to the environment. The bonobo is not *trying* be more complex or be non-ergodic. It's just doing what it does to get on in the world but that eventuates [...]

Stu: Let me throw something back at you guys that people say in evolutionary biology that I partially understand. Either the organisms [...] As evolution happens, organisms incorporate their environment and make models of their environment.

Cary: Yeah. That's what Luhmann calls "re-entry." The system–environment relationship is reentered into the system itself. Think about law. Let's say you're doing tort law or just pick whatever subspecialty of the law you want. The environment for that legal specialization is the law itself. So you get a re-entry of the system–environment relationship within the system itself, which drives the internal differentiation of that system. Same is true in higher education, right? In higher education we're trying to be more and more responsive to changes in our environment that have to do with so-called new social movements like feminism, or "Oh, wow, we're surrounded by non-human animals," etc. And so what you get is a proliferation of increasingly differentiated sub-disciplines [...] you know, cultural studies, animal studies, critical race studies, comparative ethnicity studies, gay and lesbian studies, and so on. You get an internal differentiation within education that's trying to respond to environmental complexity, changes in the environment. And so you get subspecialties within those disciplines. And there's a Foucauldian version of this, of course. Within the different social systems you have the same logic; you build up internal complexity under the pressure of environmental complexity, right?

Gaymon: Can I just add a couple variables in here?

Cary: I'm just giving a kind of a mini-description, Stu, of how Luhmann would think about this.

Gaymon: This is good because it's like we're – this is good, because we're recursively synthesizing things we've talked about before and putting it together, and in that spirit, a couple of other variables. I think once you start paying attention to the fact that these systems are not just autopoietic, but also non-prestatable [...]

Stu: Yup [...]

Gaymon: Then it no longer becomes interesting just to show how a given example, like an education system, reproduces a set of macrodynamics. Rather, if it's non-prestatable, then you actually have to go into specificities, it's this education system here rather than some other one, and we have to understand that it's these sets of actors rather than those sets of actors, embedded in these histories rather than some other histories, and this is where we get then to the question of what are the styles of reasoning that are afforded when a kind of scientific disposition and a humanist disposition come together in the manner of, the two cultures manner that Stu was pointing to [...]

Gaymon: That's one. I think the non-prestatable or non-algorithmic aspect of autopoiesis means that the demands of inquiry are different, that you have to pay attention to things at the level of, I like to say at the level of proper nouns, in a way that you wouldn't otherwise.

Stu: Could you restate that again?

Gaymon: You have to pay attention to these dynamics at the level of proper nouns. I mean by that what you were saying earlier about historical specificity. You have to tell a story relative to what's going on, and these patterns of generality, the dynamics, the sort of meta-dynamics are actual, but they're actual in a way that drives you toward the particularities. They don't provide your answer for you as to what's going on. They just parameterize the conversation in a certain way, and it seems to me that it's the autopoiesis *plus* the non-prestatable character of this that demands a certain style of inquiry.

Cary: That's right.

Stu: Can I ask you something, well, something I've wondered about for a long time. Did you use the phrase "story"?

Gaymon: Ah, I may have.

Stu: Or "narrative." The reason is that the proper noun account is a narrative, right? It's a story.

Gaymon: It's a narrative in the sense that particular things are happening, and that in order to account for them, you have to account for those particular things. You have to find some way of providing an account of those particularities and their interactions. Narrative might be one way of doing that.

Cary: But you see this in law all the time. I mean, I don't know enough about the history of law, but you see this so clearly in the law all the time, where it's like well, some guy in this particular case went over here and made this brilliant argument and it completely changed the kinds of rulings that could be made for the next forty years, even though they all feel kind of counterintuitive and they maybe don't make sense, but that's the narrative. It's like okay, how is the systematicity of the law's autopoiesis operating under constraint at that moment, and how did that lead to, but not determine, a whole history of rulings [...]

Gaymon: And just to pick up something that Mike was pushing last night is once you have an evental ontology, now you can start paying attention to particular transformations that are happening. This is coherent with a non-prestatable sensibility. Things happen in sets of relationships that have effects both local and global. The autopoietic plus the non-prestatable is one I just wanted to flag. Another one I wanted to flag is that these dynamics don't always just drive towards complexity. Some of the niches reduce complexity within a certain zone. If I'm [...]

Cary: Well that's what a niche is, in a way, right? It's an attempt [...]

Gaymon: If I'm Cargill, and I'm an autopoietic system, if you want to imagine Cargill in that way, I want to take enough control of enough variables that I now can exercise power in such a way that I can begin to anticipate the near future and minimize risk relative to my own power in the world. That matters to me for lots of reasons, but it seems to me that one of them that has come up with this group is that these links between zones of constraint and the exercise of power are having effects on what adjacent possibilities consist in. One of the political demands of the day then is to ask the question, "which adjacent possibilities are being foreclosed and opened, and how is that a function of the way in which certain powerful actors in the world are constraining possibility by way of constraining complexity?" You know, we could tell some story about the fact that they're not actually constraining complexity, it's popping up in other places in different ways, but nonetheless, there's this way in which there's a kind of, to use the language, a mono-culturing of certain cultural niches wherein certain things don't become possible.

Gaymon: For my work around biology and biotechnology, that becomes quite significant in that the most powerful actors in high tech have an algorithmic view of reality, and are now colonizing biotechnology such that the spaces of adjacent possibility in the scientific imagination among bioengineers is being governed by a philosophy of living things that's fundamentally algorithmic, and therefore on some level that means lots of stuff they try doesn't work, because it turns out living things don't like to play nicely with algorithmic rationalities. But on another level, they have enough *social* power that they can make *some* of it work *some* of the time, and then eliminate all of these other spaces of adjacent possibility in which somebody would try something less algorithmic and more vitalistic.

Stu: Right.

Gaymon: That's an example of the ways in which, I think these closures and constraints, these efforts to reduce complexity by certain powerful systems or powerful actors, are themselves a kind of site of inquiry within the proliferation of complexity. It's just my way of saying let's pay attention to places where complexity's being reduced and not just propagated. That was just a third thing to just add in here. I think the paper, the stuff you guys have been working on around the ontological status of *potentia*, for me, and this is a function of the way in which we've had these conversations. For me, it takes this seminal insight around constraint autopoiesis and non-prestatability and suggests that that insight is not only generative for thinking up into the complexity of the universe and the possibilities of complexity, but it's also generative for thinking down. I know up and down don't quite work here, for thinking down in that once you have these autocatalytic or autopoietic characteristics in the universe, you begin to understand something about the universe. This is a universe that has the potential for experience, it has potential for being alive in this manner, and that's not just true about what it can drive forward.

Gaymon: It also then, at least epistemically, allows you look backward or look downward and see that the fundamental characteristics of reality are such that you'll eventually get autopoietic systems. That's both philosophically and social-scientifically, that's quite profound, because it means then those things in the world that we thought weren't alive are actually capable of experience in a certain kind of way that *anticipates* the sorts of living things, the sorts of things we might otherwise put in the bucket of living things.

Cary: I want to read you a passage that's relevant to this. You know Russell Winslow? He lives in Santa Fe. I did a blurb for his book, *Organism and Environment: Inheritance and Subjectivity in the Life Sciences*. We should connect with this guy while we're here. I was going to wait and see if you knew him, Stu. He teaches philosophy at St John's College.

Stu: St John's College is about a mile and a half from here.

Cary: Yeah, so I did a blurb for this book, and I'm kind of re-reading it in relation to my stuff, but I just want to read a passage from this that's really relevant to what you were just talking about, and this is on the biological side. He says, "while the standard theory of evolution attempts to explain the internal configuration of the forms of living organisms – their adaptive qualities – strictly in terms of the natural selection pressures of their *external* environments which are inherited genetically by offspring, niche construction theory suggests that, insofar as organisms construct their environments in a variety of ways, they also actively contrive selection pressures in their milieu *which then select them*." He's talking here about John Odling-Smee. He says, number one, "standard evolutionary theory explains evolutionary change and organisms as a function of the relation between organisms and environment; and it explains change in environments strictly as function of the relation between the environment and itself – that is to say autonomously."

Cary: "Two, niche construction explains evolutionary change in organisms as a function of the relation between organisms and environment, and explains change in environments as a function of the relationship between organisms and environment [...] That is to suggest, the organism modifies the selection pressures of the environment and then passes these modifications along to the next generation in the form of DNA *and* milieu. That much is clear. But as profound as that is, there's something more profound happening as this calculus unfolds: there is a way that the environments of organisms become *selected*; they change in accordance with the change of organisms: *the space of the living being evolves and processes*. The meaning of the biological space of niche construction theory changes in such a way as to be other than an external environment composed by a mere deterministic flux and flow of mechanics. It is rather an organismic space [...]" – this goes back to what you were talking about, Stu [...]

Cary: "[...] In niche construction theory, however, the relationship between genome and milieu exhibits far more interrelation, more complication. Such complication illuminates a reconfiguration of space and time" (*Organism and Environment: Inheritance and Subjectivity in the Life Sciences*, Lexington, 2017, 120–21) – and then he goes on to elaborate how that happens. That is what you were talking about, Stu – what's the point of niche construction? It's like well, I'm a beaver and I build these dams, I can create an environment that's more inviting as a constraint upon my form of life and not others. Then that changes the environment [...]

Gaymon: That's right, and Monsanto [...]

Cary: You get flooding over here, right, because of this [...]

Gaymon: That's right, it has these non-comm effects [...]

Cary: Yeah, yeah yeah, so that's already a much more complex dynamic [...]

Mike: So what's interesting is when a system itself gets to decide whether or not a particular self-imposed constraint should be exceeded or when the balance between increased *potentia* and restricted *potentia* is wrong. The system itself gets to decide, "Hey, this particular constraint is no longer relevant or no longer beneficial." You use the word algorithm and yeah, you're right. We're an algorithmic culture increasingly, it seems to me. I hate it. Why are we so open to it? I think we're open to it because it's pitched to us as it will be *good* for us to be reductively constrained.

Gaymon: Well, it's non-constraint, that it's pitched to us as non-constraint [...]

Mike: Yes, it's pitched to us as it's a way of *liberating* ourselves, right, but in fact, it's not. Algorithmic reduction is constraint by definition. It's like 9/11 and the Patriot Act – liberation from terror through additional constraint. America's all about liberty vs. law. It's restrictions of our liberties when it's beneficial to us and it's the extension of our liberties when we feel too constrained. And it's always a tug of war when we've gone too far one way or the other. The Patriot Act was a particularly dramatic example. We had to get used to a new level of constraint that we hadn't really had to deal with before. But it's good for us because it keeps us safe. That phrase, I hate it. It's used so often now in politics. "Keep us safe." Before 9/11, I never heard that phrase the way we do now – like some national mantra. I never walked around worrying about my safety, and the idea, "Oh, please constrain me, because it keeps me safe!" That's a new concept, and we've welcomed it.

Cary: Exactly, *hygienically*. As you're describing that I have this picture: outside of every elevator there's hand sanitizer [...]

Stu: Is there really?

Cary: Oh yeah.

Gaymon: We're killing ourselves through sanitation, so these hygienic regimes of keeping ourselves safe in fact are creating these outsides, which are ultimately going to destroy the insides.

Cary: Well, and this is where the immunitary/autoimmunitary core of biopolitical thought is absolutely spot on, right? Biologically, this is where the food allergy thing with kids comes from. When I was a kid, there were no food allergies.

Stu: Can I come back to this thing that you just read?

Cary: Yeah, yeah.

Stu: That's right on and it's big, right? I hadn't realized it, and I'm only dimly realizing this right now having heard it, but this notion of niche construction is that organisms create their worlds that they then live in, but they co-create new worlds as they co-evolve with one another. The worlds of organisms, that's right, is utterly non-random.

Cary: That's right.

Stu: The same thing's true for corporations, right? They create their worlds, they do niche construction. It's kind of funny to say it, but isn't it right, that Cargill and Monsanto engage in niche construction.

Gaymon: They do. Apple and Google and Facebook do too. The trouble is that we think of niches as quite specialized, localized sorts of things, but in fact, these are big cultural niches where at first they don't just create the niche, but they co-create, as you just said, with a drive toward maximizing their ability to control the variables in the niche. One of the things that came up last night that Cary was pointing to is this creates an economy in which other niches begin to get populated in a compensatory relationship to the problems created by this sort of niche construction. I hate to live under the regime of Google, as it were, and so now I'm going to have to exit and meditate, or the medical apparatus is not able to deal with the autoimmune problems, so you begin to get a new niche around alternative medicine that has a functionally connected relationship to this niche construction.

Cary: Or with foodways: because you get Cargill and Tyson and Monsanto doing their thing, what do you get, you get "The Omnivore's Dilemma." You get these entire niches that are their own economies and have their own logics.

Gaymon: And their own ethos.

Cary: And their own ethos, right, right.

Mike: But isn't it true that Cargill and Google and all these entities that we keep going to when we ask the question, "Where did this constraint come from? Who authored this constraint? What was the intention?" [...] My feeling is that none of those things would happen were it not for the fact that the individual decides "I'm ready for a new constraint!" or "I'm ready for the elimination of a prior constraint!" It's the individual who decides. The question I have is why? What is it that motivates an individual to make that decision? I don't know. Somehow we decide that it increases our own fitness, or it is to our immediate advantage to adopt this new constraint. Like somebody had to say, "Gee, a self-driving car would be great!" Who? Who came up with this stupid idea in the first place?

Gaymon: Well, somebody came up with the idea, but back to this adjacent possibility: part of the reason a company like Google started thinking about all of this is because they had opened up spaces of possibility, into which you can throw an imagination of a future into that adjacent possibility and you pursue it.

Mike: Right, but now there's been a pushback, I guess is what I'm trying to say. You see it more frequently now. Maybe it's because the Russians were involved in 2016 or whatever, but people are now demanding new levels of constraint when it comes to say, the freedom of expression via a platform like Twitter or Facebook. We're looking suspiciously at those platforms now, whereas before it was like, all they do is "make the world a better place." All they do is increase the *potentia* for communication and understanding globally for anyone who participates in these networks. Now the language has changed. Now we look at these platforms as publishers. We say Facebook is a publisher, and therefore it should be constrained in the same way that any other mass media publication is constrained legally.

Mike: We know how Facebook feels about it. They don't like it. But how does the *individual* who plays in these networks feel about it? The average human beings on social media, how do they feel about it? I have no freaking idea.

Gaymon: Yeah, and of course, there *are* no average human beings.

* * *

santa fe, ii: from biosemiotics to biodynamics and the "eco-" of economies

Stu: Okay, we were talking about niche construction. Right?

Cary: Yes.

Stu: That idea is that organisms create their worlds. Then they live in the worlds that they create. Then they co-create it with one another, and they co-evolve in weird ways to make ever flowering worlds that become and inter-mesh in all sorts of complicated ways. The same thing is true for the economy, and so on. A funny branch of biology is called biosemiotics.

Cary: Yeah, I know about biosemiotics.

Stu: Yeah, so biosemiotics has to do with the notions that organisms have signs. So here it is. Take a bacterium, and it's got receptors on its surface for ten things out in the world. Oxygen, and pH balance, and photons, or [...] Ten things. So, just think of the ten receptors, on or off, bad or not bad. So the world of that organism consists in two to the tenth possible worlds. That's it.

Stu: So, the organism has created its world that it's responding to, and it screens out everything else. Doesn't care about everything else. That's precisely, I think, that's the same thing as what you were saying about ignoring much of the environment, but paying attention to some of the environment, is the way you were putting it before. Constraints of simplifying. Simplifying the world. It only pays attention to a thousand different worlds, not a zillion different worlds. But notice that, that's because the specific receptors that it happens to have evolved to put on its surface.

Cary: Yes.

Stu: Otherwise [...]

Gaymon: It has a semiotic body.

Stu: It has a semiotic body, but it might have had a different semiotic body, had it evolved different receptors.

Cary: Of course, yes.

Cary: That's right. This all, the biosemiotic stuff that goes back to Jakob von Uexküll's discussion of the tick.

Stu: Which, I don't know if know [...]

Cary: [...] yeah but that's the *locus classicus*, and that's why Agamben said [...]

Stu: Can I just finish what I was going to say?

Cary: Yeah. Yeah. Sure, go ahead.

Stu: But, now including that, that organism one can evolve [...] So I want to say, two things:

organism one can evolve receptors to notice organism two. Okay? The bacterium can notice the paramecium that's coming to eat it. And vice versa. So, they mutually create worlds that include one another by having whatever you need as a receptor to pick that up. Now they're co-creating their worlds with one another. And there's something else that I can say, but I know what I mean but I can't really say it.

Stu: Organisms play incredibly complicated games with one another. They behave with one another in all kinds of complicated ways. For example, once there's predator and prey, the prey can evolve camouflage to avoid the predator. But you've got to have a predator for it to matter to evolve camouflage. Well, rocks don't evolve camouflage. Organisms do. There's something about an increasingly complex world that organisms make in which they can then evolve [...] oh my goodness [...] new strategies. Right? We evolve new strategies with one another. That therefore creates new niches, which creates new environments, which creates [...] Okay. Now I'm losing the word. It creates niche construction, but you're part of my niche. We're all part of one another's niche.

Cary: That's right.

Stu: We're co-creating it, and we become that way so that the world [...] a billion years later, or a thousand years later, or a hundred years later [...] has all these different things in it. That all got constructed by this, and it's all being sucked into the opportunity. So, now that's the same thing that you were saying before, that ties it to social systems.

Cary: Well, and I would add, a super important part of this is: this is all non-representational.

Stu: Absolutely.

Cary: So with the paramecium, the amoeba does not need – and in fact it's extra baggage to even try to have – a theory of the paramecium coming toward it. All it needs to know is the minimum thing that it needs to know about that thing and being eaten. So, it doesn't need a representation of the paramecium. The same [...]

Gaymon: Can we slice that a little more thinly?

Cary: Yeah.

Gaymon: Which is via Peirce on this stuff. Where I think lots of it comes out of Peirce's Indexicality.

Cary: Oh, yeah. Of course.

Gaymon: It's sort of biological indexicality. We have semiotic bodies. I can know things about the world because we send and we see signs. That, there are in fact representations, but it turns out they're non-symbolic representations. Because my internal states change as a result of the fact that I know you're trying to eat me.

Cary: Yes.

Gaymon: And I can remember it. So, the epigenetic stuff.

Cary: Yeah, but my only point is that there's a difference between *that*, what you just described, and any question of representational accuracy that would map on to a third-party point of view of what's going on with the paramecium.

Gaymon: That's right.

Cary: Right?

Gaymon: This is embodied perspective [...]

Cary: That's right.

Gaymon: It's very semiotic, in this indexical sense.

Cary: That's right. So, Bateson, in *Steps to Ecology of Mind*, has this great example about camouflage in animals, with two types of fish called the wrasse and the blenny. And his point is that, the same form of camouflage that initially served to attract animals into a certain relationship to this fish, to serve as a cleaner fish, and so on [...] can later, on the evolutionary scale, end up being exactly the opposite. It's a lure for cleaner fish who get eaten. Right? And so, the point is, the reason it's non-representational is that you can't take just the formal features of the camouflage, or the formal features of any semiotic utterance, and locate the meaning there. The meaning of it is in relation to the changing dynamic state of the system itself.

Mike: Yeah, yeah, that's exactly right [...]

Cary: *That's* where the meaning is [...]

Gaymon: This is where we were going last night [...]

Cary: [...] and that's why it's non-representational because there's nothing to represent, in that sense.

Gaymon: That's right.

Gaymon: This is like last night when we were talking around the inductive global, and the local, and the global. This is like the localized state [...] we were using the example of the wine glass as the localized state [...] but all of this becomes all the more complex when your actuality, that has a relationship with the global, is a matter of signification.

Mike: Yeah.

Gaymon: Because these systems have signification, the meaning is in these sets of relationships.

Cary: Oh, yeah yeah [...]

Gaymon: [...] and those shifting sets of relationships have shifting sets of signification. That localized signification has this effect on [...] This is how I was understanding your comment about the inductive global [...] So, now the state of the global is not just [...] you're not just perturbing local things to perceive things about the global that are just physical. You're perturbing things about the signification of the configuration of the local that tells you something about the change in the global.

Mike: Right.

Cary: No, that's right. I mean, the way Luhmann puts this in *Social Systems*, he says: look, if I get up in the morning and I read in the newspaper that the Euro has fallen by 0.2 percent, that's *information* that changes the state of the system. Right? But if I were to read the same utterance in a second newspaper two hours later, it has the same formal features but it doesn't have the same meaning as information for the system, right?

Cary: So, he makes a joke. He says, you can say "a rose, is a rose, is a rose," but that's only meaningful if changes in the system do not *always* obtain based on the formal features of that utterance, right? So that's why I sort of insist on this non-representational point. You have to have a non-representational theory of meaning, and the biosemiotics people have one way of trying to do this. But that's what Uexküll was trying to do. Uexküll was trying to say, "Look. It's not about the tick. It's about these three features, that this particular" – to go back to your example, Stu – "that this life form has that constrain its relationship to its world." And this is how it builds its world.

Stu: Let me clarify something else that I've wondered about for a long time. I'm pretty sure I'm right about organisms, like bacteria. The question is, is that also true for organizations like IBM?

* * *

Stu: In the corporation, there's a bunch of roles. They're called jobs. So the task of the corporation [...] we'll call those roles. And there's a bunch of people fulfilling the roles, right? I'm the CEO. One of you is the CFO, and somebody else is the mail clerk, all right? That thing creates an organization that sustains itself by, for example, selling products in the real world by which it gets the money to continue to exist. Right? Now, I wonder if the following might not be true.

Stu: The roles are the analog of the constraints on the release of energy. They're constraints. A role or a job is a constraint on how you should behave, and the people fulfilling it are fulfilling those roles. That is the constrained release of human energy into particular, specific tasks. That might be right, so let me try it again: the jobs are the analogs of the constraints on the release of energy. They're the analogs of the canon. It's directing where the energy should go. I should file things or I should be CEO and do CEO things and so on.

Stu: The idea is the jobs that are being done in a corporation constitute the constraints, and the people fulfilling the jobs are doing the constrained release of energy or the analog of the constrained release of energy. They're specific human actions, and people could do anything, but in fact, you're filing stuff in the filing room, okay, because that's your job. That's the thought. If something like that is right, and I don't know how to think about the legal part, the laws that enable the corporation, then maybe we could say social systems really are autopoietic systems.

Stu: If we could say that, then we get to where – we were talking about this this morning – these things co-evolve with one another, create their *umwelt*, their environment, create their adjacent possibility, come into their adjacent possible, always in unprestatable ways. They propagate. They propagate and construct themselves, which is sort of saying [...] so like Monsanto has propagated like mad and it's extended its power to control all over the place. Okay, that's what I wanted to say.

Adam: Well, this is really interesting. But a couple things to note. One thing would be the meaning of the job in this context, because what you're talking about here is not a simple social system. But what you're referring to is the distribution of work in a techno-social system, right?

Stu: Yeah.

Adam: I mean, increasingly, the kind of work that's happening within an organization is actually happening through automated technologies. I think that has to be part of the equation. The social conditions of work are fundamentally changing. So I wonder how that figures into what you're saying. That's the first thing. The second thing to add to the equation relates to the question of law. I think [...]

Stu: [...] of law?

Adam: [...] of law indeed. Here's the thing: you were just asking about what's generating the constraints, right? That was, as you said, your addition. I wonder how we would think about lobbying in your description. For example, it's not simply that laws create the conditions under which corporations can function, but corporations generate the laws under which corporations can function.

Stu: Right.

Gaymon: This came up this morning. We talked about niche construction and the way in which dominant players within a niche, within a social environment [...] You know, Monsanto or whoever doesn't get constrained by the law precisely because it goes out and it shapes it.

Adam: So this means that a corporation constructs its own niche – including the laws that make it possible – so that it can continue to do the work that it does.

Cary: Yeah, I mean [...] this is a good point because to go back to talking about Luhmann this morning, social systems for him – and there's a long history of arguments about this in sociology – but for him, human beings are not the constitutive elements of social systems. Communications are, functions are. Human beings can enter into, as participants in these systems, [...]

Stu: What are the two things, functions and what?

Cary: Communications are actually are the constitutive elements of social systems continuing their autopoiesis. So, being able to respond to their environment in ways in which information that comes from the environment is processed by and changes the state of the system in a positive way for the autopoiesis of the system. So I think that's one reason to think of it that way: that these functions that maintain the autopoiesis of the system in relation to its environment can be fulfilled in a number of ways. But human beings actually are not constitutive of the system. And you can easily imagine – and I'm sure there are plenty of them that exist – corporations *without people* that are nevertheless responding to environmental change and processing that environmental change in a way that continues the autopoiesis [...]

Adam: Well, the way this is going, it means that humans actually become *noise*. They're noisy elements in the system.

Cary: Yeah, exactly [...]

Adam: They're clunky, right?

Phil: I thought your slip was really interesting when you went from communications to functions.

Cary: Yeah, well it's because communications *are* functions within that scheme, right?

Phil: Right, but would we define them as functions and not necessarily communications. They end up being much more thermodynamic in the sense that Stu was talking about [...]

Cary: Yeah, yeah that makes sense [...]

Stu: Could I ask you something and then ask *you* something? An autocatalytic set has the following properties: you define the function of a peptide in an autocatalytic set as catalyzing the reaction that makes the next peptide, but it's irrelevant whether or not it jiggles water on the Petri plate. Functions are a subset of the causal consequences – claim one.

Cary: This is a huge part of your book.

Stu: Yeah. Claim two is an autocatalytic set achieves functional closure [...]

Cary: [...] that's right [...]

Stu: Now a question about the definition, for example, of a firm in terms of functions. Does it achieve functional closure?

Cary: Well, I mean, if you're going to stay with the line of thinking you're proposing, the answer has to be yes.

Stu: OK.

Cary: It has to be.

Gaymon: This is a genuine question and part of what's tricky about it is, is it a question in search of an answer that's going to confirm it? I'm just trying to imagine, ethnographically, some of the biotech companies I've worked with. You know, they're actors in the world that unleash forces and they're shaped by forces, and you can kind of name them but naming them becomes kind of tricky business because people involved in the construction of those companies are engaged in a practice of self-identity. That is to say they're claiming ownership of themselves, and they actualize themselves through those processes. I begin by thinking are corporations [...] do they have enough self-enclosure and self-identity to be thought of as self-making, autopoietic? So, that's one [...]

Gaymon: Then in relationship to that, there are ways of describing a corporation as a kind of assemblage that belies the presumed integrity, the performative integrity of the corporation.

So, just to pick one company that I've interacted with: Amyris Biotechnologies was created by this guy Jay Keasling in the early 2000s. It's going to take a pathway that produces a precursor to malaria medication Artemisinin. They're pretty good at that.

Gaymon: The company's in part Jay Keasling's personality, and he's a good manager. But it's in part Jay Keasling being a member of the molecular and cell biology department at UC Berkeley at a time in which, if you're not starting corporations, eyebrows are being raised at you. This is, like, 2000. If this had been twenty years earlier, his department wouldn't have had intellectual property lawyers but now they have intellectual property lawyers so he's meeting with the intellectual property lawyers. He gets this going.

Gaymon: The Gates Foundation becomes very interested in it because now they can tell a story about scalability of biotechnological interventions into major social problems, so there's a major influx of Gates' attention to this, which has this permutational effect on the way in which global health funding is going into these domains. So NGOs now start thinking about their relationship to biotech companies. Amyris Biotechnologies begins to roll forward [...]

Gaymon: They realize they're not going to be able to make it work just on the pharmaceutical stuff, so they discover that the pathway that they engineer is also useful for a precursor to butane as a jet fuel. So now they begin to tell a story about biofuels, but that's in this post-9/11 moment, and so they're telling a story on the one hand about American securitization, on the other hand about global climate change, and they're going to have these international relationships with big fuel producers in Brazil, okay, the story goes on and on [...]

Gaymon: There are ways of telling the story of Amyris that doesn't seem like it has self-enclosure, despite the fact that it has these sort of bootstrapped moments of self-propelling. And so, the question I'd want to ask is sort of, what kind of entity is this?

Cary: Right.

Gaymon: How does the ontology of that entity change given its state in its own life cycle? Does it have a life cycle?

Cary: Right [...]

Gaymon: [...] because Amyris Biotechnologies is not Monsanto, so what's the ontology of Monsanto? Is it autopoietic or – this is the last point, I've said too much about this – but in that Deleuzian style, is this in part a function of what we're grasping as the thing we're attaching to the name Monsanto? Can you imagine it [...]

Cary: [...] right [...]

Gaymon: [...] both as an autopoietic thing as well as a distributed assemblage?

Cary: Right, and so the question would be what would the more restricted definition of what the company is, what kind of purchase would that get you in understanding the relationship between the company's ability to do what it does and turn a profit in relation to all these environmental factors [...] So everything you just described, from an autopoiesis point of view, those are all environmental changes in the [...] – including the guy's personality, by the way, but also what's going on at Berkeley, et cetera – those are all changes in the environment of the company that could cut for better or for worse in terms of the company refining its functionality.

Gaymon: But this requires a conceptual judgment about the difference between what counts as the environment and what counts as the thing itself.

Cary: Precisely so, right? So the question is – the pragmatic questions to me would be: ok, if you can use these different descriptions (and we could use more descriptions to look at this), what kind of purchase do you gain by figuring out, for example, what the fuck are you talking about when you're talking about a company? How much of this stuff is *essential* to the company doing what it does or not?

Gaymon: They seem poetic. They seem non-prestatable. They seem to be major players in the construction of social niches such that those niches begin to favor their way of being in the world and other things have to conform to them. You know, like, we talked this morning about the transformation of farming practices around Monsanto's intellectual property regimes in a way that drove forward [...]

Cary: [...] right, right. But [to Stu] it sounds like what you're [...] Your desire underneath everything you're saying is for a kind of a natural law of companies, is what [...]

Stu: Well, no [...]

Cary: If you could actually come up with [...]

Stu: What I'm wanting is something like the following. So this morning, I brought up this idea from this book that I haven't read, the Ancient Greeks thought in terms of order and chaos, where order was the celestial spheres and chaos was the earth where [...] whatever. Don't know that that's right. Trying to make the claim that order is where you find law, like Newton and quantum mechanics and stuff, and the earth is where you don't find laws. So what I want is, an unprestatable [...]

Stu: [...] I want to know when can you have law and when can't you. And I want to say that history enters in the non-ergodic universe, and I want to say that the two cultures meet when one wants to explain, for example, how Monsanto did what it did, which is the specific historical becoming of a thing that can propagate organization. Monsanto propagates its own organization and so does an autocatalytic set that creates the world of companies co-evolving with one another. So it's not that I want a law. In fact, I don't want a law. I want a historical becoming, but carriers of organization [...]

Cary: [...] yeah yeah, sure, I understand that.

Adam: I think what we're getting at is something like, and I could be wrong here, but something like corporations are particular kinds of organizations that historically inscribe themselves [...] Well, if we're talking about corporations as social structures, then autopoiesis is a historical moment for a corporation [...]

Stu: Is a what?

Adam: [...] is a historical moment. In other words, I think that what we're doing is like detective work [...] where we're hunting down ontologies. I mean this is sort of a regional ontology, if you like, or something that [...] Maybe regional ontology is not quite right, but corporations become or resemble autopoietic systems within particular historical conditions, right? And sometimes they are autopoietic, and sometimes they're not? Maybe I'm wrong, but [...]

Gaymon: We're saying that, in this regional way, there are moments in which they can be described as having autopoietic dynamics [...]

Stu: Let's draw – Maturana and Varela do this – let's draw a distinction between a system that is autopoietic and *maintains* itself. Further, it can also reproduce. You don't have to have reproduction to have autopoiesis. I don't think that firms reproduce. I think they maintain themselves.

Adam: But Stu, you're actually getting [...] or rather, you said you want to move away from this idea of a law and you want to talk about the historical becoming – you can actually begin to talk about the historical becoming of things like autopoiesis. The autopoiesis of a corporation is not something that's given. It's something that's become possible given certain historical conditions.

Phil: I think this is a really fascinating discussion because I think this is what we bring to the table that second-order systems theory doesn't do yet, right? Second-order systems theory is – and Cary, please, correct me – is excellent at thinking about provisional closure and self-reference [...]

Stu: Thinking about what?

Phil: Provisional closure.

Gaymon: [...] having achieved provisional closure.

Phil: It's not so good about thinking about "can we locate some type of formation, some type of consistency?," before you get that closure? Matter of fact, Simondon is not good at thinking about that either. Both are much more interested in the pragmatic equivalents that happen afterwards when the question that's really interesting here is much more of a political question.

Cary: Right, and that was my point about what purchase do you gain in using the kind of restrictive sense of a company's autopoiesis that we started out with.

Phil: That's right.

Cary: How does that help you in terms of being able to look at a big assemblage and say, "Yeah, all this shit's going on [...]

Gaymon: [...] and yet [...]

Cary: [...] but what are we talking about?" The bottom line is, can the company deal with all this in the services of growing itself?

Phil: Correct [...]

Cary: [...] in refining its functionality, right? So [...]

Gaymon: Cargill doesn't need to be a centered being in order to act like one.

Cary: No, no, no. Exactly. And with the Monsanto example, the difference between a startup and Monsanto is Monsanto can massively control and predict its environment in a way that a small mom and pop corporation can't. That's why they spend all this fucking money to do that, right?

Gaymon: So let's flag work, which I think is quite important here. Maybe not jobs. I'm thinking about Adam's point on jobs, and I think jobs are maybe too internal to the life of the organism to be the constraint that drives it. I don't know. We'd have to think more about it, but there's clearly work being done. I'm very much interested in the kind of provocation that autopoiesis itself needs to be historicized and detailed, such that it gets enacted in ways that are non-prestatable. That means that lots of people and processes and organizations and forces have to do work in [...]

Gaymon: [...] it's not as though Monsanto has a kind of substantive ontology that will just sit there in the world and continue to exist if it's left alone. It constantly has to reanimate itself as a thing in the world. Providing a historicist description of that kind of labor that allows it to maintain its "auto-" such that it could be "poietic" [...]

Phil: [...] and that often involves working *against* the other aspects of poiesis, that type of closure.

Gaymon: [...] spell that out [...]

Phil: Sometimes you need to focus on the guy who's jerking off in the basement, right? 'Cause *that's* work even if it's not work toward closure [...]

Gaymon: Right [...]

Stu: Phil, I heard what you said. Let me try this. I think it's like the function of your heart is to pump blood, but your heart makes heart sounds and jiggles water in the pericardial sac. Those are *not* the functions of your heart [...]

Cary: [...] that's the jerking off in the basement [...]

Phil: [...] that's the jerking off in the basement [...]

Adam: [...] that's the kind of unproductive work [...]

Stu: [...] that's the jiggling water in the pericardial sac [...]

Phil: That's right, that's right, but that's work that is leading to reproduction without leading to closure [...]

Cary: Right, but that's the virtue I think of the restricted sense of a corporation that we're talking about. You could simply say, "look, ideally, from the corporation's point of view, what would be ideal would be to have *no* employees" [...]

Adam: [...] yeah yeah [...]

Phil: [...] that's friction [...]

Cary: [...] and *no* physical, no "noise" [...] The completely frictionless elimination of all that crap where you've got to have the millennials sleeping together in a big dorm room and calling out for pizza and listening to music so they can have their brilliant ideas. From the restricted point of view of a corporation, the ideal would be, "Actually, we don't have any employees. We don't have to deal with anything." So there's a pure refinement of the functionality of the company's reproduction of itself. At the same time, that "noise," the millennials having their pizza party, may be a source of creativity and may become an asset for the company's functionality [...] You can't just sit still [...]

Adam: That's what capital's really good at figuring out: the points of resistance and knowing, okay, the workers are working on a thing that could become dangerous, and so what we need to do is actually invent new conditions of work to allow them to be distributed and work in coffee shops on laptops, or some other configuration, that inscribes new forms of precarity, that doesn't allow for the old forms of resistance to take place.

Cary: Yeah, but see that's where I think you can come back to Gaymon's sketch a minute ago with Amyris and say, okay, now you can circle back and say of that long list of stuff that you just itemized – which is qualitatively heterogeneous – now you can circle back and say, "okay, how does the company turn that heterogeneity into some refined functionality" [...]

Gaymon: [...] that names itself [...]

Cary: [...] that's right. And in some cases, even use and *create* this qualitative heterogeneity to refine its functionality.

Adam: So Stu, basically, what they're saying is essentially how do you take all this noise that is sort of working against the coordination of the system and how do you turn that noise into something that's productive for the reproduction of the system?

Cary: That's straight-up Bateson [...] that's [...]

Phil: Historically, it was important to form corporations in the first place, right? And I think that's an important, key piece [...]

Cary: [...] that's boundary formation, yeah [...]

Phil: This is exactly where I see your stuff [to Cary] on autoimmunity actually coming into relationship to this, dealing with a similar type of fundamental discordance with the organisms, right? To proliferate or to specialize [...]?

Cary: Yeah, and if a corporation is just a state within the immunity/autoimmunity paradigm [...] If corporations over-purify, then they undergo a transition state from immunity to autoimmunity.

Gaymon: Yeah [...]

Cary: If they over-refine, what happens? They become brittle. They lose touch with the world [...]

Gaymon: And notice when, just in the spirit of that, when you get the dominance of niche construction, if you begin to work on the constraints of the niche such that you can survive, you've stopped doing the vigilant work of self-maintenance such that you're actualizing your own ontology in the world and get sloppy. GE becomes a great example, or Oracle right now. Even Apple has become quite conservative in the sense that it wants to make a world filled with people with the desire for itself such that it doesn't actually want to innovate. It just wants to refine the aesthetics of its products such that it can reproduce these regimes.

Stu: The biological example I think is [...] You all know that you have about 500 different bacterial species in your gut, right? Were you aware of this?

Cary: I would've guessed more, but [...]

Stu: [...] might be a couple thousand, but anyway. Raise the following: most of them are not competing with one another, experimentally. So now raise the question, so what are they doing for one another, okay? It might be the case that one bacteria makes a waste product that's food for another. It might be the case that one bacteria makes a surface over which another one can crawl. Think that there are some huge number of distributed functionalities in this thousand or so bacterial species in your gut that allows them to continue to exist as a community. That's somehow the analog of a bunch of corporations making their way with one another in the world, and it can be made even more precise [...]

Stu: [...] I'm kind of amused to say this. It turns out that there's an analog of price and price formation. It's going on in such a community, it might be worth taking a second to say so. Suppose you've got two yeasts. One fails to make one of the amino acids, say alanine. The other fails to make glycine. Well, neither can grow alone, but if you grow them together, the one that can't make alanine makes glycine and the one that makes glycine can't make alanine. They feed one another. Imagine plating them together.

Stu: Imagine the following. I came up with this about two years ago, and Paul Samuelson had come up with it forty years ago. He said the same thing, so I'll quote Paul Samuelson or what I imagine he said. Imagine that you have a bunch of mutant yeast that tune how fast they secrete each amino acid, low to high. Imagine co-plating all possible pairs, amino acid one, squirting low. Squirting low, squirting middle, squirting high. Amino acid, yeast squirting low, just do all possible combinations.

Stu: Come back a day later, one particular pair of those yeast with some intermediate level of squirting each amino acid will outgrow all the others, right? That ratio of secreting the two amino acids is the analog of price. It's two of my A for one of your B. It's price formation with a reinvestment because the bacteria are growing as well. It's the analog of, I just said it, it's price. The 500 bacteria in your gut are in fact an economic system, quite literally.

Stu: If we now ask where would we like to head with the idea that corporations are somehow, sometimes, autopoietic systems that have some kind of ontology, which is individuated in their worlds where they're co-creating their world, they're co-creating their world with one another just like the bacteria in your gut are. The bacteria in your gut might evolve to make different kinds of things but continue to coexist with one another.

Phil: This is especially true historically, post-World War II, as companies brought marketing and consumption practices into how they started selling the things they were making. A good example is the computer industry. They actually had to get consumers incorporated into the companies to figure out how they could be helping each other out – to do the "squirting" they couldn't do themselves. That's how they could make and sell more complex machines.

Stu: Somehow that sounds dirty [...] (laughing) [...]

Phil: [...] I thought it was innocent (laughing) [...]

Gaymon: On some level, we want to recognize the historicist nature of the ontologies of these autopoietic moments in these entities which have enough individuation that they can dominate the certain spaces they live in in the world. But in part, in naming that – this is to get back to something that Cary said yesterday that I mentioned this morning as well – it's like, then, other things are opened up in the world in response to not only the existence of the corporation but the dominating forces of the corporation.

Gaymon: Some of those things are – Mike mentioned this this morning – you get Facebook becoming too dominant and then people want to move in and regulate it and reimagine its ontology as publishing, such that they can marshal a certain regime of regulation. But some of them are just the opening up of adjacent spaces that are functionally linked to the world that this corporation domination creates such that something compensatory now exists within a broader adjacent space [...]

Phil: The reason why I like this as a historian of biology is this gets you out of the form vs. function debates that you've had in biology for hundreds of years, right? Because it's no longer about the holism of the organism, because the organism itself is fundamentally antagonistic with itself, in a certain way. And so functions, in that way, end up *becoming* forms in a way that I don't think a lot of biologists have really grasped in the way that you're trying to get at here, Stu. So I think that's cool.

Stu: Could you restate the last thing you said? I didn't understand it.

Phil: Yeah. I think what's interesting now is, with some of the science that I'm seeing, is a fundamental antagonism at the level of the organism as a whole, right? There is some complementarity of cell function that's going on the whole time, but there's also the ability – this is why we get cancer – there's also still the availability to proliferate, right? Somehow, the organism needs both, but we've too often had debates only at the level of the whole organism, that once it divides these into either what is its form – to think about this as a formal issue – or what is its function – to think about this as an adaptational issue.

Phil: I think the way you posed your question earlier about notions of work in relationship to programs, functions that could happen within this, if you hold that level and you see how that can still be fundamentally antagonistic, you come up with a whole set of different issues that's no longer just about form vs. function because those are no longer antagonistic. What's much more interesting is proliferation vs. specialization.

Cary: Yeah, which we did talk about some this morning, yeah [...]

Phil: I think that's a fundamentally different perspective [...] especially from a historian's point of view, because they're still writing about form and function [...]

Gaymon: Whereas if you're interested in specifying sets of relationships that end up having some coordinative dynamics to them such as they can level and complexify and [...]

Gaymon: [...] but nonetheless then have a kind of hypostasis. But that's an interactive ontology rather than the totality providing the context within the [...]

Phil: The total ontology [...]

Gaymon: You can interpret the element or the reductive inversion of that, which is to say,

"Oh we have a set of functional mechanisms in which we have an integrated totality [...]"

Phil: That's the other option that we've seen in biology.

Cary: Right. Right.

Adam: Whoa, okay.

* * *

Stu: You know, I'm realizing that we are making good on something we said to one another in our first meeting. Remember the idea of this "post-complexity" science? We were trying to talk about something that's after complexity science. I know complexity science really well I mean I [...]

Cary: You should! (general laughter) [...]

Stu: I should. We are post-complexity science because complexity science, in one way or another, is algorithmic. And it's prestatable. Even an agent-based model, you have this rich behavior in an agent-based model but you're the one who created the agent-based model. Now you see all this stuff that happened and isn't that cool? Okay, we're all buying unprestatable becoming in which the things in the world of interact, corporations or organizations, create their, their environment, that they co-create with one another then become into all these ways we've been saying.

Stu: This is beyond complexity. We're making good on what we said in our first meeting. That's a big thing that we're doing.

note

1 Because we did not originally intend for the Ontogenetics Process Group meetings to yield specific outcomes (like a publishable roundtable conversation), many conversations went unrecorded. We would like to pay tribute to those individuals who were essential to the development of the Ontogenetics Process Group, but whose utterances are not transcribed here. These individuals include: Erin Espelie, Helga Wild, Giuseppe Longo, Patricia Pisters, Wim Hordijk, and Peter Sloot.

Index

Note: Figures are indicated by *italics*. Endnotes are indicated by the page number followed by 'n' and the endnote number e.g., 20n1 refers to endnote 1 on page 20.

Actor Network Theory 130, 133, 138, 141
acts of evacuation 86–7
actualized facts 106
actualized (individuated) outcome 114
actual occasion of experience 33
adaptability drivers 141
Adjacent Possible 16, 17
aesthetics 57–9
agricultural revolution 18
Alaimo, Stacy 132–3
algebraic qualities 66
algebraization 122
All is Number 9, 13
ambient biosemiotic ecology 70
An Autobiographical Note 24
ancient Greeks 8–9
Andersen, Thom 98
Anderson, Kayla 102
A Net to Catch the Light (film) 97
Angelaki 2
the Animal 133, 141
animal studies 165
The Annihilation of Time and Space (Solnit) 95
ante-meridiem 95
Anthropocene 19, 129, 142; Alaimo, Stacy 132–3; Anderson, Kayla 102; the Animal 133, 141; Clarke, Bruce 131–2; Clark, Timothy 132; definition 19; *Facing Gaia* 131; Latour's influential rendition 130; Sloterdijk, Peter 133
anthropocentrism 131
anthropology 3, 22–3, 43, 48
antientropic process 134
archemateriality 137
Arkin, Adam 43–4
Aspirdontus taeniatus 137
Assembling the Living 39, 40
A Thousand Plateaus (Deleuze and Guattari) 71
Australia 12
Australopithecus 18
autopoiesis 129, 132, 138, 139, 163–7, 174–7
Autopoietic unities 140

"avant-garde" 25
A World Beyond Physics: On the Origin of the Evolution of Life (Kauffman) 163
Axiom of Choice (AC) 74

The Baffler 152
Bailly, Francis 30
Baldwin effect 22, 130, 140–2
Banach, Stefan 73
Banach–Tarski monster 74
Bank of England Act 1694 93n4
Benjamin, Walter 33
The Beast & the Sovereign (Derrida) 133
Beyond Mechanism: Putting Life Back into Biology (Henning and Scarfe) 3
Big Data analytics 25
biofabs 41–6
biological systems 45; nonlinearity 27–31
Biology in the Grid (Thurtle) 55
biomedia 35n2
biosciences 26, 31, 34
biotic and abiotic systems 131
Boltzmann, L. 9
Boolean algebras 108, 110–12
Boolean local–global relations 113
Brahe, Tycho 13
bricolage 15
broken democracy 40
Bulletin of the Atomic Scientists 96

Cadwalladr, Carole 40
Canalization of Development 27
canalized 25
cancer 53, 55, 56, 96, 180; evolution of 55–7
Cantodea, Anna-Varney 57, 59
Canudo, Ricciotto 95
Capitalist Sorcery: Breaking the Spell (Pignarre and Stengers) 77n2
carbon, hydrogen, nitrogen, oxygen, phosphorus, sulfur (CHNOPS) 12
cells 11
central dogma 135

INDEX

the Central Dogma of molecular biology 31–2
chirality 102–3
CHNOPS proteins 141
cinema 95, 97–100, 103
Cinema, Nature, Ecology Conference at the University of Chicago, 2009 100
Cinema Scope (Andersen) 98
cinemetrics 98–9
circadian 96–8
Clarke, Bruce 131–2
Clark, Timothy 132
classical episteme 45
The Clock 98
closed compositing 55
collectively autocatalytic metabolic set 12
collectively autocatalytic sets 10, 11
Colli, Giorgio 122
complexity 4
complex systems 2, 5, 12, 14, 26, 27, 32
conception of communication (Serres) 33
constituting entities 65
constraint closure 140
Continuous Quantities (Gatten) 97
convolution 70
coordinate structure of individuals 110, 111
Copernicus–Kepler theory 119
cosmological inclination 45
creatio ex nihilo 88
creationism 121
CRISPR-Cas9 22
Critique of the Power of Judgment (Kant) 58
crittercams 102
Cro-Magnon museum 18
cross-veinless phenotype 24
cubic polynomial p(x) with intersections 67, *67*

"Dali Clock Face, From 'Halsman/Dali' Portfolio" 96
Darwinian mechanism 2
Darwinian pre-adaptations 15, 16, 136
data-intensive biology 26–7
Davidson, Arnold 63
Davies, Paul 30–1
deanimation 131
death 7, 51–5, 59, 121, 152
Déclaration des Droits de l'homme et du Citoyen de 1789 123
Defoe, Daniel 83
Deira Clock Tower, Dubai 95
Deleuze, Gilles 2, 31, 62, 64, 71, 73
Democritus 8
De Rerum Natura (Lucretius) 8, 19
Descartes, Rene 66
developmental biology 57
de Waal, Franz 18
dialectic subsumption 68
Difference and Repetition (Deleuze) 71
digital biology 39–41, 44, 45, 48–9
digital sublime 39–48
Dirichlet indicator function *69*

DNA 11, 12, 25, 130, 149
dogmas 123–6
Don Quixote (Cervantes) 19
doomsday 103–4
Dorsophilia 27
Dream of a Final Theory 9, 14
Drive Your Plow over the Bones of the Dead (novel) 100

ecological embeddedness 136
Ecological Poetics, or, Wallace Stevens's Birds (Wolfe) 133
ecologization 129
ecology 3
El Sueño de la Razón Produce Monstruos (The Sleep of Reason Produces Monsters) 62, *63*
emergence 3, 56, 70, 102, 129, 132–4
endosymbiosis 102
endosymbiotic structures 102
Endy, Drew 43–4
ENIAC 149, 151
epigenetic landscape 23–6, 28–33, 35, 36
Epigenetic Landscapes: Drawing as Metaphor (Squier) 22
epigenetics 22–3; complex landscape 24–7
epigenome 31
epimedia 35n2
epimediality 31–3
epimedial landscapes 23, 33–5
épistémè 125
Epperson, Michael 2
EPR-type experiments 108, 113
E pur si muove (And still it moves) 19
ergodic 9
Eros: ancient Greeks 8–9; anew 15–17; and Logos, ancient Greek 18–19; non-ergodic 9–10; rebirth of 9
Essay Upon Projects (Defoe) 83
eternal sickness 55–7
ethics of knowledge 118, 122–6
European Bioinformatics Institute (EBI) 46, 47
Excluded Philosophy 24
explicitness 121–2
externalization 132–3

Facing Gaia 130, 131, 133, 138
"falls off" 51
Fichte, Johann Gottlieb 90–2
filmmakers 98–9
Final Theory 9, 14, 17, 19
findable, accessible, interoperable, reusable (FAIR) 47, 48
finitely additive 74
fitness landscapes 26
Flat Ontology 129–30
flexible organism-in-its-environment 130
Foucault, Michel 63

Gaia 130–3, 139, 140
Gatten, David 97
Gene Ontology Consortium (GO) 47
generate entities 65
Gene Regulation Consortium (GRECO) 47

genesis 23, 31, 34, 76, 90–2, 106
genetically intensive structure of individuations 111
Genetic Assimilation 27
genetic code 11, 30
genetic program's function 124
genetic regulatory networks (GRNs) 25
genetic structure of individuations 110
geometric monsters 70–2
geometry 86
German Idealism 57
Geyrhalter, Nikolaus 101
"gheu" 49
Ginko 41–2
global Boolean algebra 108, 111–12
global economy 7
Gödel incompleteness theorems 74, 75
god of creativity 8
God's Providence 83–4
Goldman Sachs 40
gothic 52–4, 59
goth music 53–5
goth theory 4, 51–9
"goth" voice 4
Goya, Francisco 62, *63*
The Great Leveler (Scheidel) 18
"grid of intelligibility" 2
Guattari, Félix 2, 64, 70, 71
Gunning, Tom 103

Habermas, Jürgen 32
Hadrosaur *57*
Hägglund, Martin 137
Halsman, Philippe 96
Hammang, Anne 42
Haraway, Donna J. 102
harpedonaptai 88, 93n7
heterogeneity 32
histone/epigenetic code 30
History of Madness (Foucault) 63
holism 130
hominid lineage 18
Homo erectus 18
homogeneity 32
Homo habilis 18
Homo sapiens 18, 101
Horned Sphere 78n14
human beings 83
Human Genome Project 25
human hearts 10
humanism 130
humanity 7, 19
Humanity in a Creative Universe (Kauffman) 133, 162

iconicity 103
identity of identity and non-identity (Hegel) 4
Iliad 8
Illinois Parables (film) 100
imaginary number 66–8, 77
imaginary numbers 64

individuated actuality 114
individuated-contextual-actual portrait 107, 109, 114, 115
individuated facts 106
inductive limit 112
Information and Causality 43
innovation 42, 47, 66, 90, 109, 150–3, 155
Inside the Shared Life (film) 102
intelligibility 121–2
International Geosphere–Biosphere Programme (IGBP) 131
irreducible complexity 4

Jablonka, Eva 25
Jacob, François 15, 40
James, William 103
Jean-Luc Nancy's notion of community 33
John Durham Peters' theory of non-reciprocal communication 33
"just-so stories" 52

Kantian Whole 10–11, 15–17, 134, 138, 140, 141
Kant, Immanuel 58
Kauffman, Stuart 2, 30, 31, 133
Keller, Evelyn Fox 39
Kelly, Jason 42
Kelvin, Lord 102
Knight, Tom 44
Kochen–Specker theorem 107–8
Kohler, Tim 18
Krämer, Sybille 32
Kristersson, Mikael 101–2
Kubelka, Peter 97

Labroides dimidiatus 137
Lamarckism 22
Lamb, Marion J. 25
La Nascita della Filosofia (Colli) 122
Langsdorf, Martyl 96
Latour's theory 141
laws of physics 7, 15, 141
Lenton, Timothy 139
"Life" 130–1
Life: A Modern Invention (Tarizzo) 58
Life and Process: Towards a New Biophilosophy (Koutroufinis) 3
lifeless matter (Brassier) 3
light sensitivity 96
living foundries 41–2, 48
living individuals 110
Ljusår, or Light Year (film) 101
Lloyd, Harold 95
local contextuality 109
local spacetime 109–10
logical causality 111–12
logicism 124
Logos 7–20; ancient Greeks 8–9
Longo, Giuseppe 2, 31, 43
Lucretius 8

The Major Transitions in Biology (Smith) 144
Making and Breaking Mathematical Sense (Wagner) 65
Martin, Bill 12
materialism 2, 129, 134
mathematical complexity 23
mathematical formalism (Meillassoux) 3
Mathematics and the Natural Sciences: The Physical Singularity of Life (Longo and Bailly) 125
mediality 31–3
media philosophy 23, 31, 33
Meillassoux, Quentin 3
mereotopological transductive-transcontextual-relational structure 115
meridiem 95
metabiotic ecosystems 131
meta-physical isolationism 34
meta-physics of mechanism 26
metastability 109
Molecular Capture: The Animation of Biology (Nocek) 35n3
monogamy 126n4
Montévil, Maël 30
Monument (film) 97
multi-core electric cable 28
multidimensional phase space 26
Murchison 12

Nachleben 42–3, 146
narrative 7, 8, 17, 27, 98, 100, 102, 166
nature contra nature 83
Neanderthal 18
negative results 118, 122
neighboring trajectories 28
neo-Darwinian 24, 25, 27–8, 135, 139, 141, 142
neoplasms 56
Newtonian Paradigm 13–15, 17
New York Times 97
9/11 168, 175
Nocek, A. J. 35n3
no entailing law 13, 136, 138
non-dualistic theory 24
non-ergodic 9–10, 15, 17, 134, 138, 141, 162, 176
non-identity of identity and non-identity (Derrida) 4
non-linear differential equations (Khan) 29
nonlinearity, biological systems modeling 27–31
non-trivial boundary curves *71*
Nowell, Peter C. 56
Nuage Vert 100

Odyssey 8
O'er the Land (film) 100
Of Flying Cars and the Declining Rate of Profit 152
omics-wide research programs 25
Ontogenetics Process Group (OPG) 1–3
open compositing 55
open science 46, 47
operator 72
ordinary differential equations (ODEs) 27

Organism and Environment: Inheritance and Subjectivity in the Life Sciences (Winslow) 167, 168
The Organism as Dynamical System 35n4
Our Daily Bread 101

Pagus 87–8, 93n6
pantograph *66*
Pappochelys rosinae 56
papyrus 66, *66*
Patriot Act 168
Peirce, Charles S. 103
Perspectives on Organisms: Biological Time, Symmetries and Singularities (Longo and Montévil) 30
phase space 17, 29
philosophy of organism 24, 30
physical individuals 110
physico-mathematical organization 30
Pisco, Angela Oliveira 24
Platonicism 124
post-genomics era 26
post-meridiem 95
potential (preindividuated) outcomes 114
practical metaphysics 39
preindividual reality 114
Primate lineage 18
Principia 7, 17
Principles of Psychology (James) 103
problematization 62
Process and Reality (Whitehead) 25, 33, 34, 106
Promethean design (Bratton) 3
Protention and Retention 30
providence 83
"Pro Videre" 83
Psychocinematics: Exploring Cognition at the Movies 98–9
"Pure Potentials for the Specific Determination of Fact, or Forms of Definiteness" 107
Pythagoras 8–9, 13

Quantum Chromo Dynamics 14
quantum mechanics 14, 15, 68, 106–16, 117n5, 124, 158, 176

Rabinow, Paul 42, 43
Rainer, Arnulf 97
"reals" R 68
Real Time series 97
recursivity 140, 141
refactor DNA 44
relational realism 106–16
relativism 118–20
relativizing objectivity 120–1
return of epigenetics 25
RNA 11, 12, 149
Romanticism 57
rope-stretchers 88, 93n7

Safety Last! (Lloyd) 95
sample space 17
Santa Fe 1–2; economies 170–81; evolution of social forms 158–70

Saunders, Peter T. 26, 35n4
Scheidel, Walter 18
Schrödinger's equation 122
Science and the Modern World (Whitehead) 24, 33
science novo methodo (science of knowing) 91
science *vs.* ethics 122–3
scientific universals 118–20
Scottsdale: ontogenesis, biogenesis, genetics and "life" 144–9; social forms 149–58
The Screwdriver Argument 16
Second Law of Thermodynamics (Snow) 9
selfish gene theory 139, 141
semiotics of instability 54
sequence of surfaces 71–2, *72*
serial-inclusive mereotopological relatedness 110
Serres, Michel 33, 81–2, 86–9, 92
Seventeen Seconds (Cure) 55
sexual multi-celled organisms 12
Sha Xin Wei 2
Shrimp Boat Log (film) 97
Sikelianos, Eleni 103–4
Silicon Valley 44
Simmel, Georg 95
Simondon, Gilbert 2, 4, 22, 76, 106–16, 177
simply-connectedness 72
single-celled organism 12
Sloterdijk, Peter 133
Smith, John Maynard 144
Snow, C. P. 7, 9
social nature 83
Socrates 13
Solnit, Rebecca 95
Sopor Æternus & the Ensemble of Shadows 57
space-filling curves 73
speciation 28
speculative turn, humanities 3
Spheres project 133
Squier, Susan Merrill 22
Stavrianakis, Anthony 42, 43
Stein, Wilfred 35n4
Stephen Gould "exaptations" 15
Steps to Ecology of Mind (Bateson) 171–2
The Strategy of Genes (Waddington) 25, 26, 28
Stratman, Deborah 100
Summa theologicae 19
swim bladder 15–16
synthetic biology 42–4, 55, 145–8, 157

Tarizzo, Davide 58
Tarski, Alfred 73
Tathandlung 90–2
teleology 57–9
teleonomy 141
Templum 87
territorialization 85
Theoretical Biology Club in 1930s 1
Theory of Extension (Whitehead) 114
Theory of Prehensions (Whitehead) 114

The Theory of the Leisure Class (Veblen) 153
theory of translation (Benjamin) 33
Thomae's "popcorn" function T(x) *69*
Thompson, D'Arcy Wentworth 26
three-peptide collectively autocatalytic set 10
Thurtle's essay 4
Timaeus (Plato) 113
timbre 52–5, 59
tinkering 15
totalization 131, 139
trajectory physics 122
transcendental numbers 64
transcriptional clocks, humans 96
transductive-transcontextual-relational portrait 108, 111, 113–16
transfinite Axiom of Choice 79n16
Turing, Alan 26
"Two Cultures," Art and Science (Snow) 7

Umwelts (Hoffmeyer) 18, 86, 173
unchecked climate change 96
Universal Declaration of Human Rights, 1948 123
universality of theoretical principles 121–2

van Elferen, Isabella 57
Varela, Francisco J. 35n4
verum ipsum factum 90
Veyen, Paul 48
Vico, Giambattista 81–92
Virno, Paolo 81, 88–90, 92
virtualization 132
vital media 35n2
von Uexküll, Jakob 132

Waddington, C. H. 22–31, 33–4, 35n2, 35n4, 36n8, 36n10
Wagner, Roi 65
Wallin, Ivan 102
wanderers 8
Warbug, Aby 42, 146
The Watchtower Announcing Jehovah's Kingdom 123
Weinberg, Steven 14
Weinstock, Jeffrey Andrew 57
Weissm, Ron 44
Western, Educated, Industrialized, Rich, and Democratic (WEIRD) 4
What is Posthumanism? 132, 138, 140, 142
When Species Meet (Haraway) 102
Whitehead, Alfred North 3–4, 23–5, 30, 33–5, 36n1, 36n14, 57, 73, 106, 107, 111, 113–15
Whiteheadian metaphysics 25
Whiteheadian notion 109–10
Wired 40
Wissenschaftslehre (Fichte) 91
Woolf, Virginia 99
Wusi May Fourth movement 153

Xavier, Joana 12